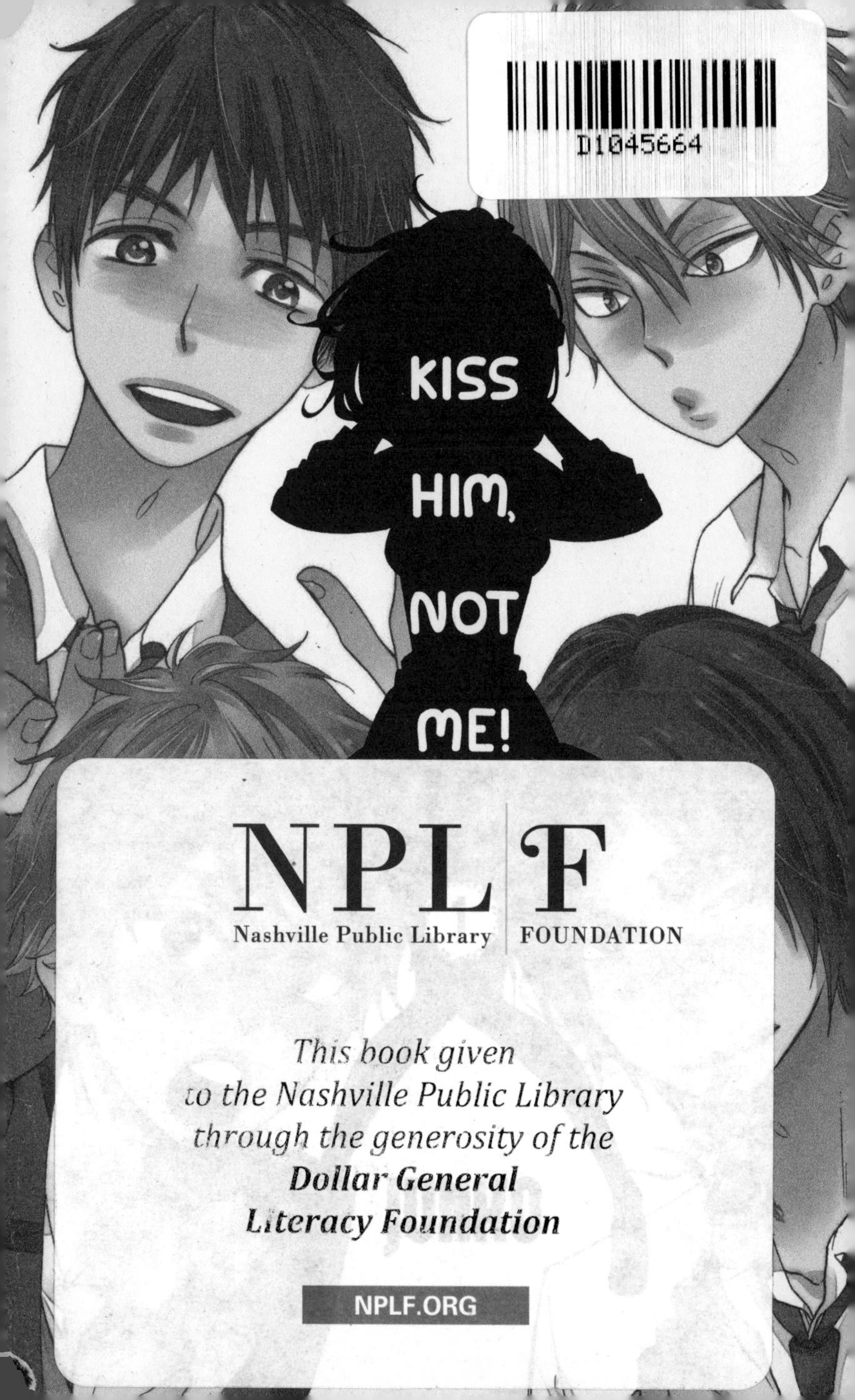
KISS
HIM,
NOT
ME!

CONTENTS

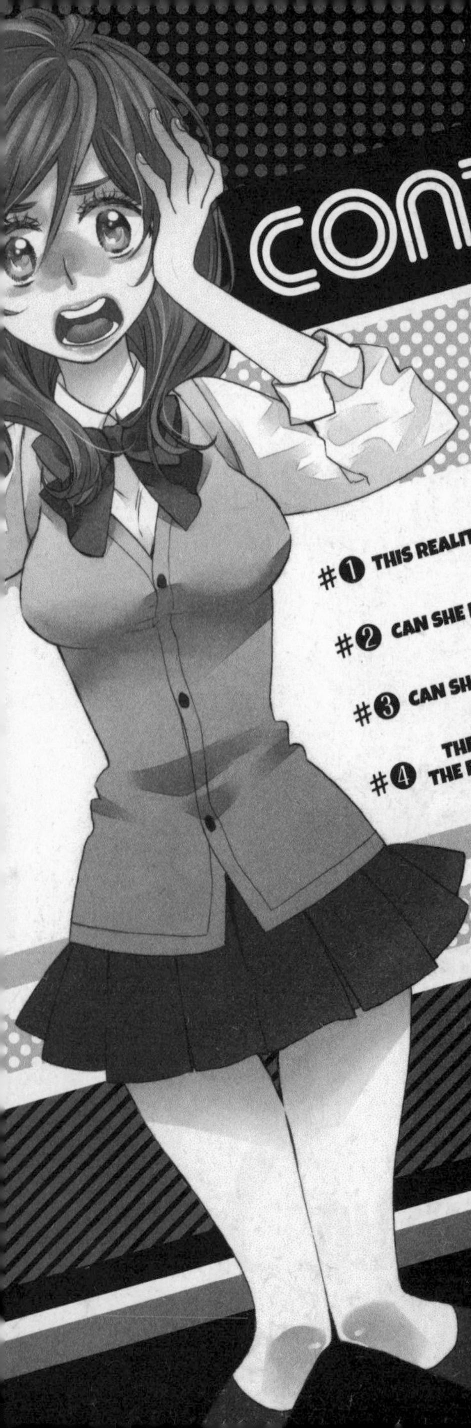

I ♥ BL

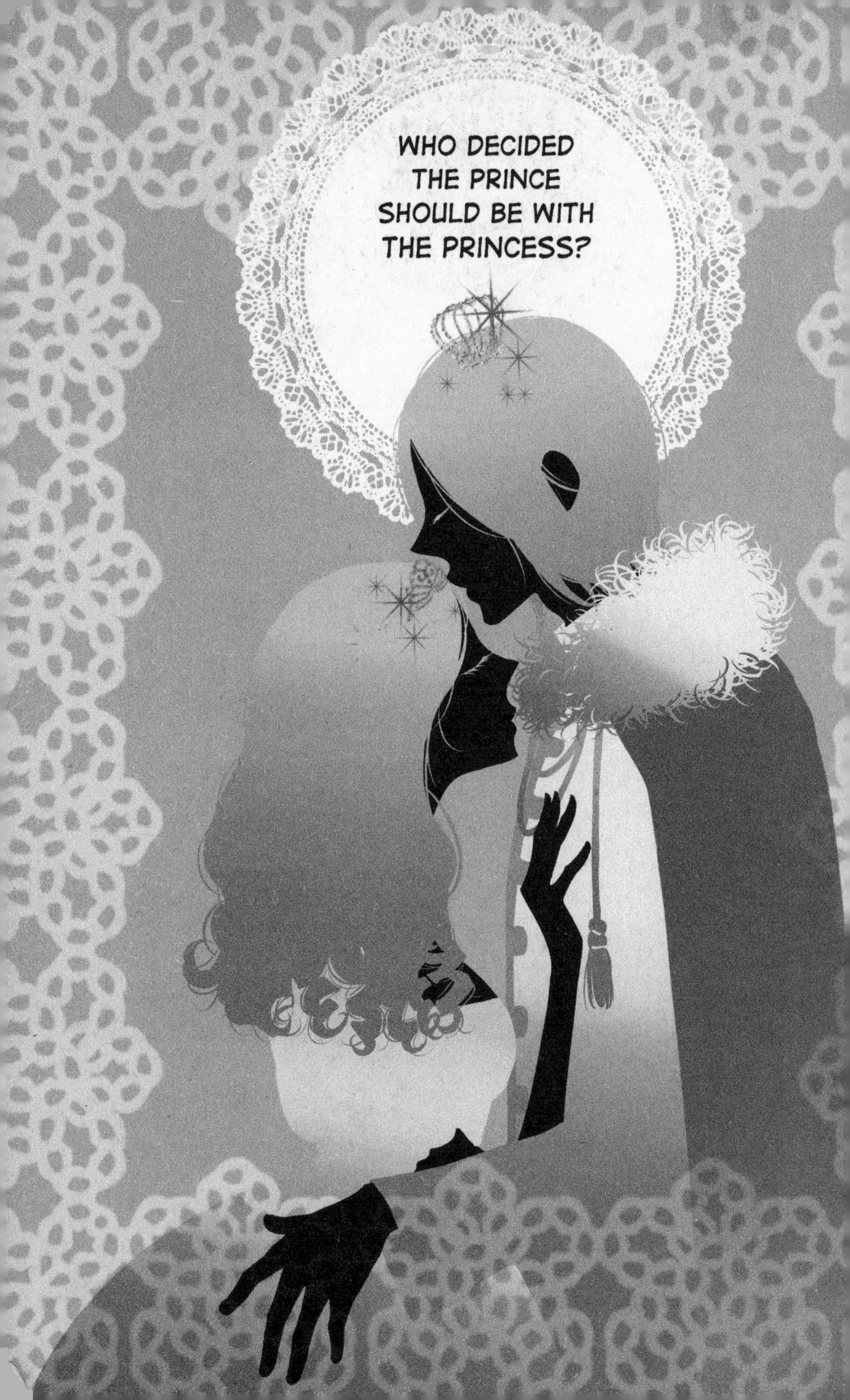
WHO DECIDED THE PRINCE SHOULD BE WITH THE PRINCESS?

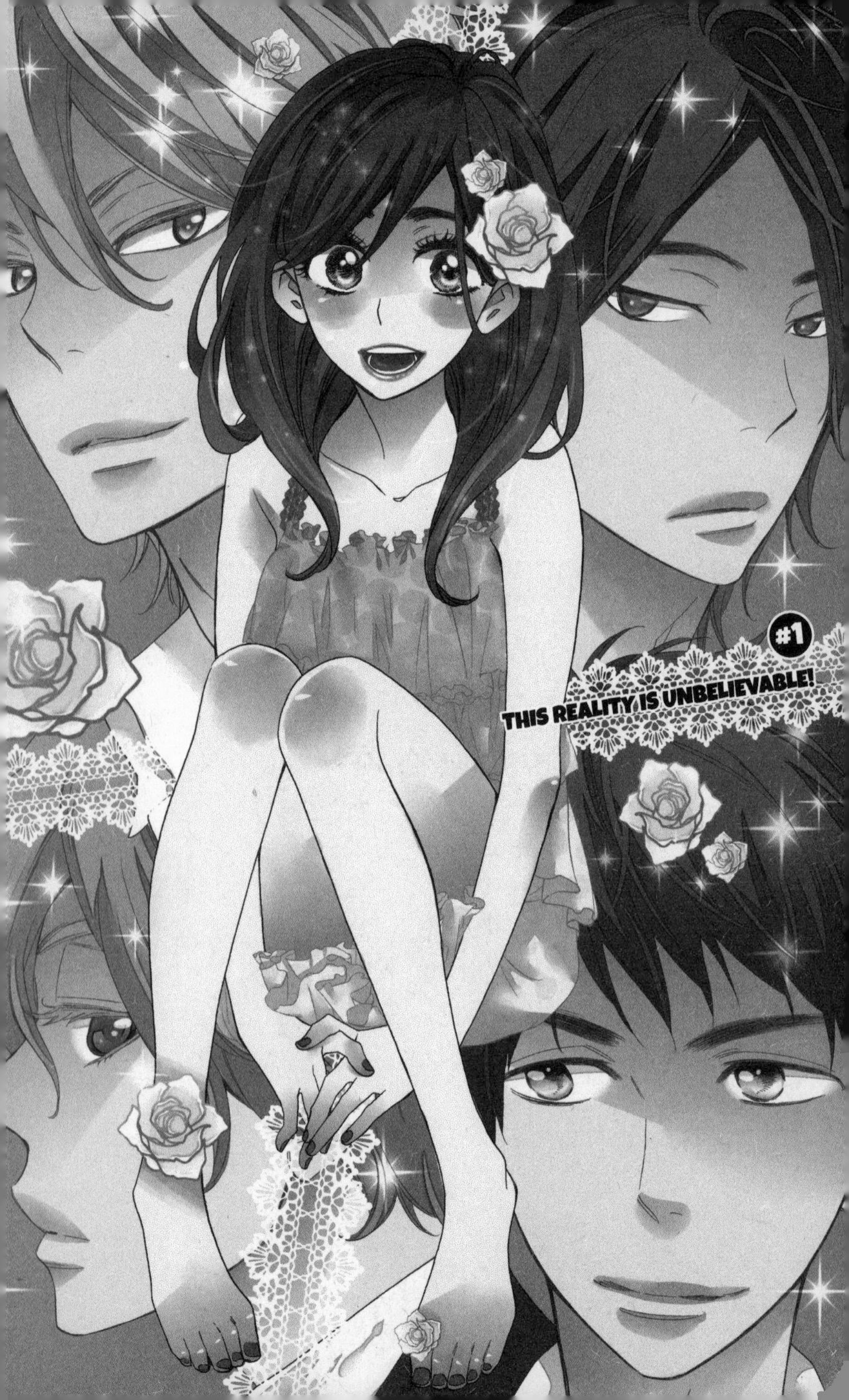
#1
THIS REALITY IS UNBELIEVABLE!

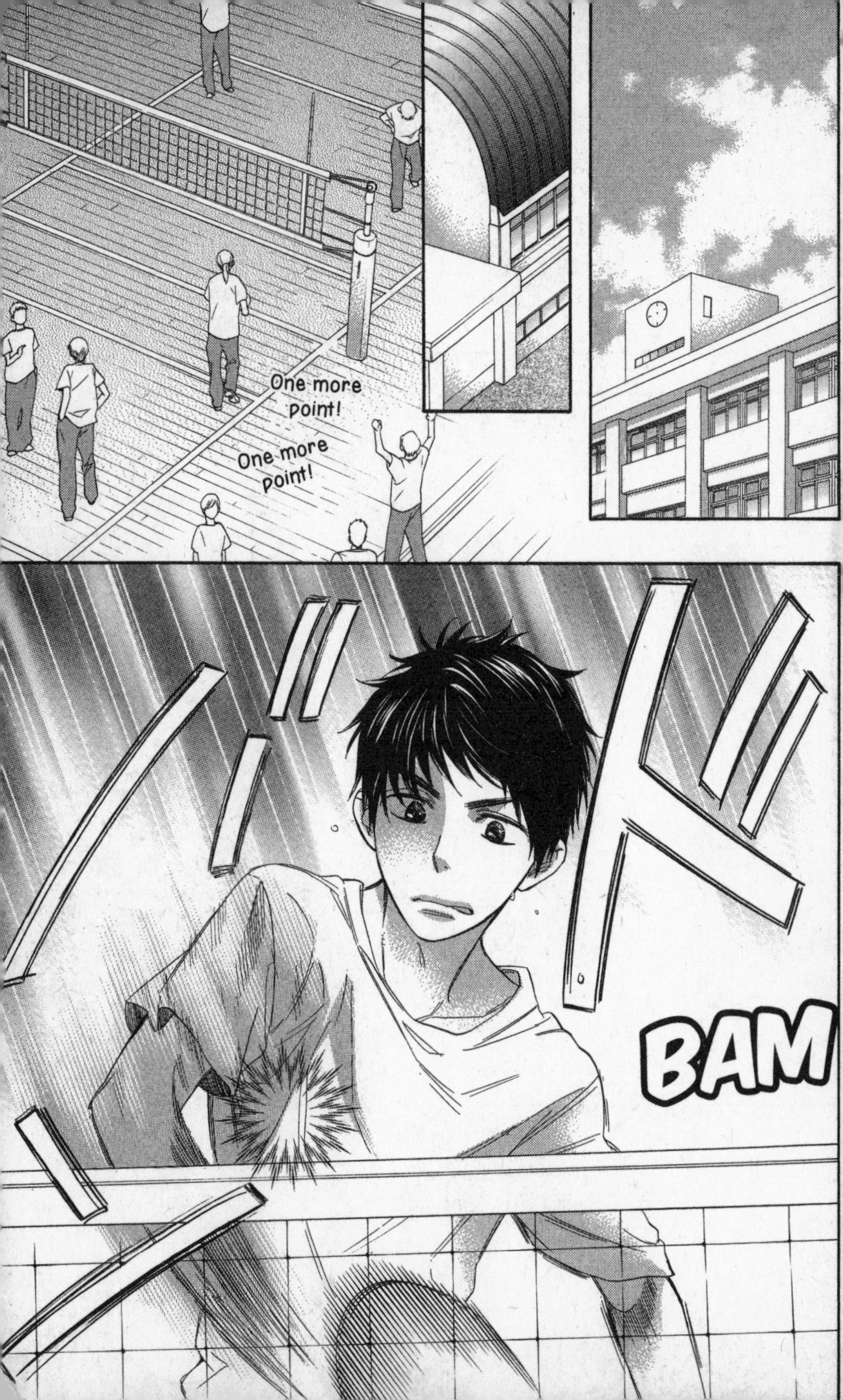
One more point!
One more point!
BAM

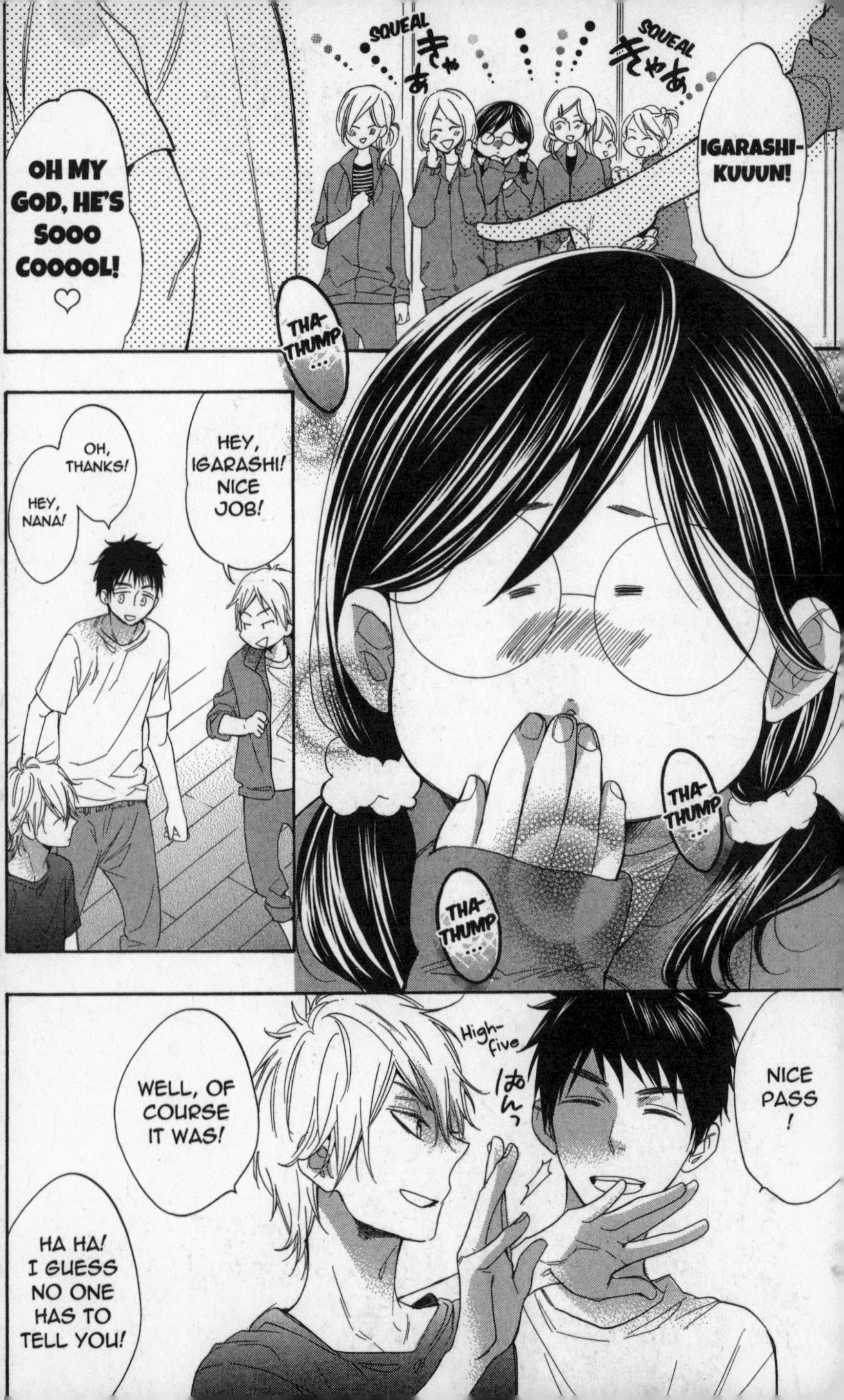

SQUEAL
きゃあ
IGARASHI-KUUUN!
SQUEAL
きゃあ
OH MY GOD, HE'S SOOO COOOOL! ♡
THA-THUMP...
THA-THUMP...
THA-THUMP...
HEY, IGARASHI! NICE JOB!
OH, THANKS!
HEY, NANA!
NICE PASS!
High-five
ぱんっ
WELL, OF COURSE IT WAS!
HA HA! I GUESS NO ONE HAS TO TELL YOU!

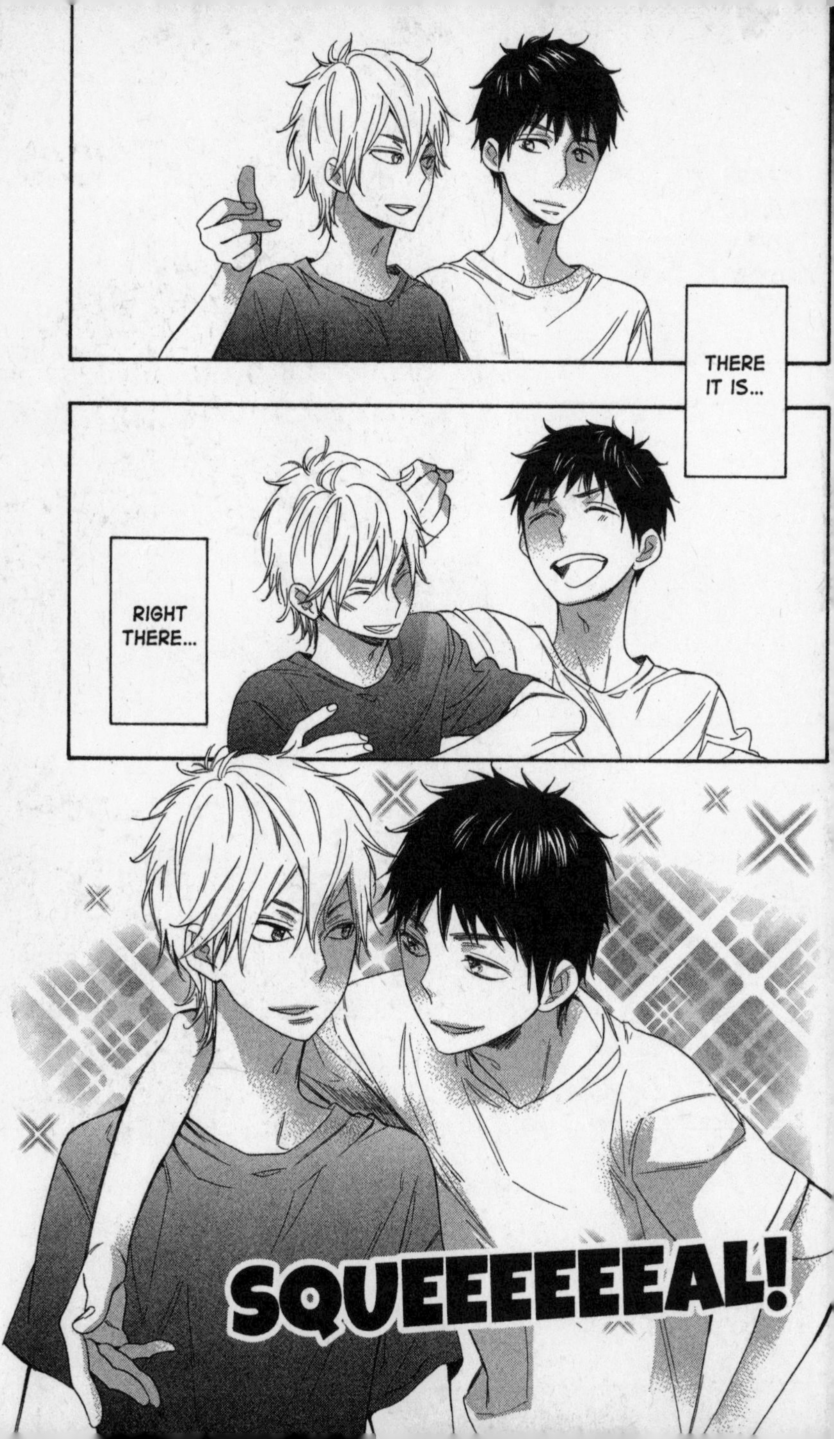
THERE IT IS...
RIGHT THERE...
SQUEEEEEEEAL!

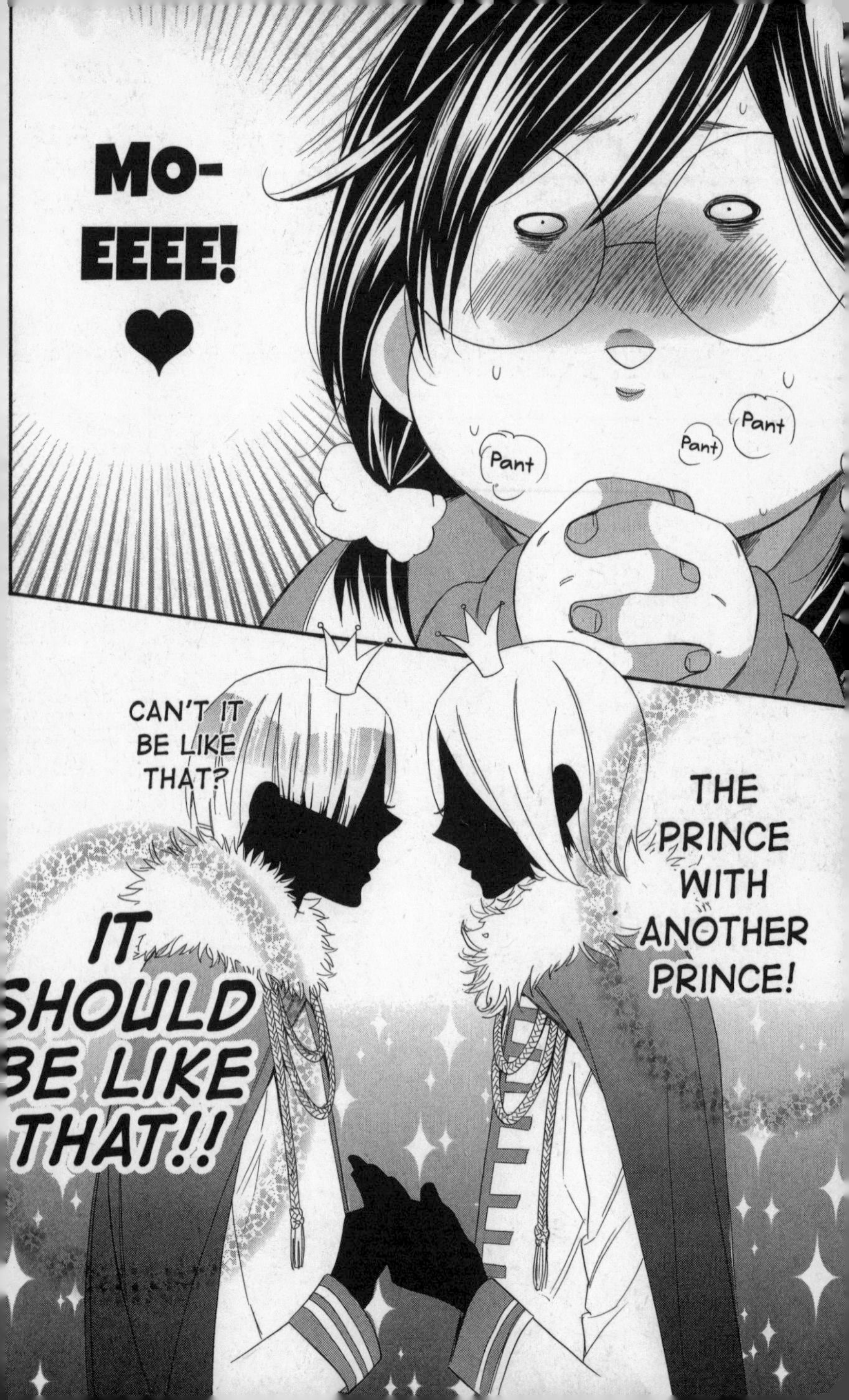
MO-EEEE! ♥
Pant
Pant
Pant
THE PRINCE WITH ANOTHER PRINCE!
CAN'T IT BE LIKE THAT?
IT SHOULD BE LIKE THAT!!

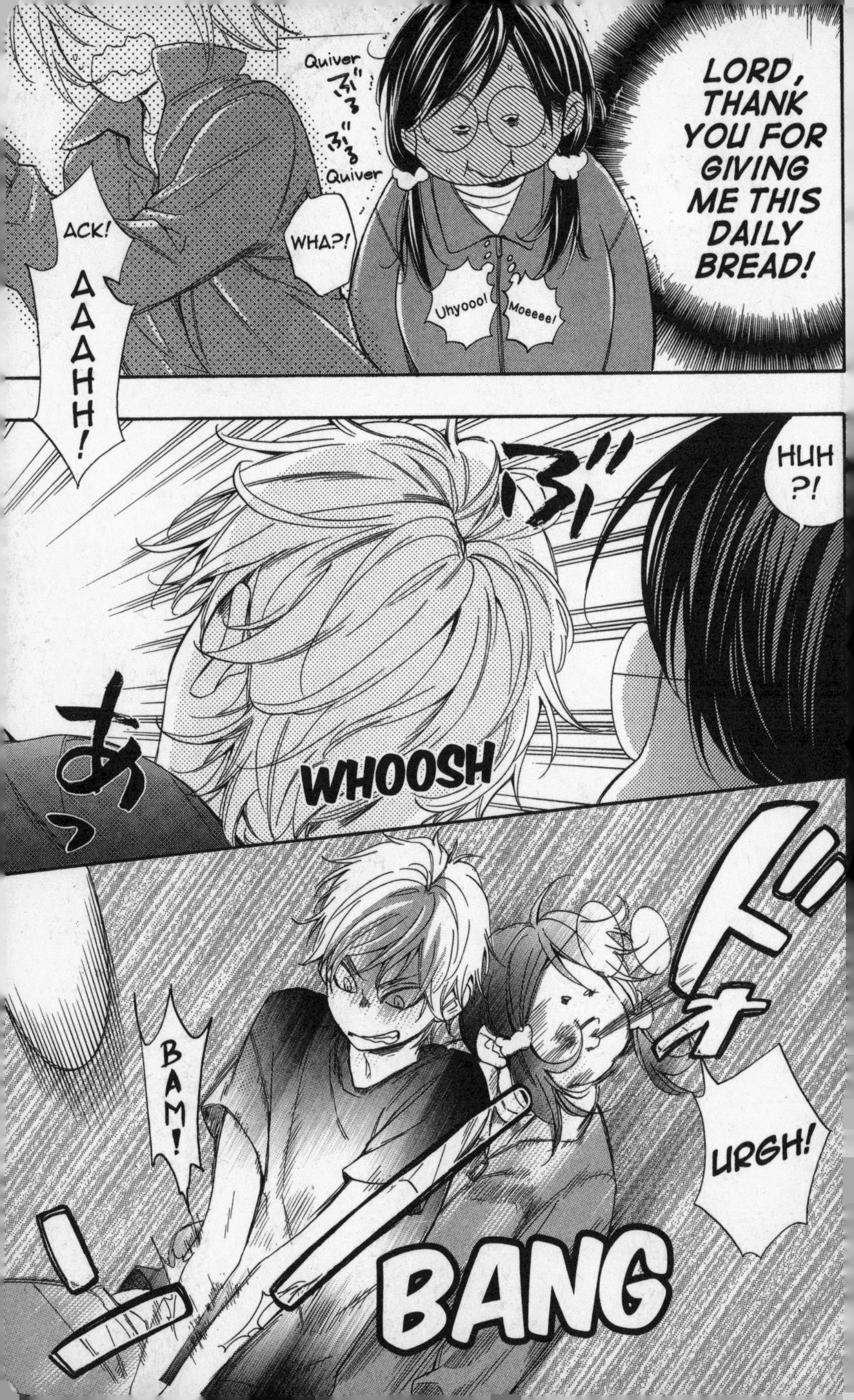
LORD, THANK YOU FOR GIVING ME THIS DAILY BREAD!
Quiver ぶる ぶる Quiver
Moeeee!
Uhyooo!
WHA?!
ACK!
AAAAHH!
HUH ?!
ぶ
WHOOSH
あっ
ドオ
URGH!
BANG
BAM!

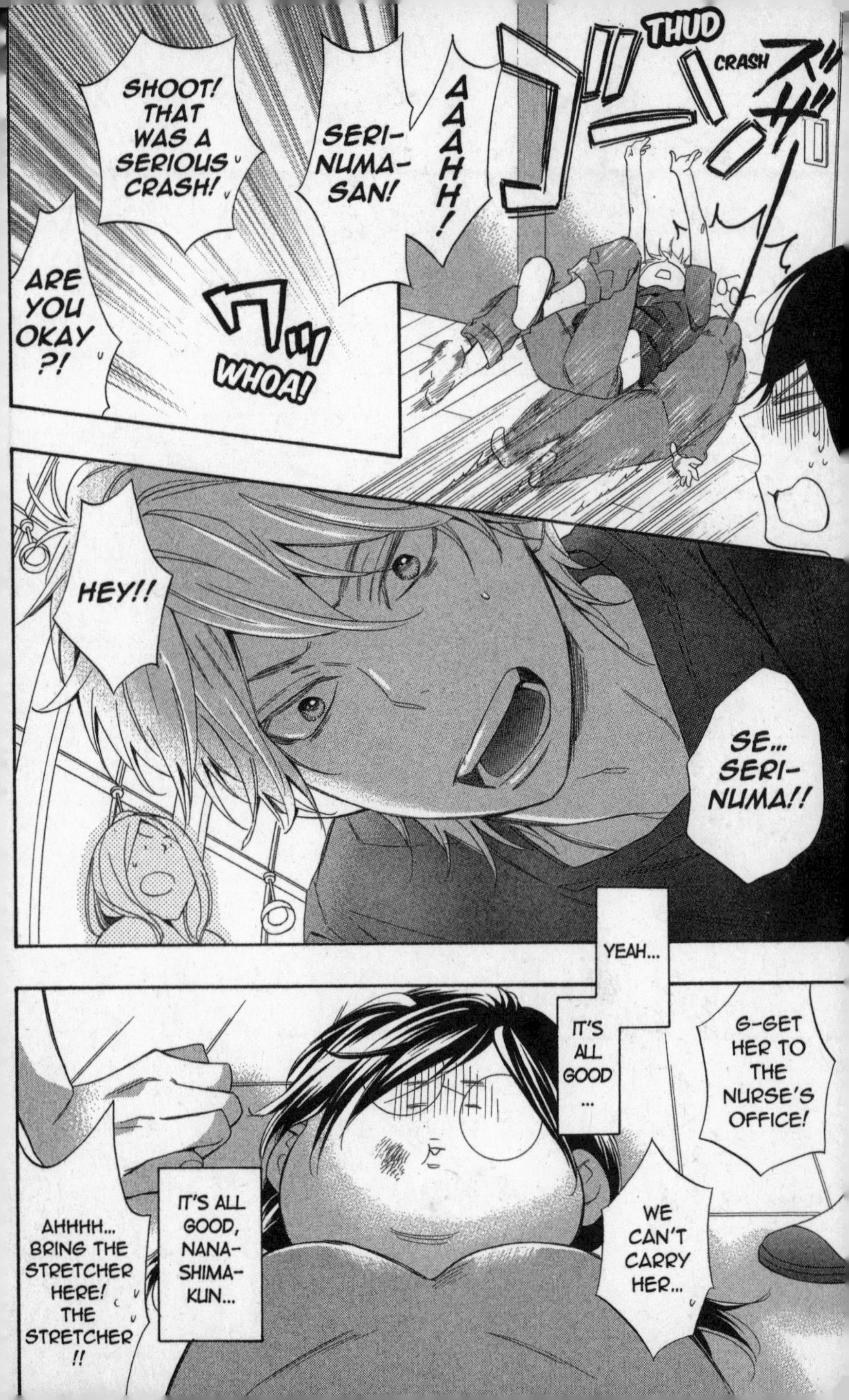
THUD
CRASH
AAAAHH!
SERI-NUMA-SAN!
SHOOT! THAT WAS A SERIOUS CRASH!
WHOA!
ARE YOU OKAY?!
SE... SERI-NUMA!!
HEY!!
G-GET HER TO THE NURSE'S OFFICE!
YEAH...
IT'S ALL GOOD...
WE CAN'T CARRY HER...
IT'S ALL GOOD, NANA-SHIMA-KUN...
AHHHH... BRING THE STRETCHER HERE! THE STRETCHER!!

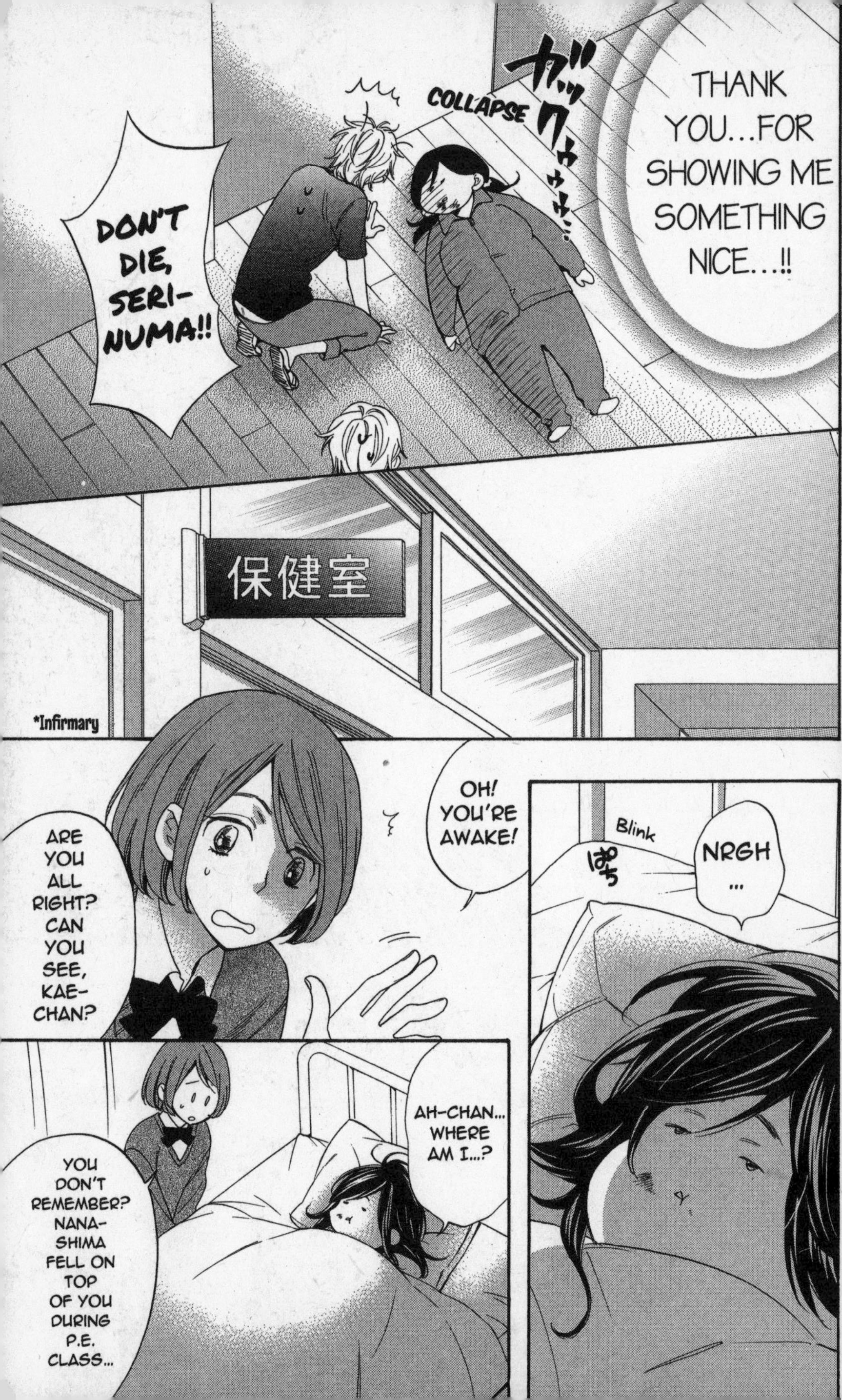
THANK YOU…FOR SHOWING ME SOMETHING NICE…!!
COLLAPSE
DON'T DIE, SERI-NUMA!!
保健室
*Infirmary
Blink
ぱち
NRGH …
OH! YOU'RE AWAKE!
ARE YOU ALL RIGHT? CAN YOU SEE, KAE-CHAN?
AH-CHAN… WHERE AM I…?
YOU DON'T REMEMBER? NANA-SHIMA FELL ON TOP OF YOU DURING P.E. CLASS…

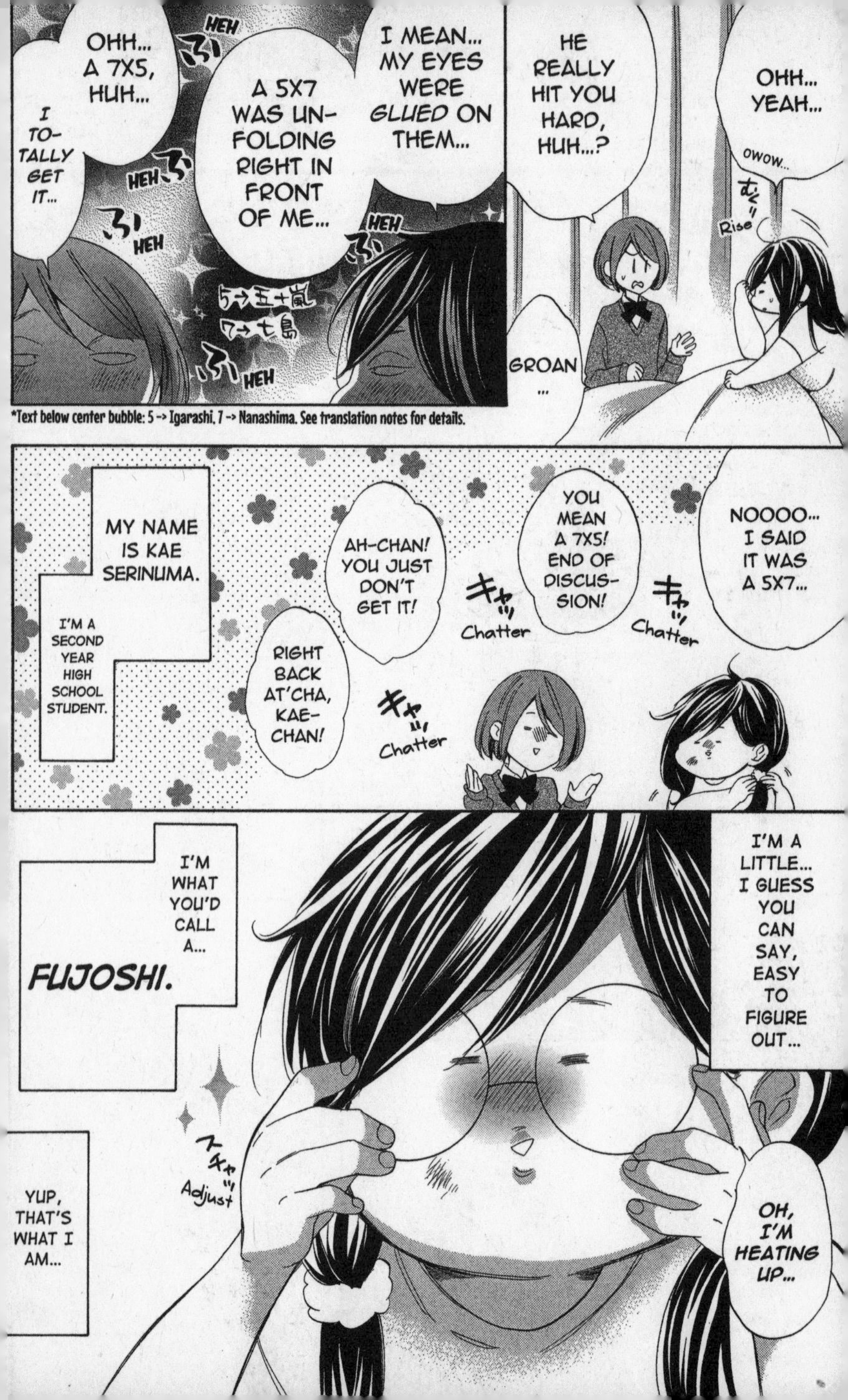
OHH... YEAH...
OWOW...
むく Rise
HE REALLY HIT YOU HARD, HUH...?
GROAN...
I MEAN... MY EYES WERE GLUED ON THEM...
A 5X7 WAS UN-FOLDING RIGHT IN FRONT OF ME...
OHH... A 7X5, HUH...
I TO-TALLY GET IT...
ふ HEH
ふ HEH
ふ HEH
ふ HEH
ふ HEH
5→五十嵐
7→七島
NOOOO... I SAID IT WAS A 5X7...
キャッ Chatter
YOU MEAN A 7X5! END OF DISCUS-SION!
キャッ Chatter
AH-CHAN! YOU JUST DON'T GET IT!
キャ Chatter
RIGHT BACK AT'CHA, KAE-CHAN!
MY NAME IS KAE SERINUMA.
I'M A SECOND YEAR HIGH SCHOOL STUDENT.
I'M A LITTLE... I GUESS YOU CAN SAY, EASY TO FIGURE OUT...
OH, I'M HEATING UP...
Adjust
I'M WHAT YOU'D CALL A...
FUJOSHI.
YUP, THAT'S WHAT I AM...

*Text below center bubble: 5 -> Igarashi, 7 -> Nanashima. See translation notes for details.

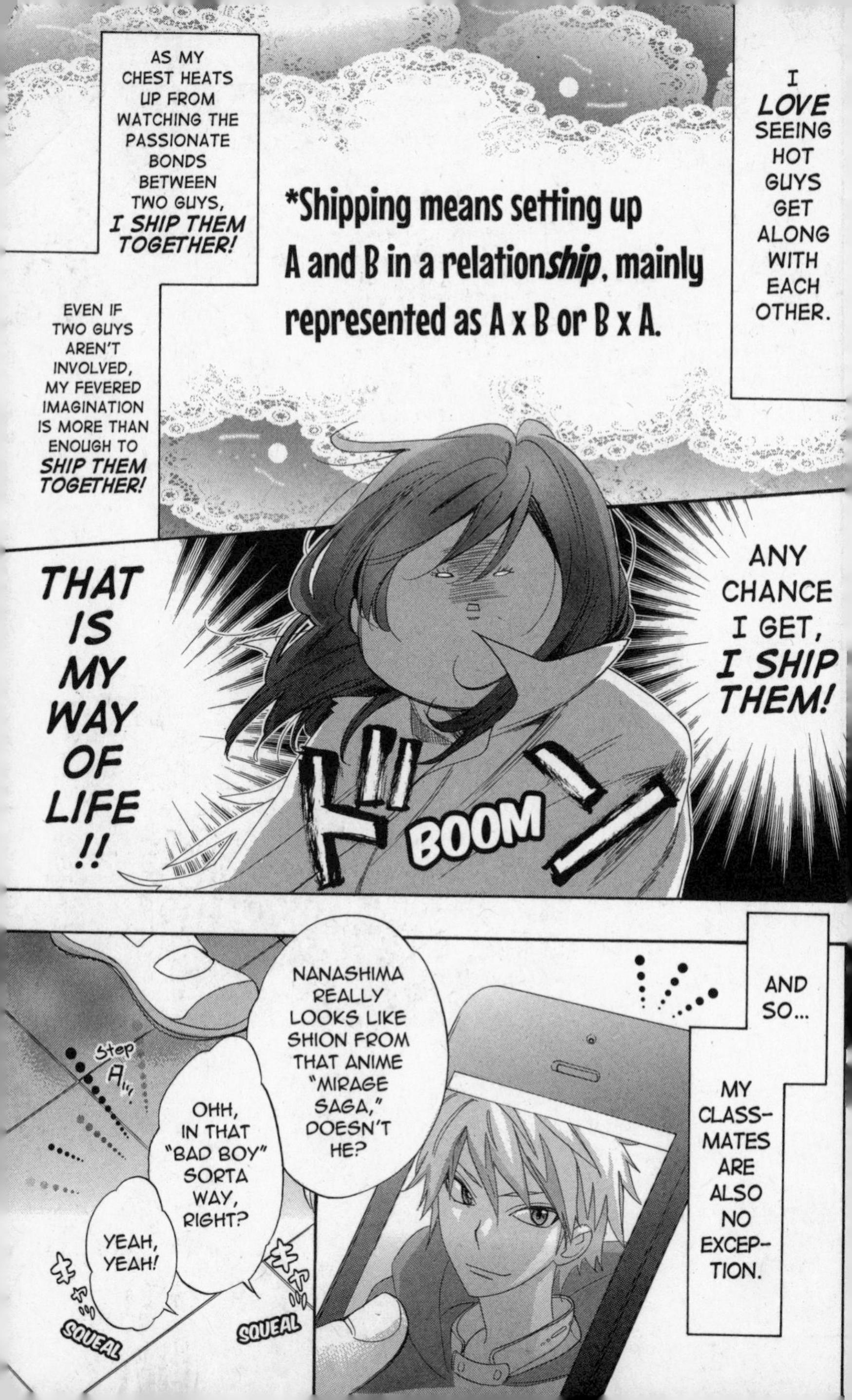
I LOVE SEEING HOT GUYS GET ALONG WITH EACH OTHER.
AS MY CHEST HEATS UP FROM WATCHING THE PASSIONATE BONDS BETWEEN TWO GUYS, I SHIP THEM TOGETHER!
*Shipping means setting up A and B in a relationship, mainly represented as A x B or B x A.
EVEN IF TWO GUYS AREN'T INVOLVED, MY FEVERED IMAGINATION IS MORE THAN ENOUGH TO SHIP THEM TOGETHER!
ANY CHANCE I GET, I SHIP THEM!
BOOM
THAT IS MY WAY OF LIFE!!
AND SO...
MY CLASSMATES ARE ALSO NO EXCEPTION.
NANASHIMA REALLY LOOKS LIKE SHION FROM THAT ANIME "MIRAGE SAGA," DOESN'T HE?
SQUEAL
OHH, IN THAT "BAD BOY" SORTA WAY, RIGHT?
YEAH, YEAH!
SQUEAL
Step

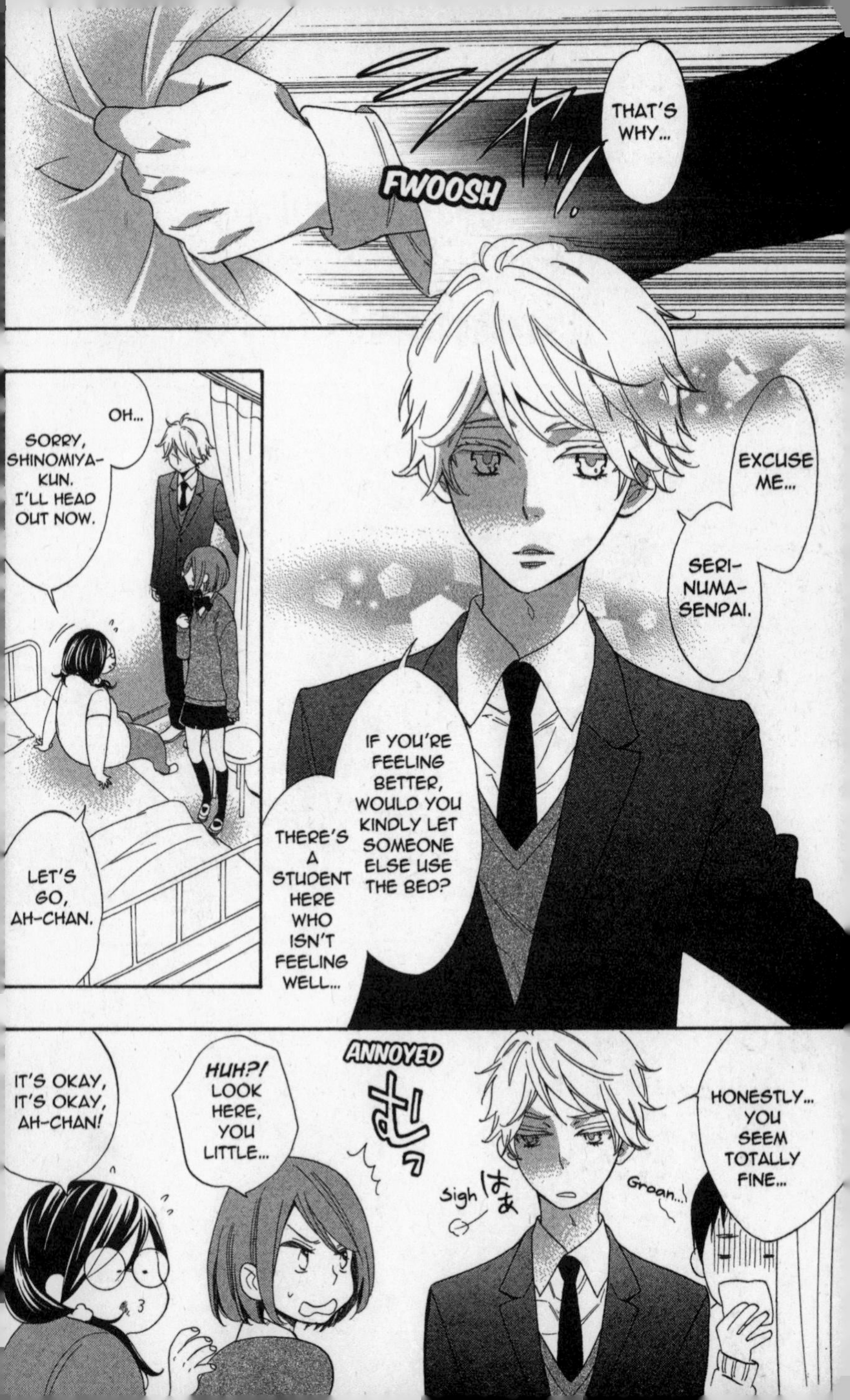
THAT'S WHY...
FWOOSH
EXCUSE ME...
SERI-NUMA-SENPAI.
IF YOU'RE FEELING BETTER, WOULD YOU KINDLY LET SOMEONE ELSE USE THE BED?
THERE'S A STUDENT HERE WHO ISN'T FEELING WELL...
OH...
SORRY, SHINOMIYA-KUN. I'LL HEAD OUT NOW.
LET'S GO, AH-CHAN.
HONESTLY... YOU SEEM TOTALLY FINE...
Groan...!
Sigh
はあ
ANNOYED
むっ
HUH?! LOOK HERE, YOU LITTLE...
IT'S OKAY, IT'S OKAY, AH-CHAN!

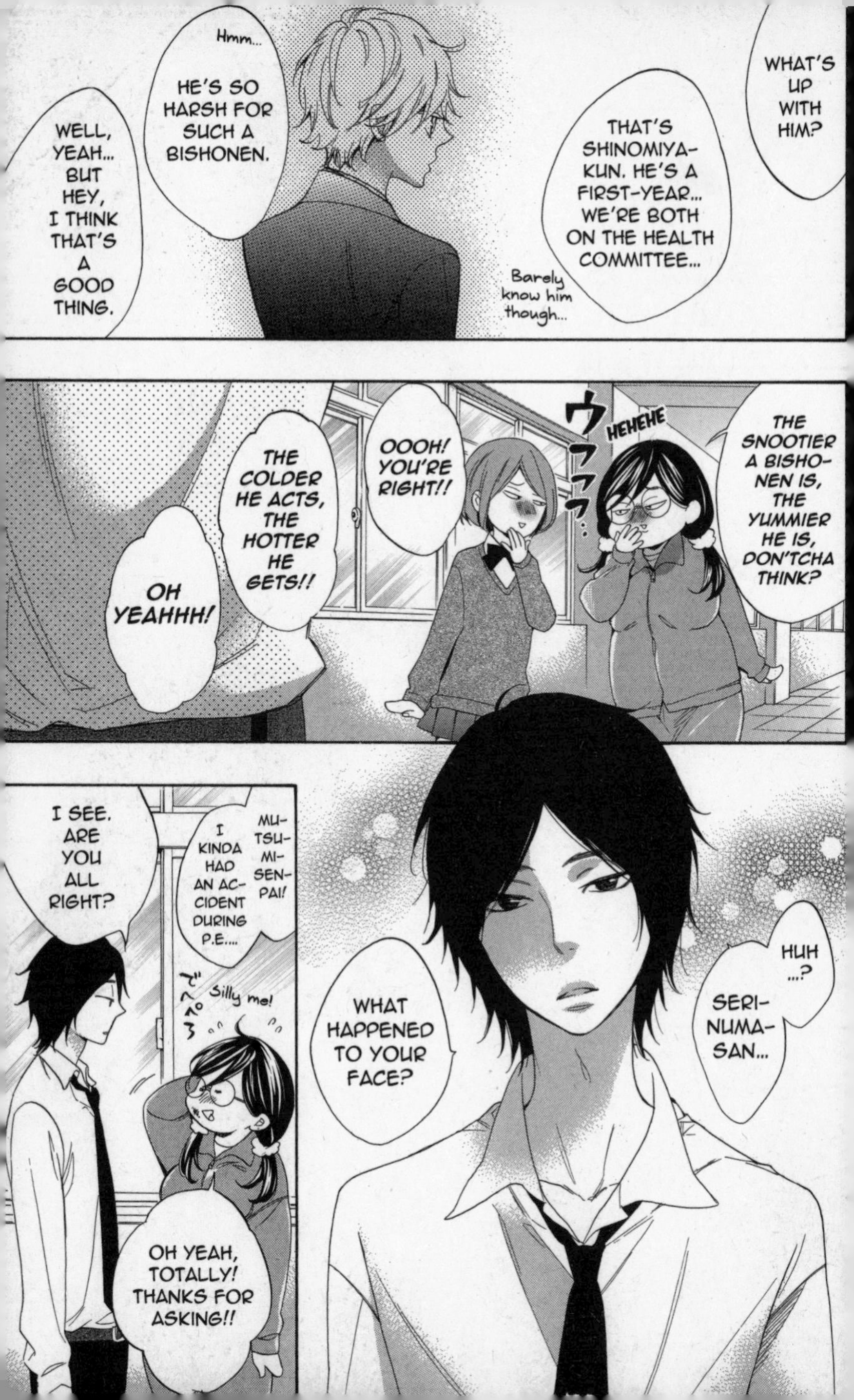
WHAT'S UP WITH HIM?
THAT'S SHINOMIYA-KUN. HE'S A FIRST-YEAR... WE'RE BOTH ON THE HEALTH COMMITTEE...
Barely know him though...
Hmm...
HE'S SO HARSH FOR SUCH A BISHONEN.
WELL, YEAH... BUT HEY, I THINK THAT'S A GOOD THING.
THE SNOOTIER A BISHO-NEN IS, THE YUMMIER HE IS, DON'TCHA THINK?
ウフフ…
HEHEHE
OOOH! YOU'RE RIGHT!!
THE COLDER HE ACTS, THE HOTTER HE GETS!!
OH YEAHHH!
HUH ...?
SERI-NUMA-SAN...
WHAT HAPPENED TO YOUR FACE?
MU-TSU-MI-SEN-PAI!
I KINDA HAD AN ACCIDENT DURING P.E....
I SEE. ARE YOU ALL RIGHT?
Silly me!
OH YEAH, TOTALLY! THANKS FOR ASKING!!

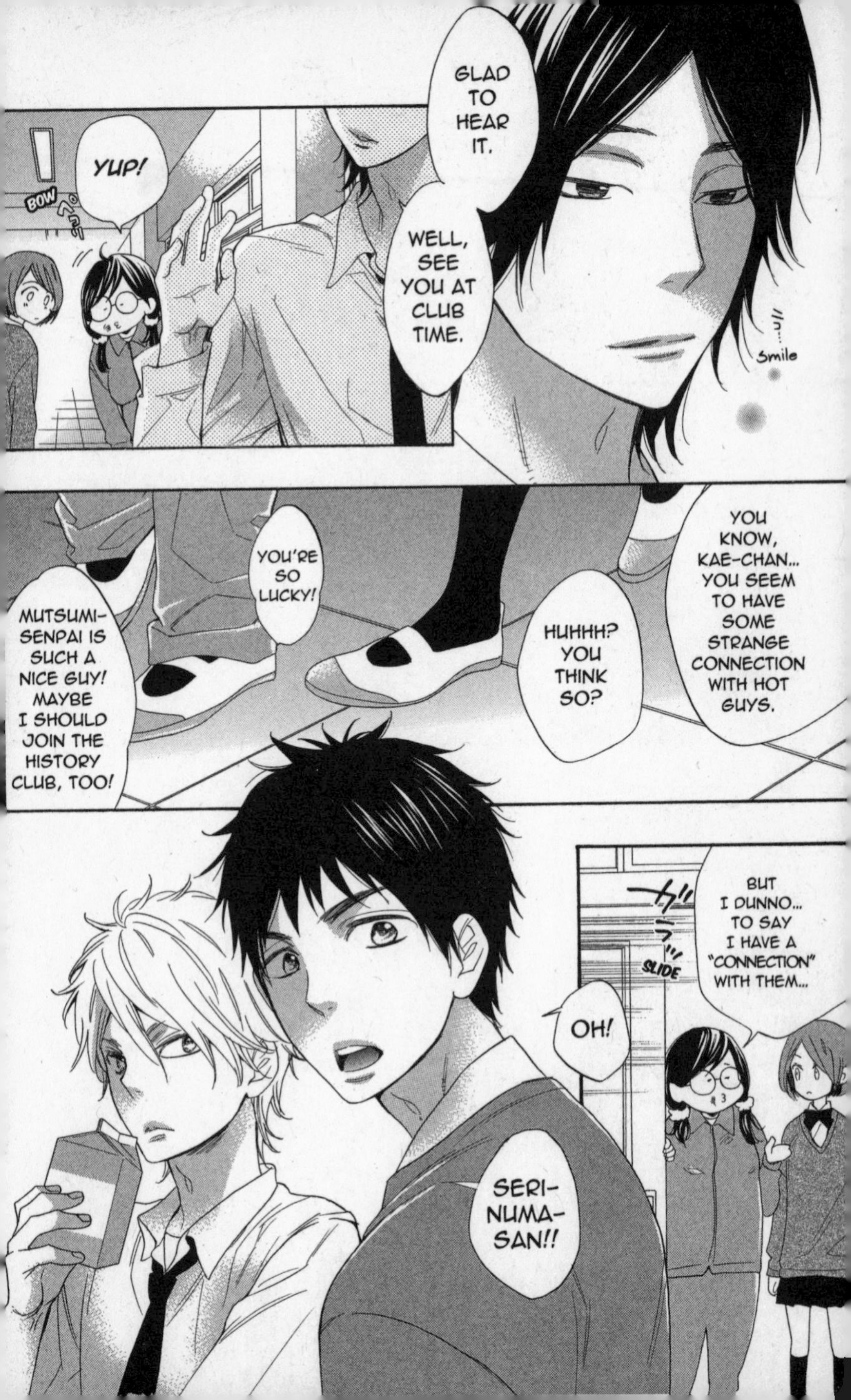
GLAD TO HEAR IT.
WELL, SEE YOU AT CLUB TIME.
Smile
YUP!
BOW
YOU KNOW, KAE-CHAN... YOU SEEM TO HAVE SOME STRANGE CONNECTION WITH HOT GUYS.
HUHHH? YOU THINK SO?
YOU'RE SO LUCKY!
MUTSUMI-SENPAI IS SUCH A NICE GUY! MAYBE I SHOULD JOIN THE HISTORY CLUB, TOO!
BUT I DUNNO... TO SAY I HAVE A "CONNECTION" WITH THEM...
SLIDE
OH!
SERI-NUMA-SAN!!

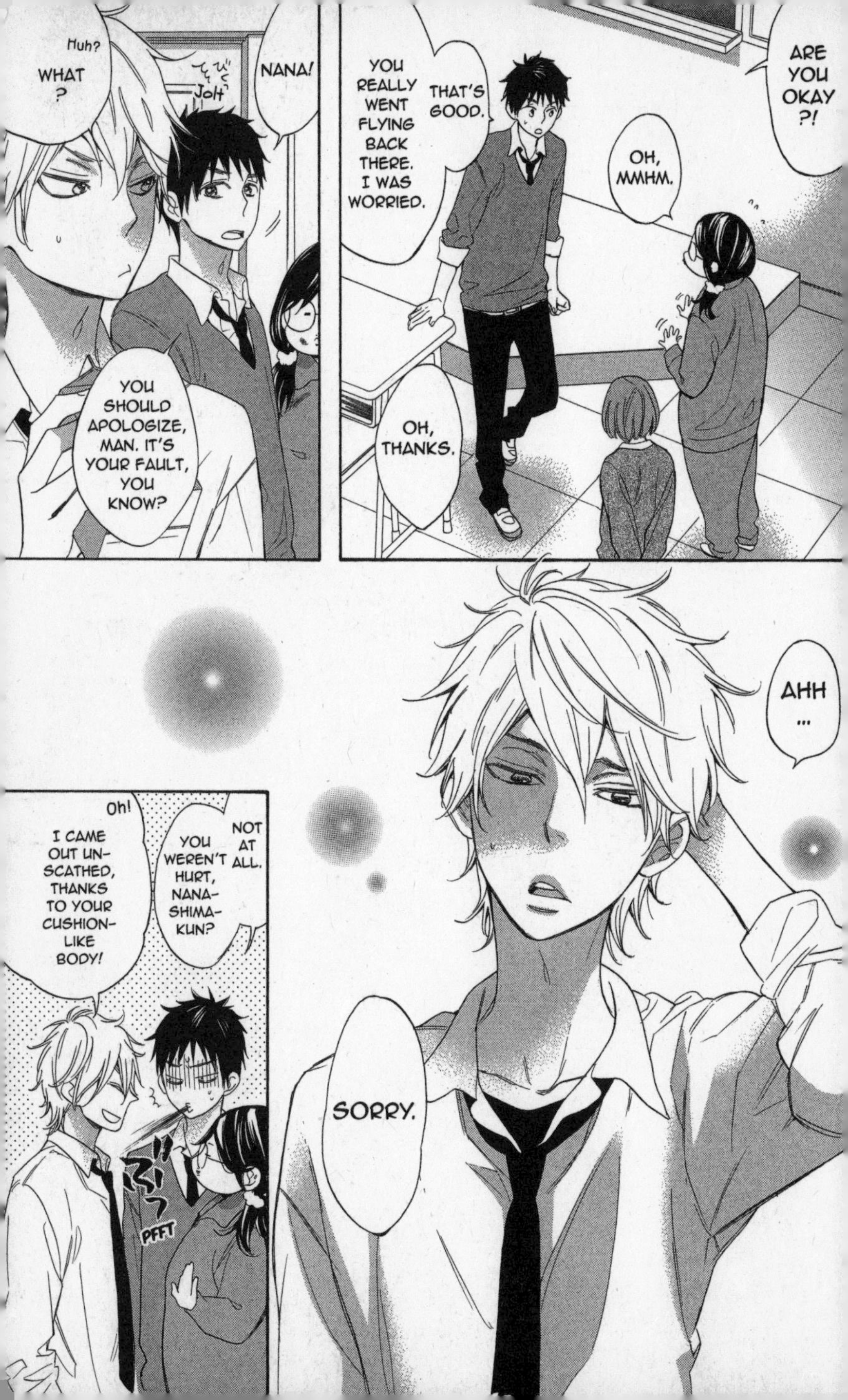
ARE YOU OKAY?!
OH, MMHM.
THAT'S GOOD.
YOU REALLY WENT FLYING BACK THERE. I WAS WORRIED.
OH, THANKS.
NANA!
Jolt
Huh? WHAT?
YOU SHOULD APOLOGIZE, MAN. IT'S YOUR FAULT, YOU KNOW?
AHH ...
SORRY.
NOT AT ALL.
YOU WEREN'T HURT, NANA-SHIMA-KUN?
Oh! I CAME OUT UN-SCATHED, THANKS TO YOUR CUSHION-LIKE BODY!
PFFT

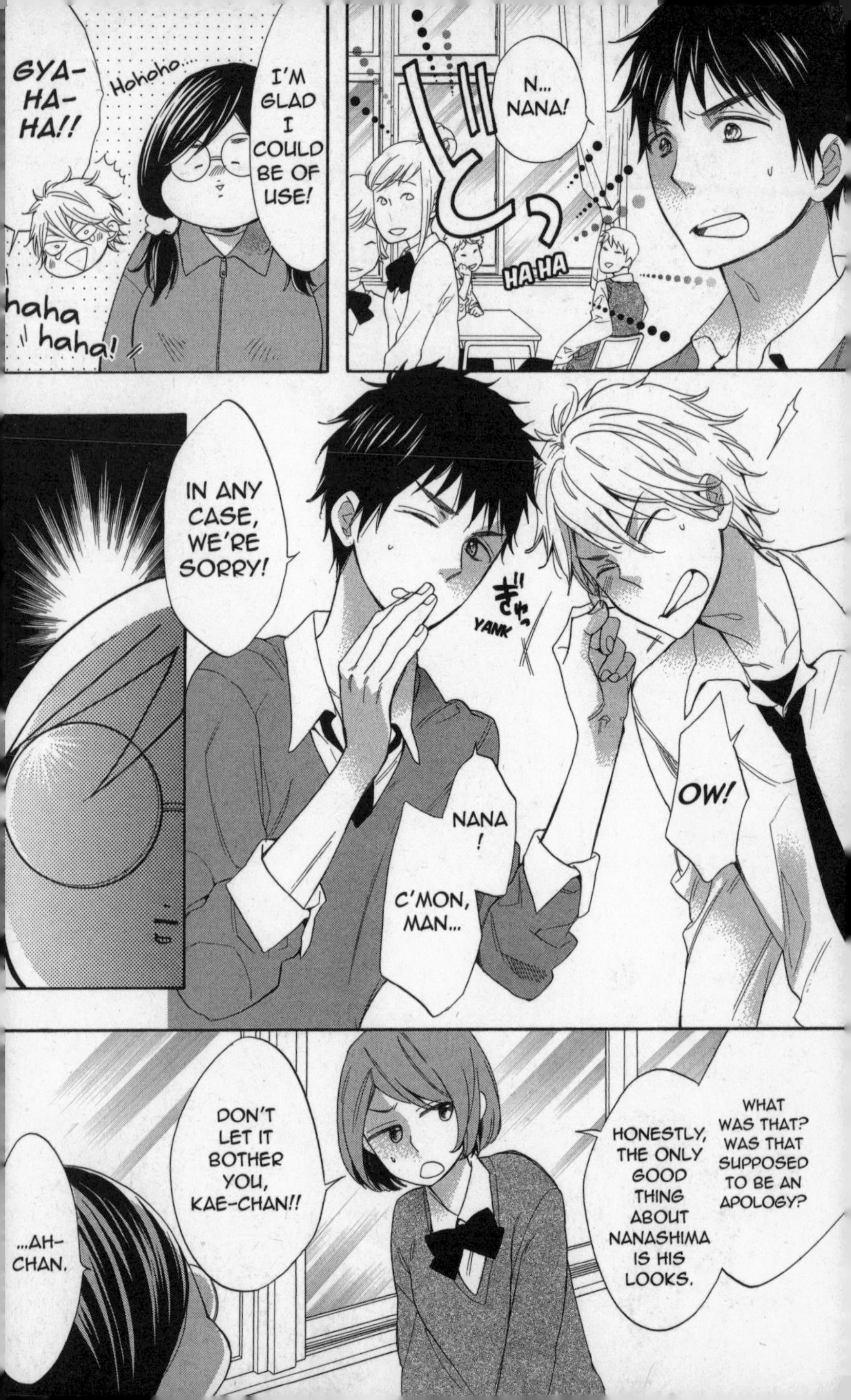
N... NANA!
とっ
HA HA
I'M GLAD I COULD BE OF USE!
Hohoho...
GYA-HA-HA!!
haha haha!
ぎゅっ
YANK
OW!
NANA!
C'MON, MAN...
IN ANY CASE, WE'RE SORRY!
WHAT WAS THAT? WAS THAT SUPPOSED TO BE AN APOLOGY?
HONESTLY, THE ONLY GOOD THING ABOUT NANASHIMA IS HIS LOOKS.
DON'T LET IT BOTHER YOU, KAE-CHAN!!
...AH-CHAN.

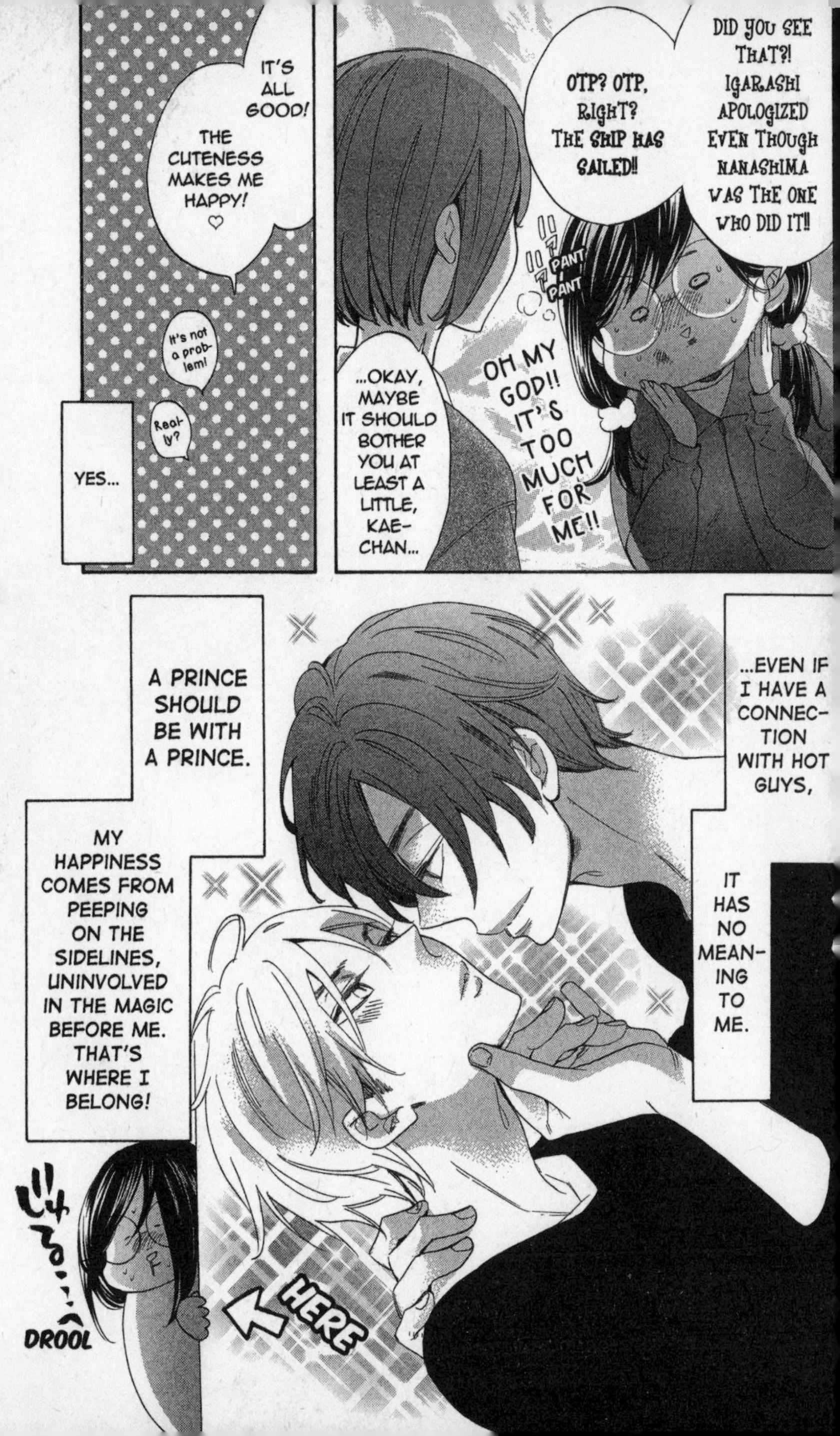
DID YOU SEE THAT?! IGARASHI APOLOGIZED EVEN THOUGH NANASHIMA WAS THE ONE WHO DID IT!!
OTP? OTP, RIGHT? THE SHIP HAS SAILED!!
PANT PANT
OH MY GOD!! IT'S TOO MUCH FOR ME!!
...OKAY, MAYBE IT SHOULD BOTHER YOU AT LEAST A LITTLE, KAE-CHAN...
IT'S ALL GOOD! THE CUTENESS MAKES ME HAPPY! ♡
It's not a problem!
Really?
YES...
...EVEN IF I HAVE A CONNECTION WITH HOT GUYS,
IT HAS NO MEANING TO ME.
A PRINCE SHOULD BE WITH A PRINCE.
MY HAPPINESS COMES FROM PEEPING ON THE SIDELINES, UNINVOLVED IN THE MAGIC BEFORE ME. THAT'S WHERE I BELONG!
HERE
DROOL

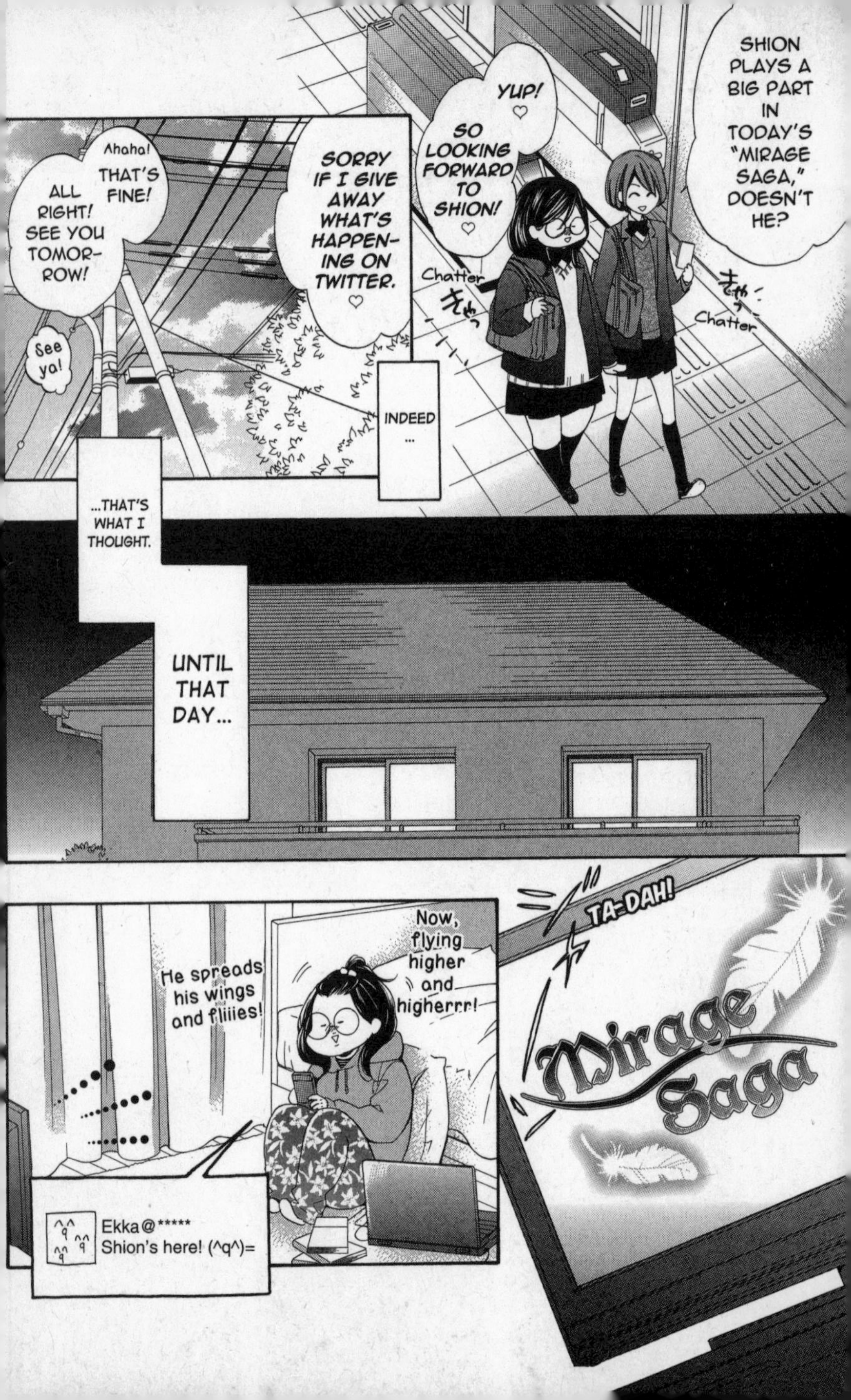
SHION PLAYS A BIG PART IN TODAY'S "MIRAGE SAGA," DOESN'T HE?
Chatter
YUP! ♡
SO LOOKING FORWARD TO SHION! ♡
Chatter
SORRY IF I GIVE AWAY WHAT'S HAPPEN-ING ON TWITTER. ♡
Ahaha!
THAT'S FINE!
ALL RIGHT! SEE YOU TOMOR-ROW!
See ya!
INDEED ...
...THAT'S WHAT I THOUGHT.
UNTIL THAT DAY...
TA-DAH!
Mirage Saga
Now, flying higher and higherrr!
He spreads his wings and fliiies!
Ekka@*****
Shion's here! (^q^)=

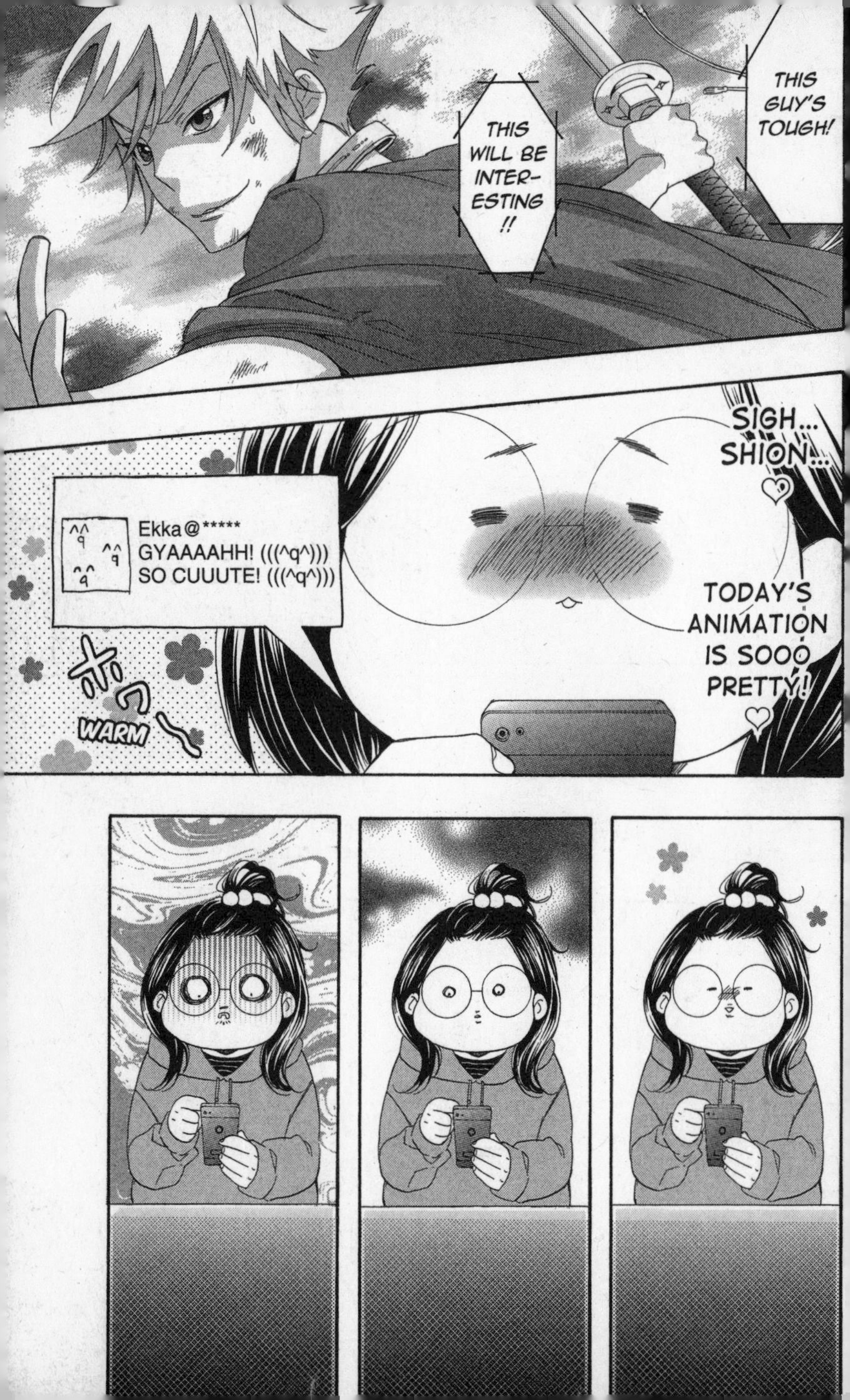
THIS GUY'S TOUGH!
THIS WILL BE INTERESTING!!
SIGH... SHION...
TODAY'S ANIMATION IS SOOO PRETTY!
Ekka@*****
GYAAAAHH! (((^q^)))
SO CUUUTE! (((^q^)))
WARM

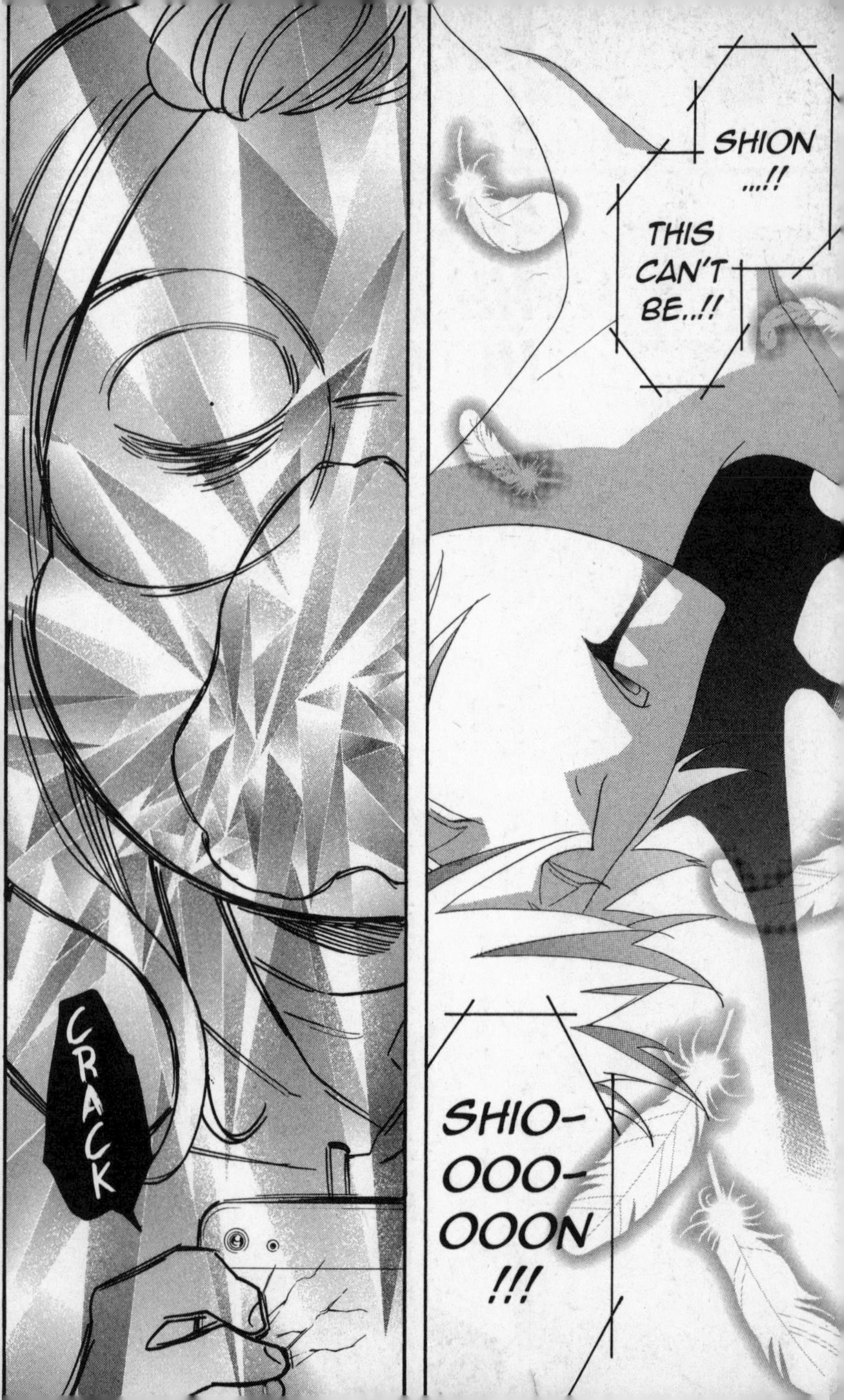
SHION ...!!
THIS CAN'T BE..!!
SHIO-OOO-OOON !!!
CRACK

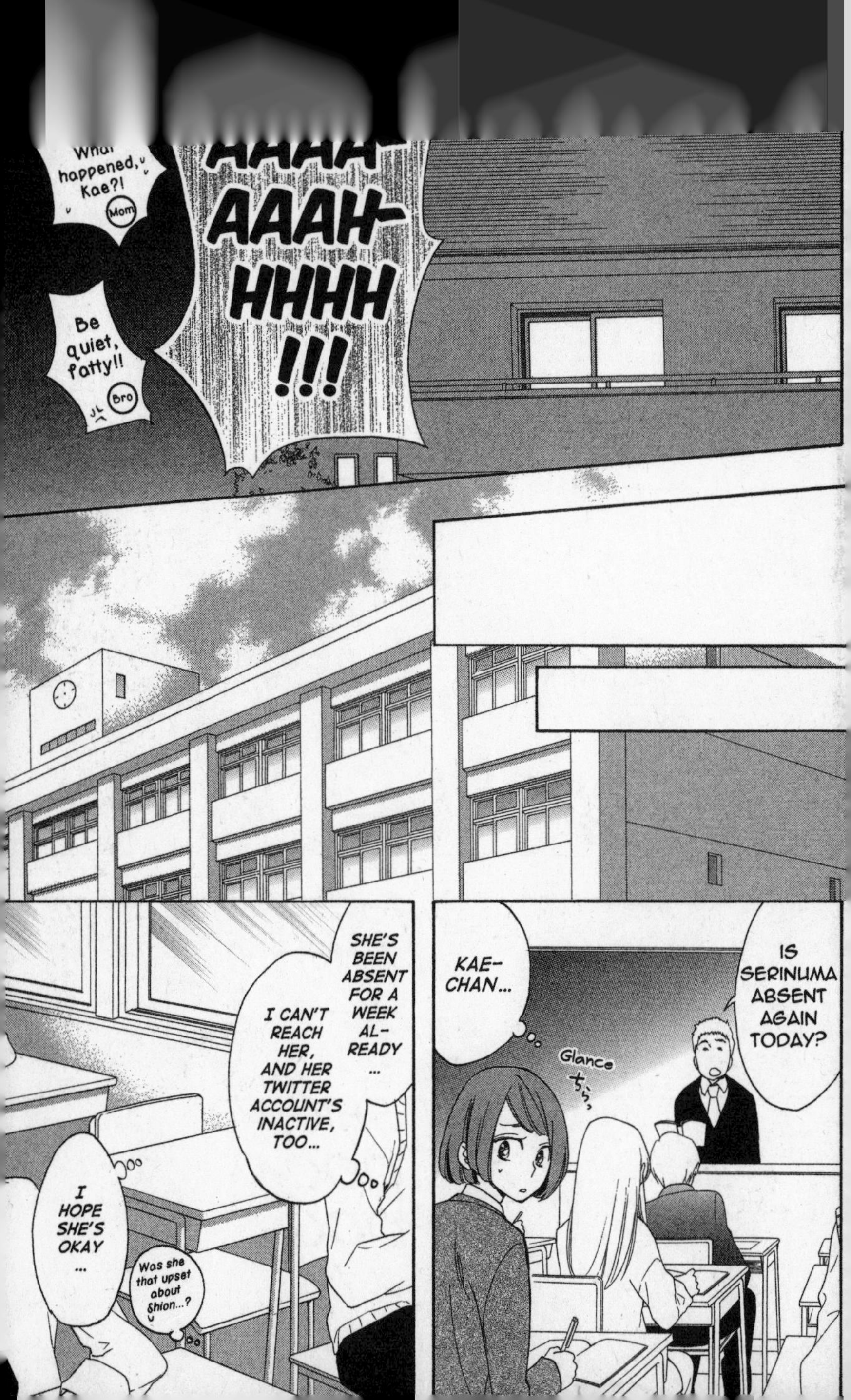
AAAH AAAH-HHHH!!!
What happened, Kae?!
Mom
Be quiet, fatty!!
Bro
IS SERINUMA ABSENT AGAIN TODAY?
KAE-CHAN...
Glance
SHE'S BEEN ABSENT FOR A WEEK AL-READY...
I CAN'T REACH HER, AND HER TWITTER ACCOUNT'S INACTIVE, TOO...
I HOPE SHE'S OKAY...
Was she that upset about Shion...?

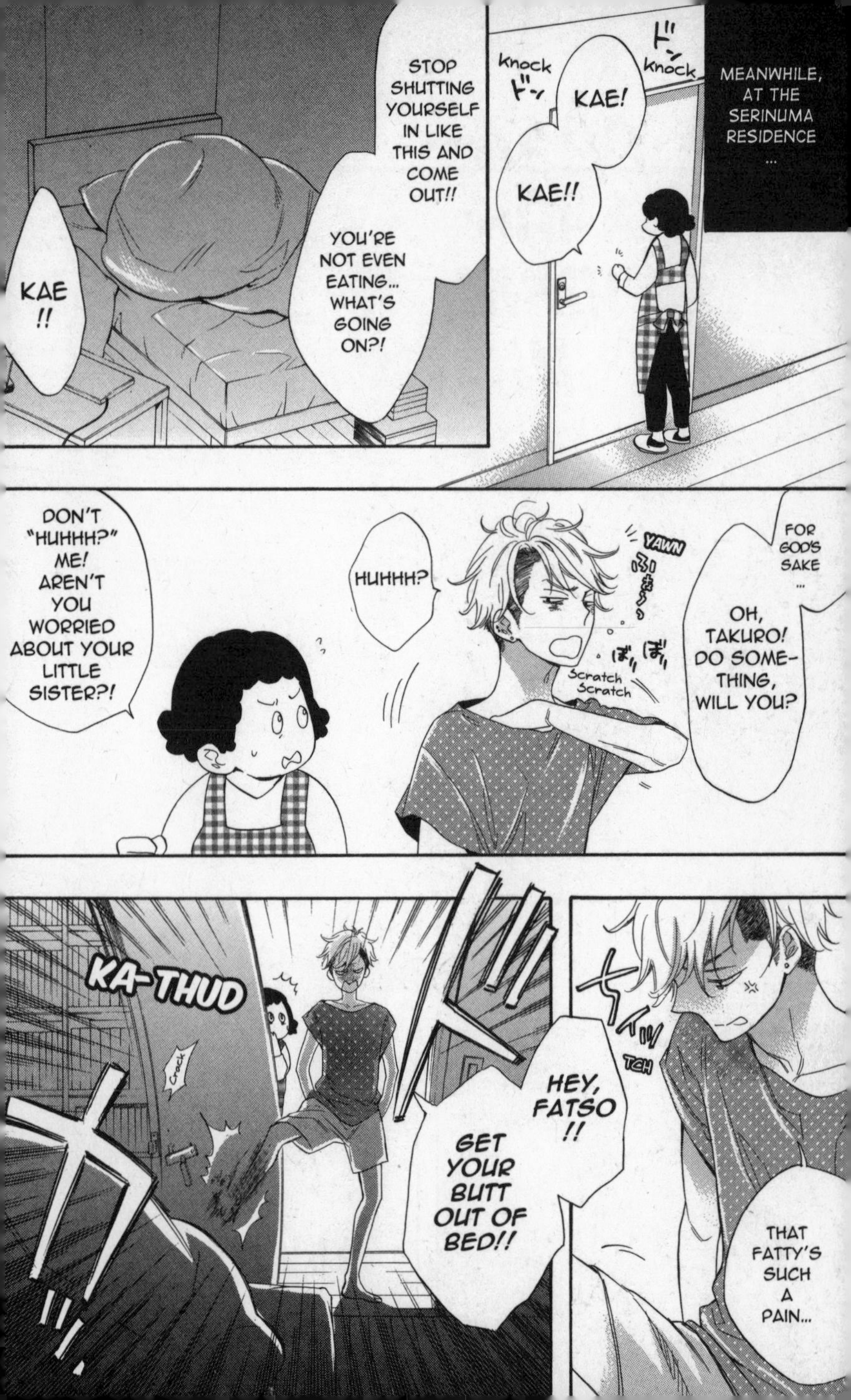
MEANWHILE, AT THE SERINUMA RESIDENCE ...
knock
knock
KAE!
KAE!!
STOP SHUTTING YOURSELF IN LIKE THIS AND COME OUT!!
YOU'RE NOT EVEN EATING... WHAT'S GOING ON?!
KAE !!
FOR GOD'S SAKE ...
OH, TAKURO! DO SOME-THING, WILL YOU?
YAWN
Scratch Scratch
HUHHH?
DON'T "HUHHH?" ME! AREN'T YOU WORRIED ABOUT YOUR LITTLE SISTER?!
TCH
THAT FATTY'S SUCH A PAIN...
HEY, FATSO !!
GET YOUR BUTT OUT OF BED!!
KA-THUD
Crack

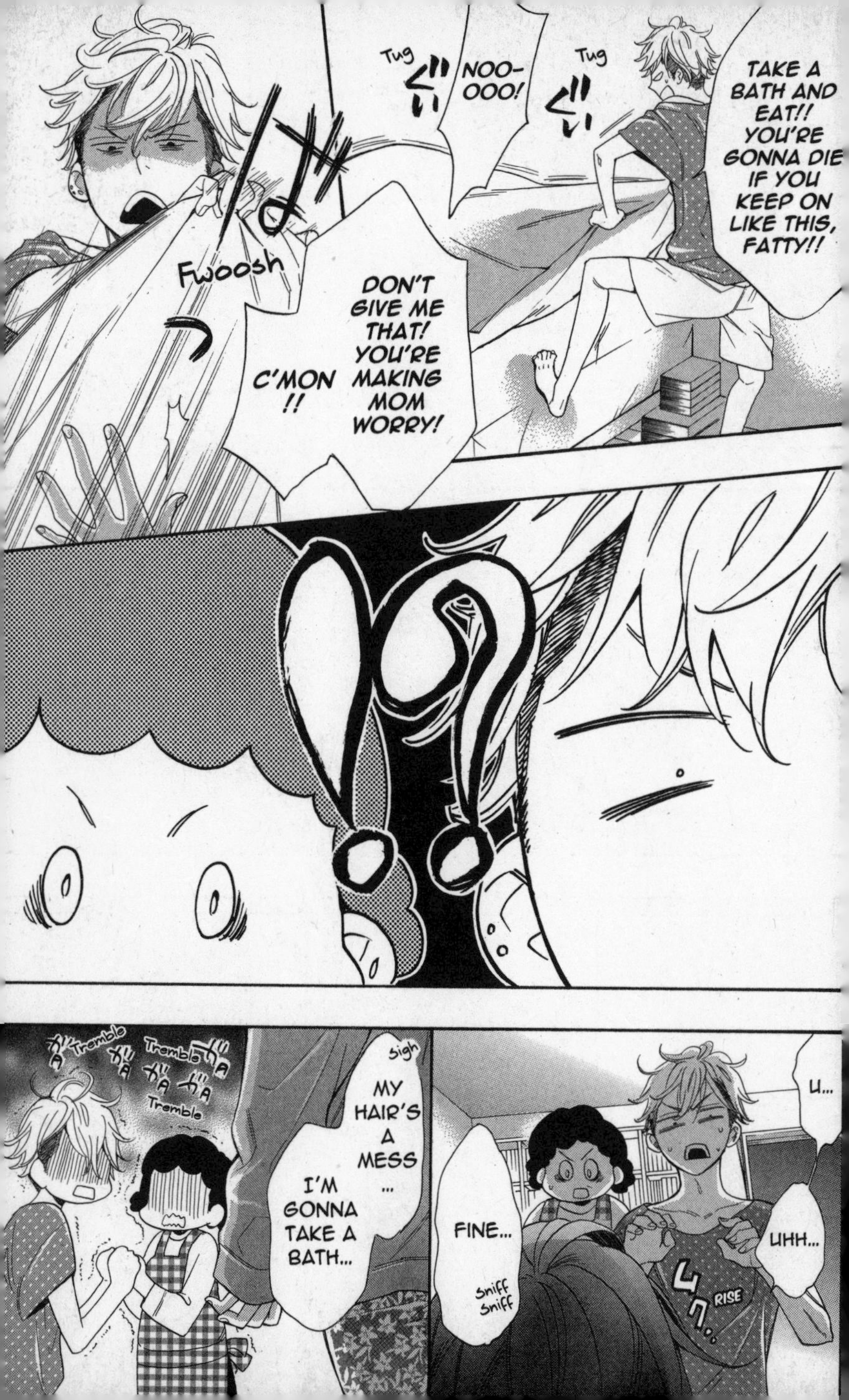
TAKE A BATH AND EAT!! YOU'RE GONNA DIE IF YOU KEEP ON LIKE THIS, FATTY!!
Tug
NOO-OOO!
Tug
DON'T GIVE ME THAT! YOU'RE MAKING MOM WORRY!
C'MON !!
Fwoosh
U...
UHH...
RISE
FINE...
Sniff Sniff
sigh
MY HAIR'S A MESS ...
I'M GONNA TAKE A BATH...
Tremble
Tremble
Tremble

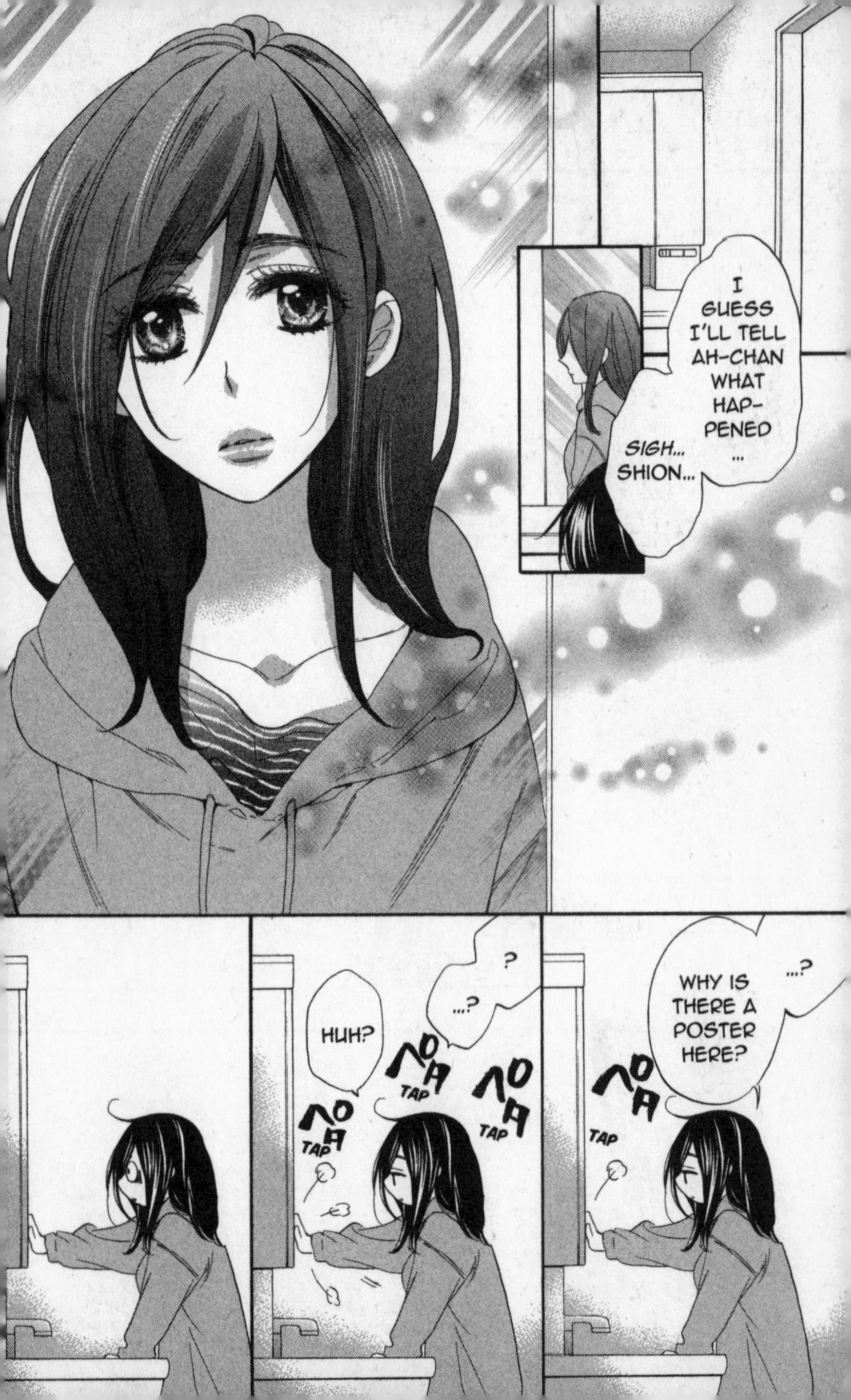

I GUESS I'LL TELL AH-CHAN WHAT HAPPENED ...
SIGH... SHION...
...?
WHY IS THERE A POSTER HERE?
TAP
?
...?
TAP
HUH?
TAP
TAP

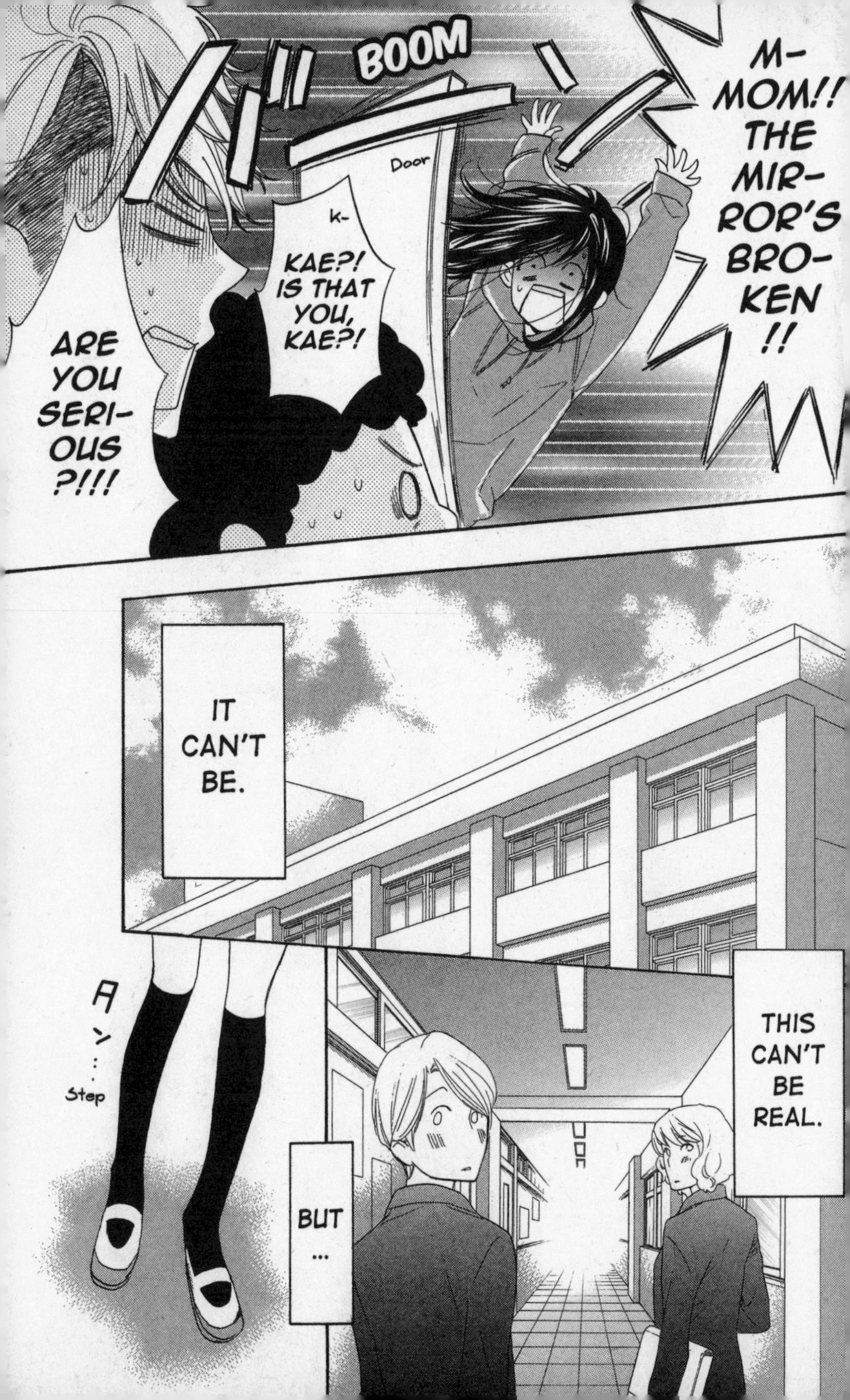
M-MOM!! THE MIRROR'S BROKEN!!
BOOM
Door
k-
KAE?! IS THAT YOU, KAE?!
ARE YOU SERIOUS?!!!
IT CAN'T BE.
THIS CAN'T BE REAL.
BUT...
Step

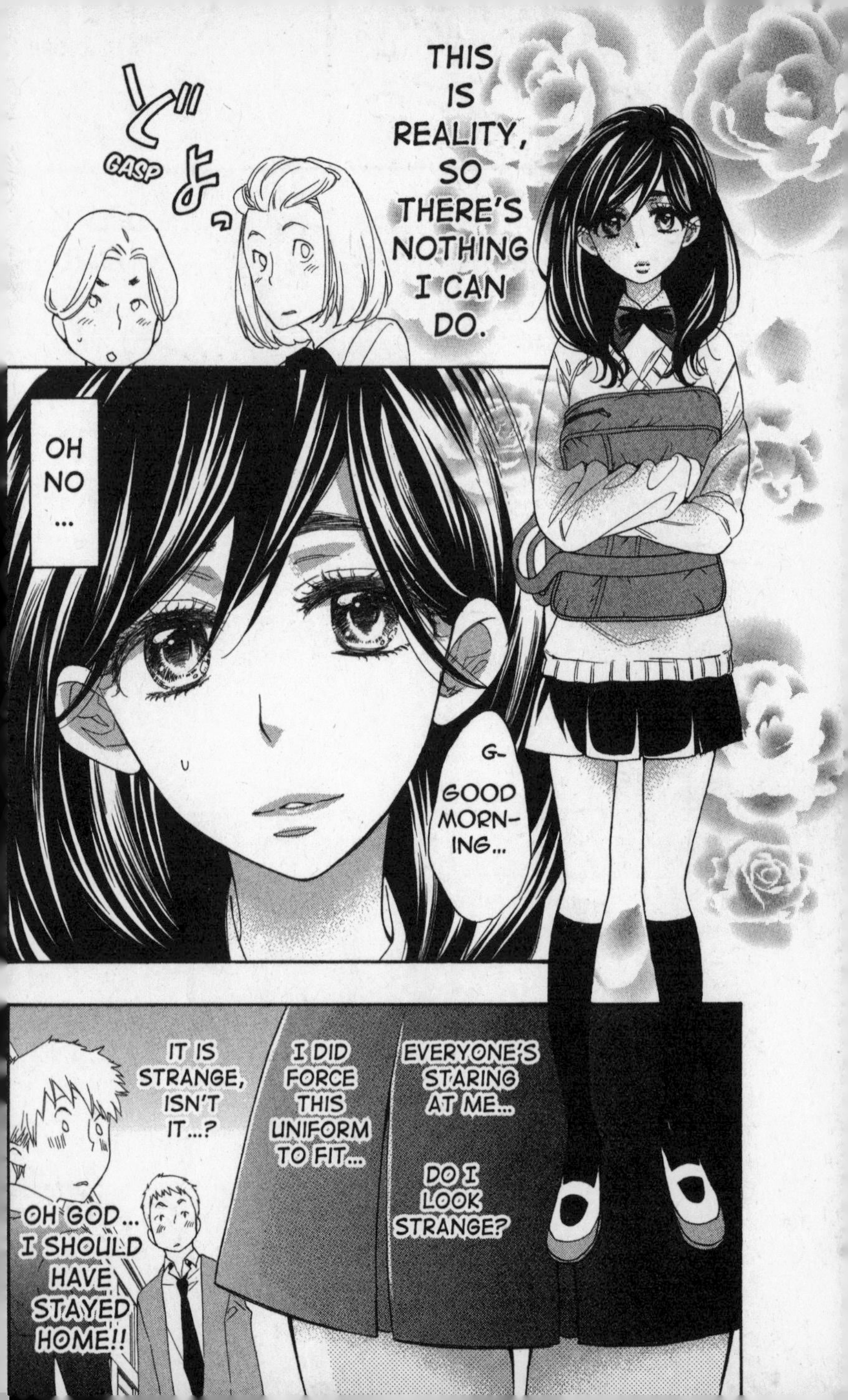

THIS IS REALITY, SO THERE'S NOTHING I CAN DO.
どよっ
GASP
OH NO ...
G- GOOD MORN- ING...
EVERYONE'S STARING AT ME...
DO I LOOK STRANGE?
I DID FORCE THIS UNIFORM TO FIT...
IT IS STRANGE, ISN'T IT...?
OH GOD... I SHOULD HAVE STAYED HOME!!

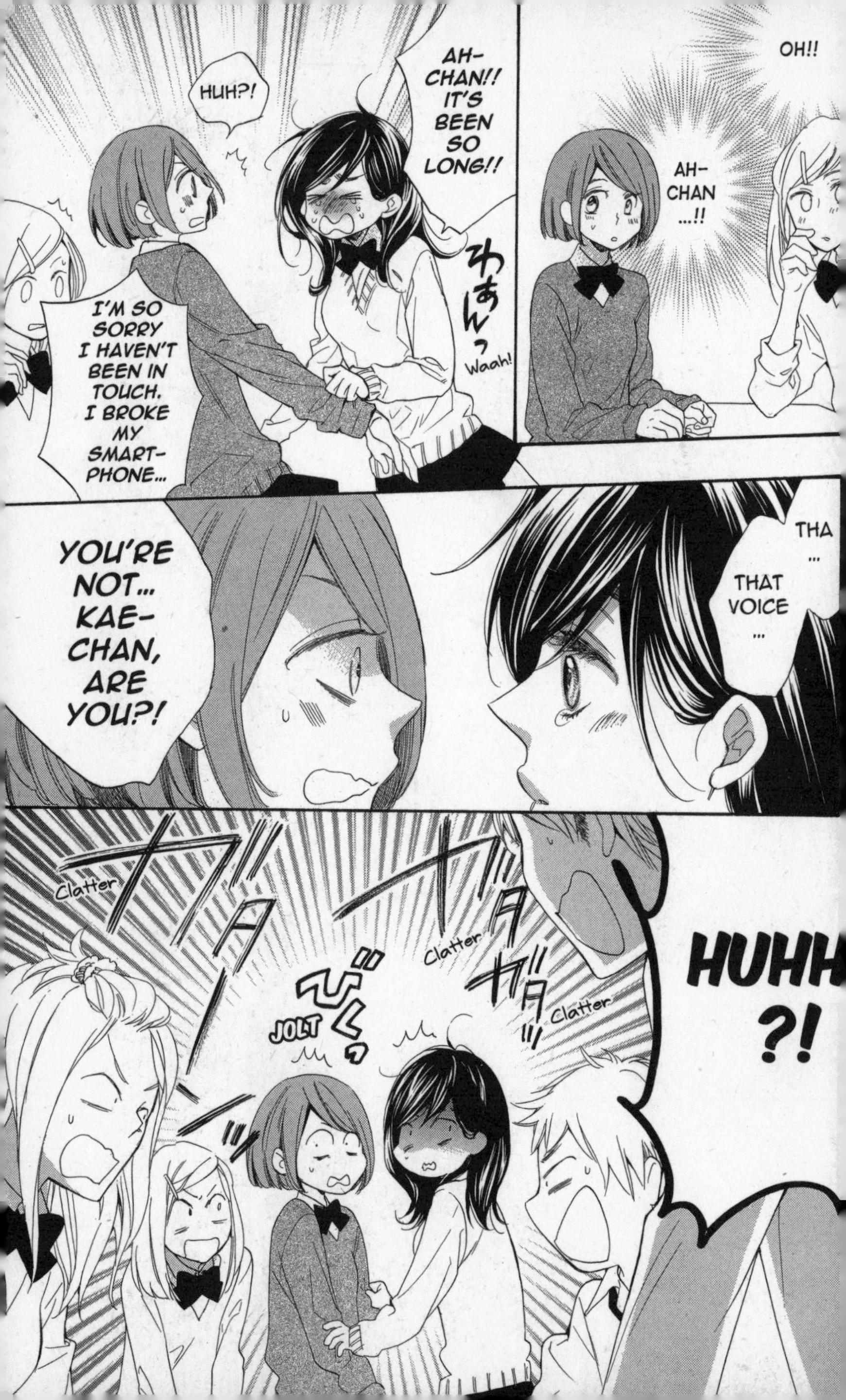
OH!!
AH-CHAN ...!!
AH-CHAN!! IT'S BEEN SO LONG!!
わあんっ
Waah!
HUH?!
I'M SO SORRY I HAVEN'T BEEN IN TOUCH. I BROKE MY SMARTPHONE...
THA ... THAT VOICE ...
YOU'RE NOT... KAE-CHAN, ARE YOU?!
HUHH ?!
Clatter
Clatter
Clatter
びくっ
JOLT

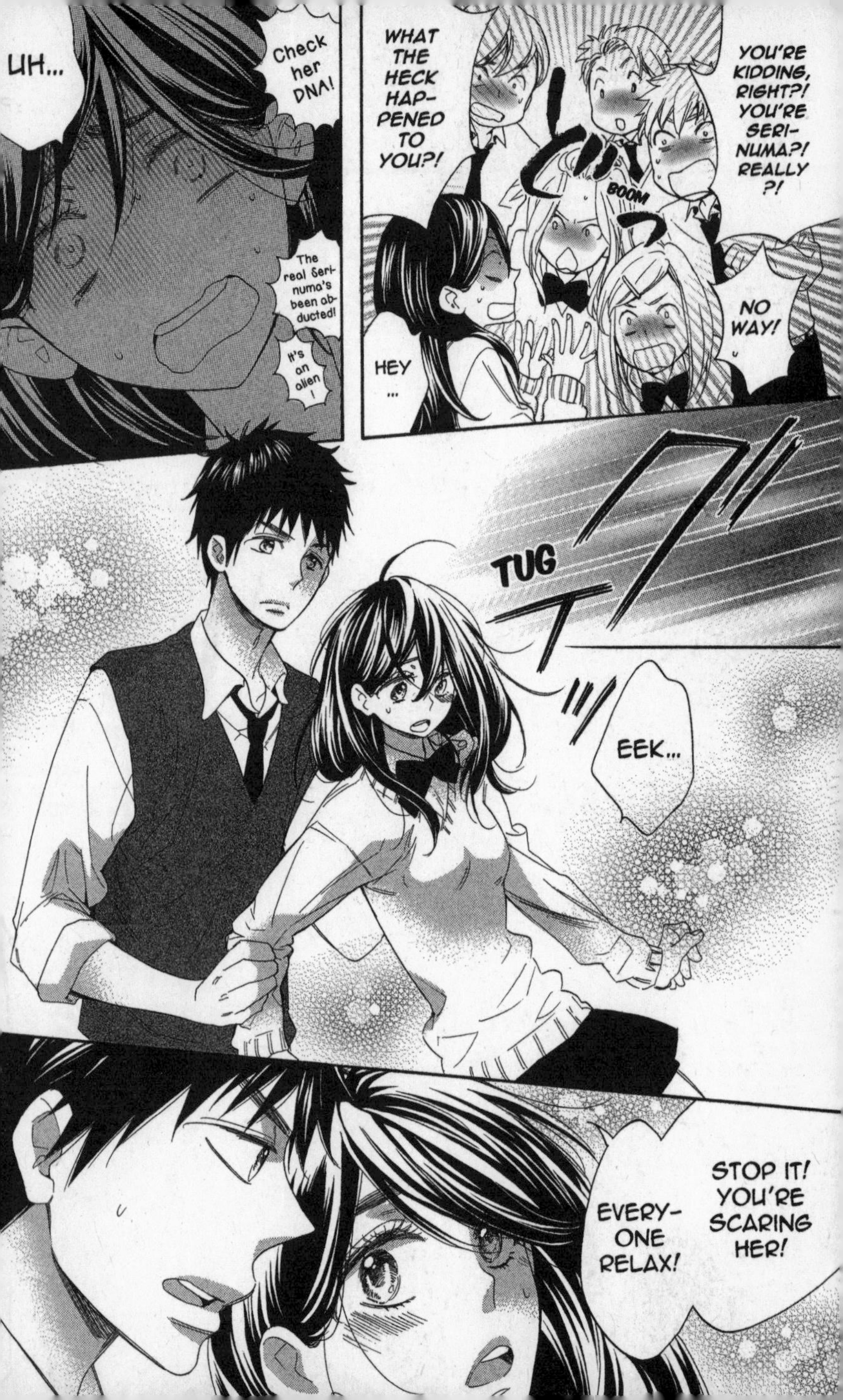
YOU'RE KIDDING, RIGHT?! YOU'RE SERI-NUMA?! REALLY?!
WHAT THE HECK HAP-PENED TO YOU?!
BOOM
NO WAY!
HEY...
Check her DNA!
UH...
The real Seri-numa's been ab-ducted!
It's an alien!
TUG
EEK...
STOP IT! YOU'RE SCARING HER!
EVERY-ONE RELAX!

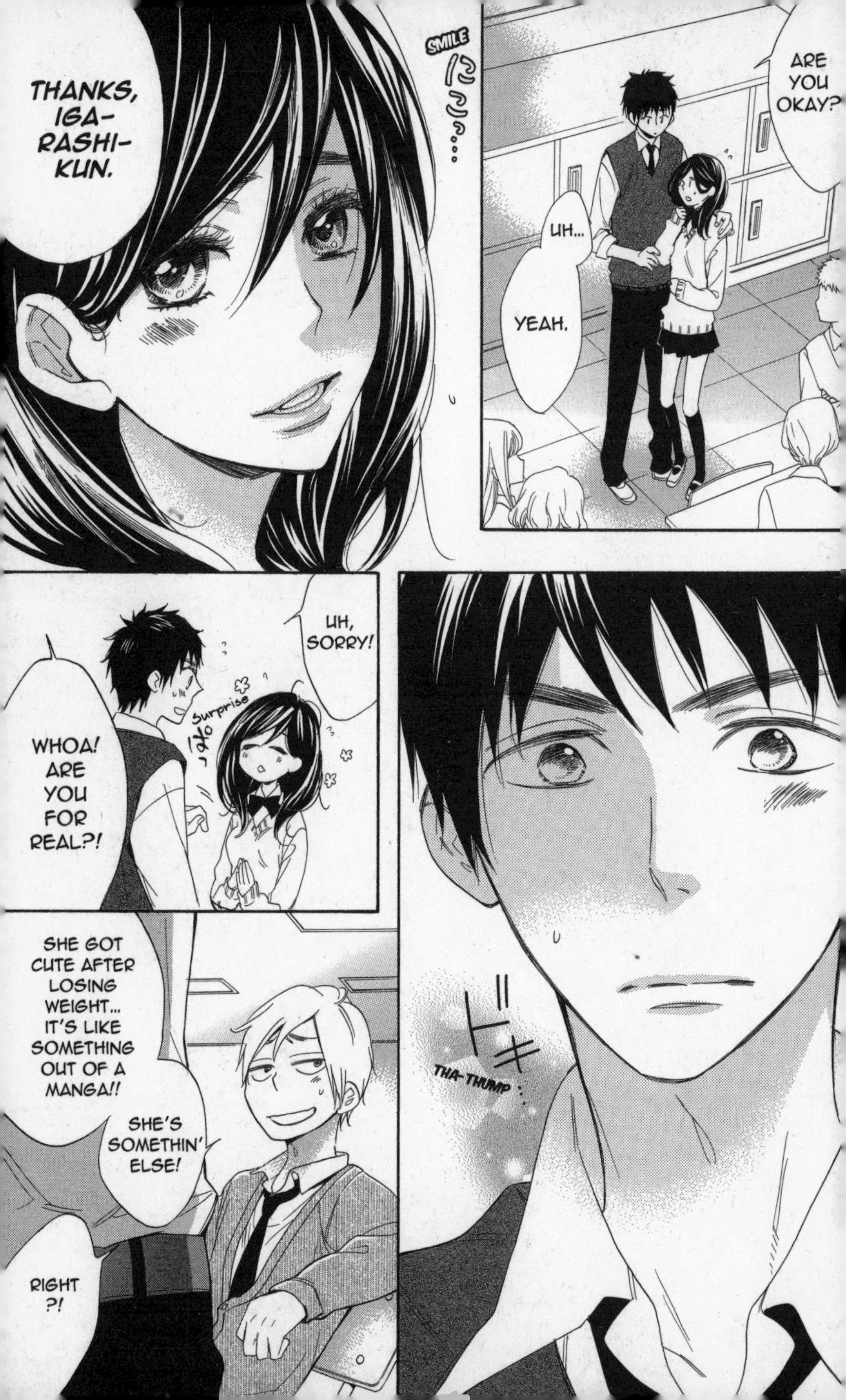

ARE YOU OKAY?
UH...
YEAH.
SMILE
THANKS, IGA-RASHI-KUN.
THA-THUMP
UH, SORRY!
Surprise
WHOA! ARE YOU FOR REAL?!
SHE GOT CUTE AFTER LOSING WEIGHT... IT'S LIKE SOMETHING OUT OF A MANGA!!
SHE'S SOMETHIN' ELSE!
RIGHT?!

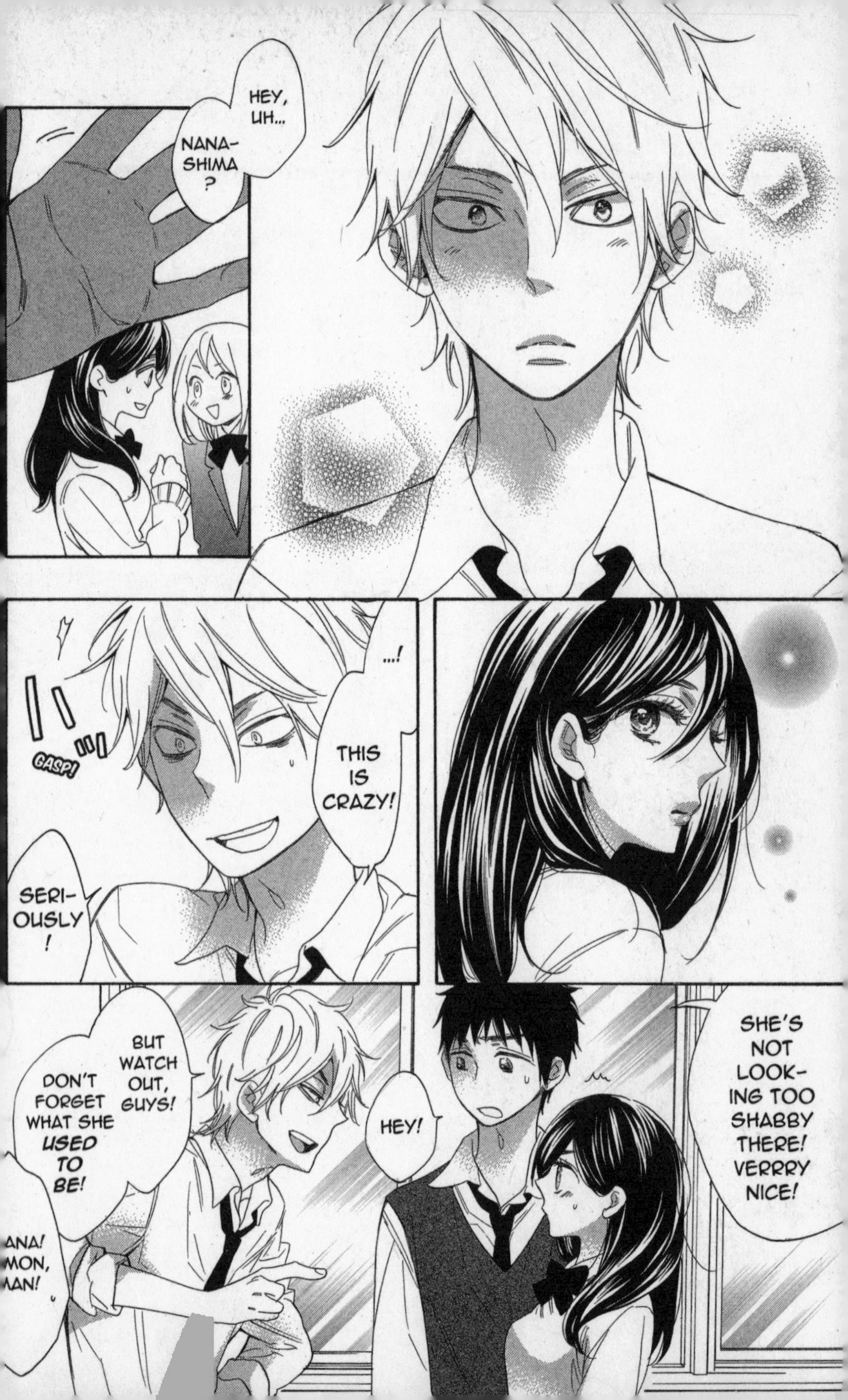
HEY, UH...
NANA-SHIMA?
GASP!
...!
THIS IS CRAZY!
SERI-OUSLY!
SHE'S NOT LOOK-ING TOO SHABBY THERE! VERRRY NICE!
HEY!
BUT WATCH OUT, GUYS!
DON'T FORGET WHAT SHE USED TO BE!
ANA! MON, MAN!

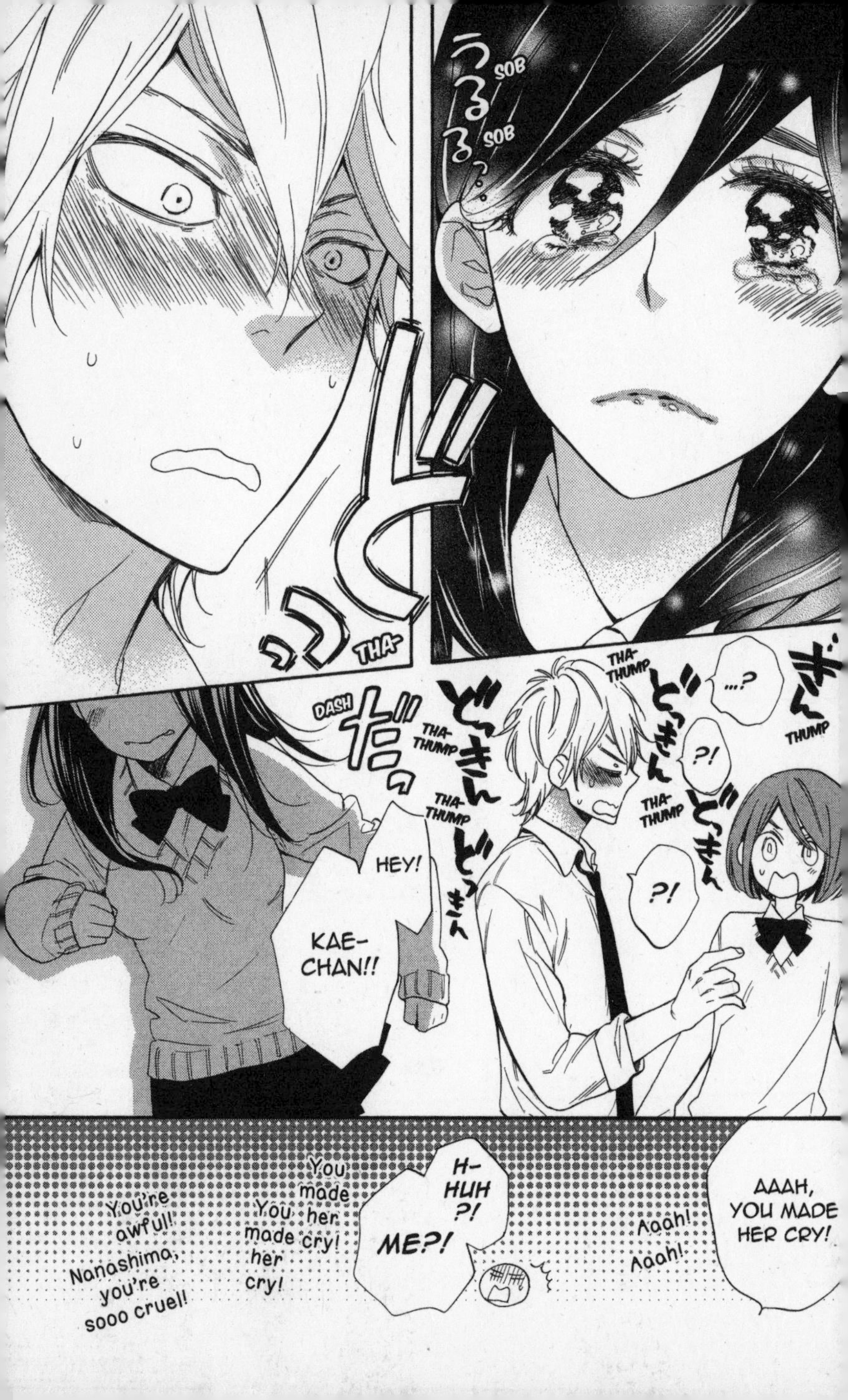

SOB
SOB
THA-
THUMP
...?
THA-THUMP
?!
?!
THA-THUMP
DASH
THA-THUMP
THA-THUMP
HEY!
KAE-CHAN!!
AAAH, YOU MADE HER CRY!
Aaah! Aaah!
H-HUH?!
ME?!
You made her cry!
You made her cry!
You're awful! Nanashima, you're sooo cruel!

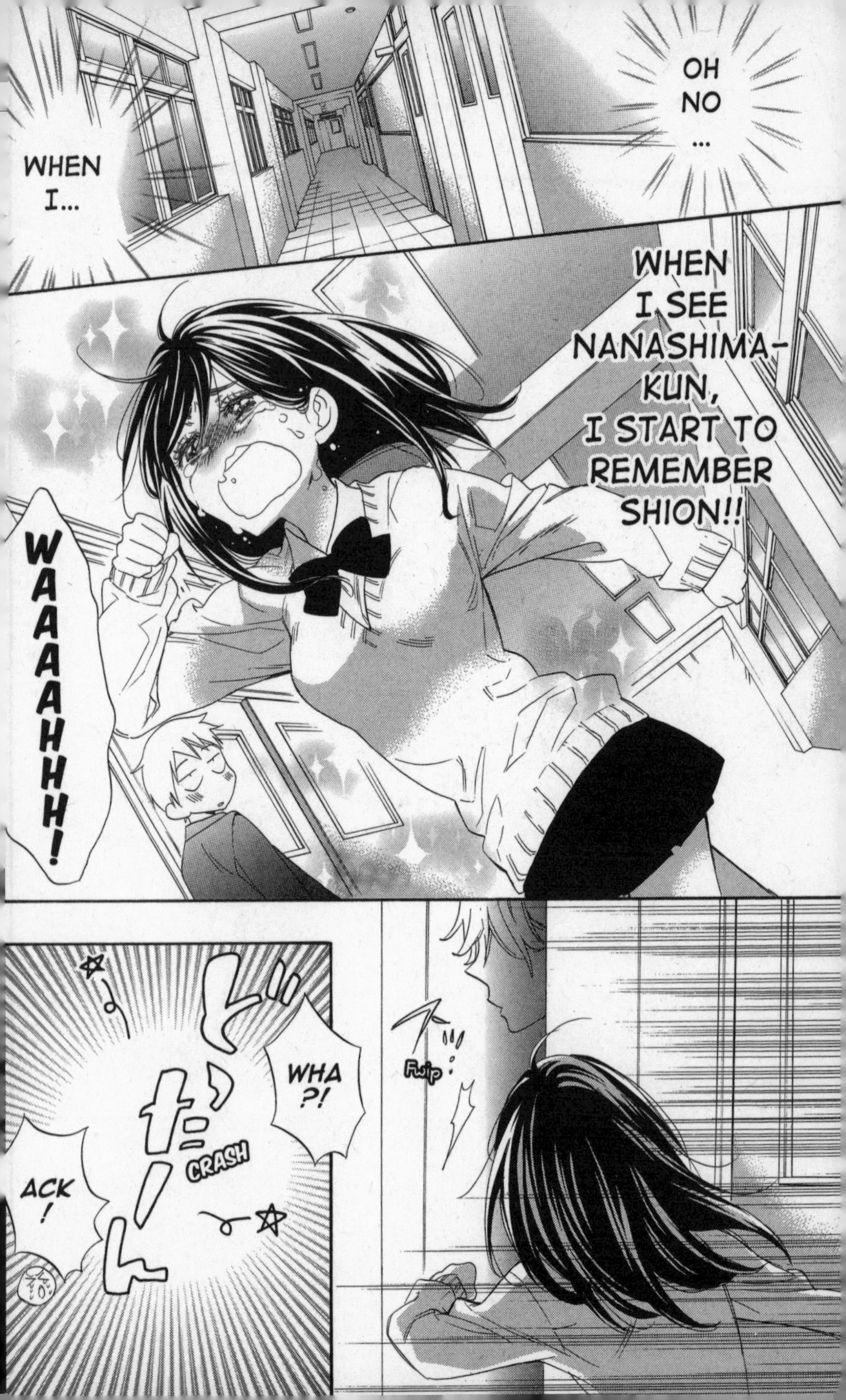

OH NO ...
WHEN I...
WHEN I SEE NANASHIMA-KUN, I START TO REMEMBER SHION!!
WAAAAAHHHH!
Fwip
WHA?!
CRASH
ACK!

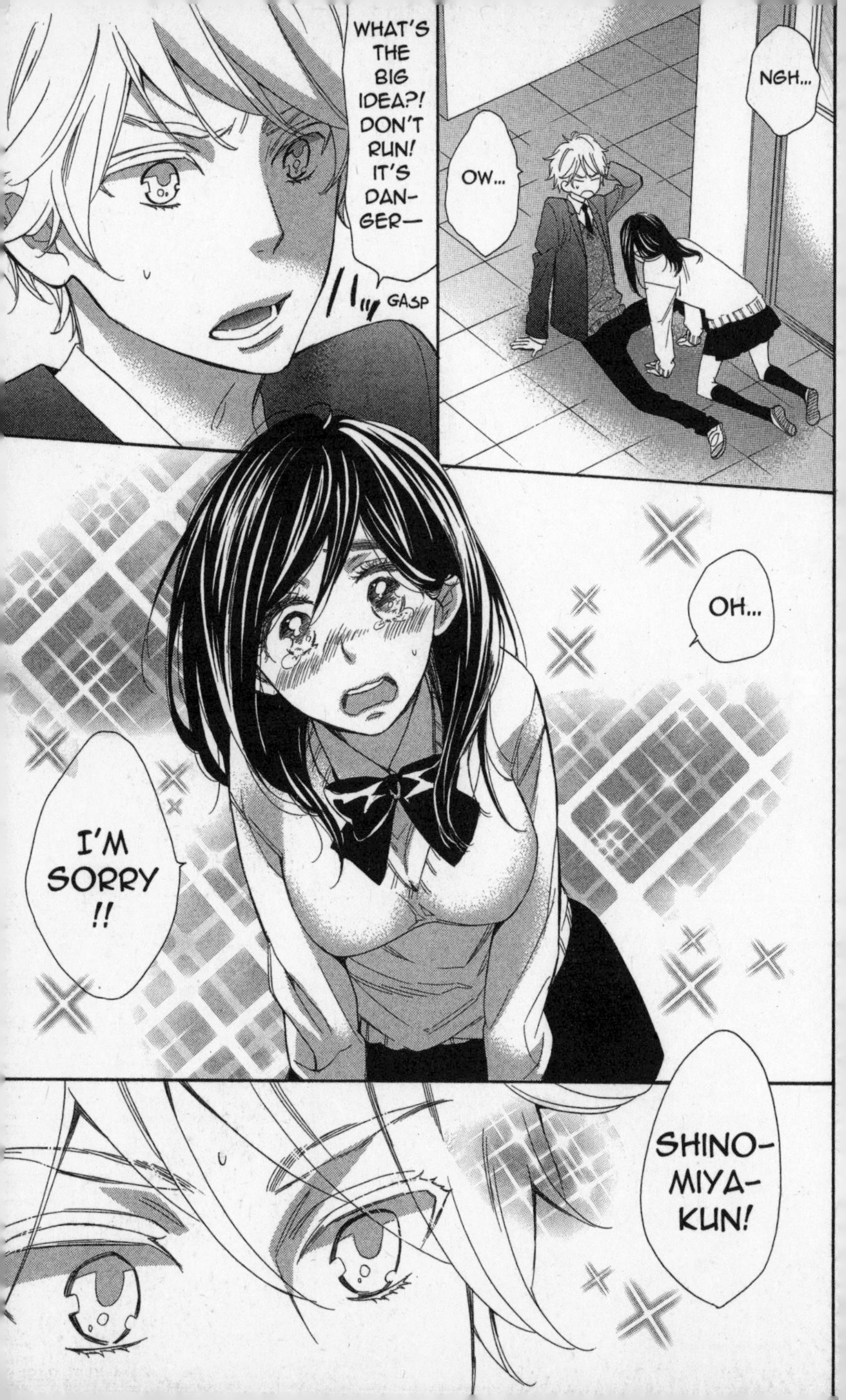
NGH...
OW...
WHAT'S THE BIG IDEA?! DON'T RUN! IT'S DAN-GER—
GASP
OH...
I'M SORRY!!
SHINO-MIYA-KUN!

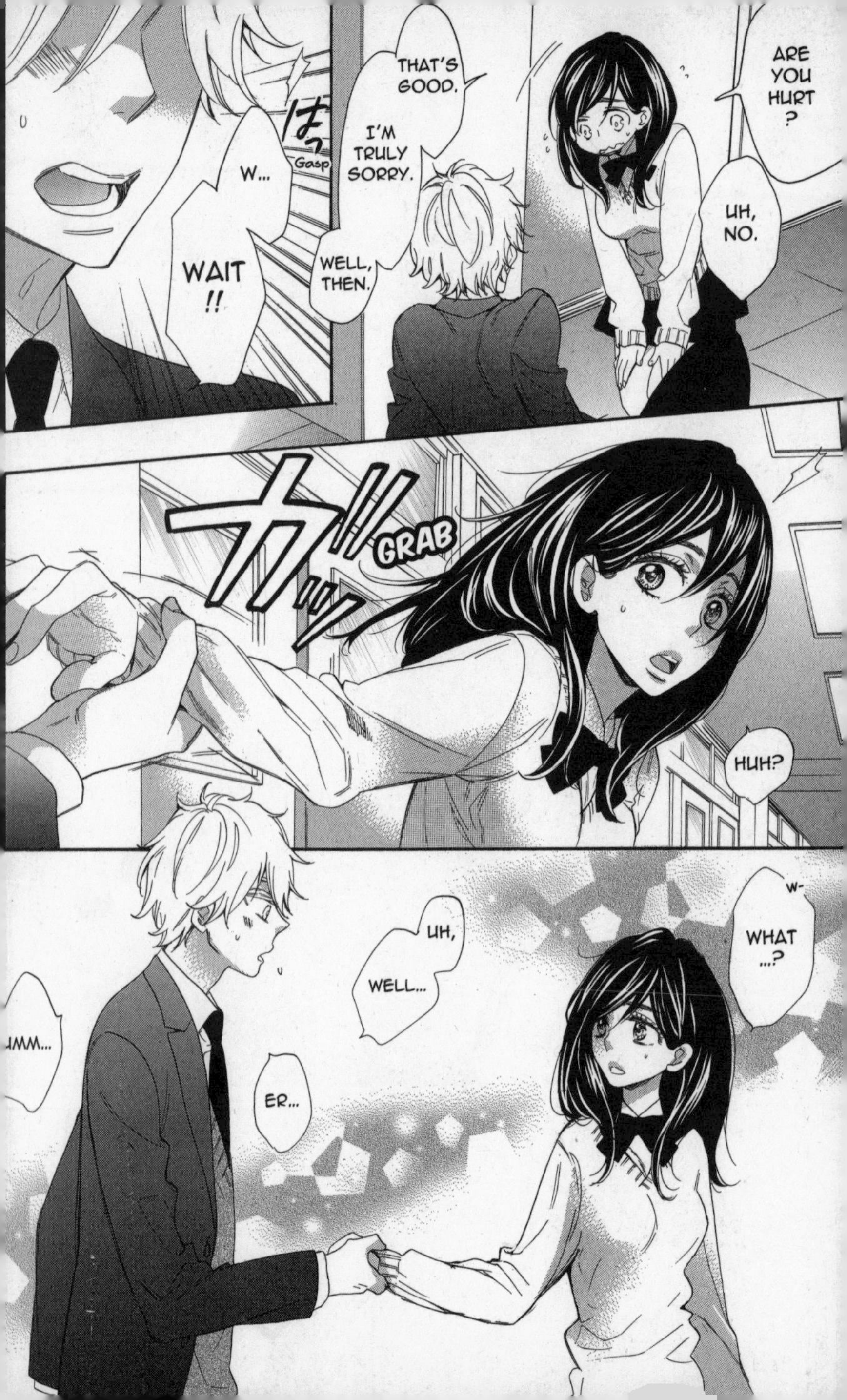

ARE YOU HURT?
UH, NO.
THAT'S GOOD.
I'M TRULY SORRY.
WELL, THEN.
はっ
Gasp
W...
WAIT!!
カッ
GRAB
HUH?
W-WHAT...?
UH, WELL...
ER...
MM...

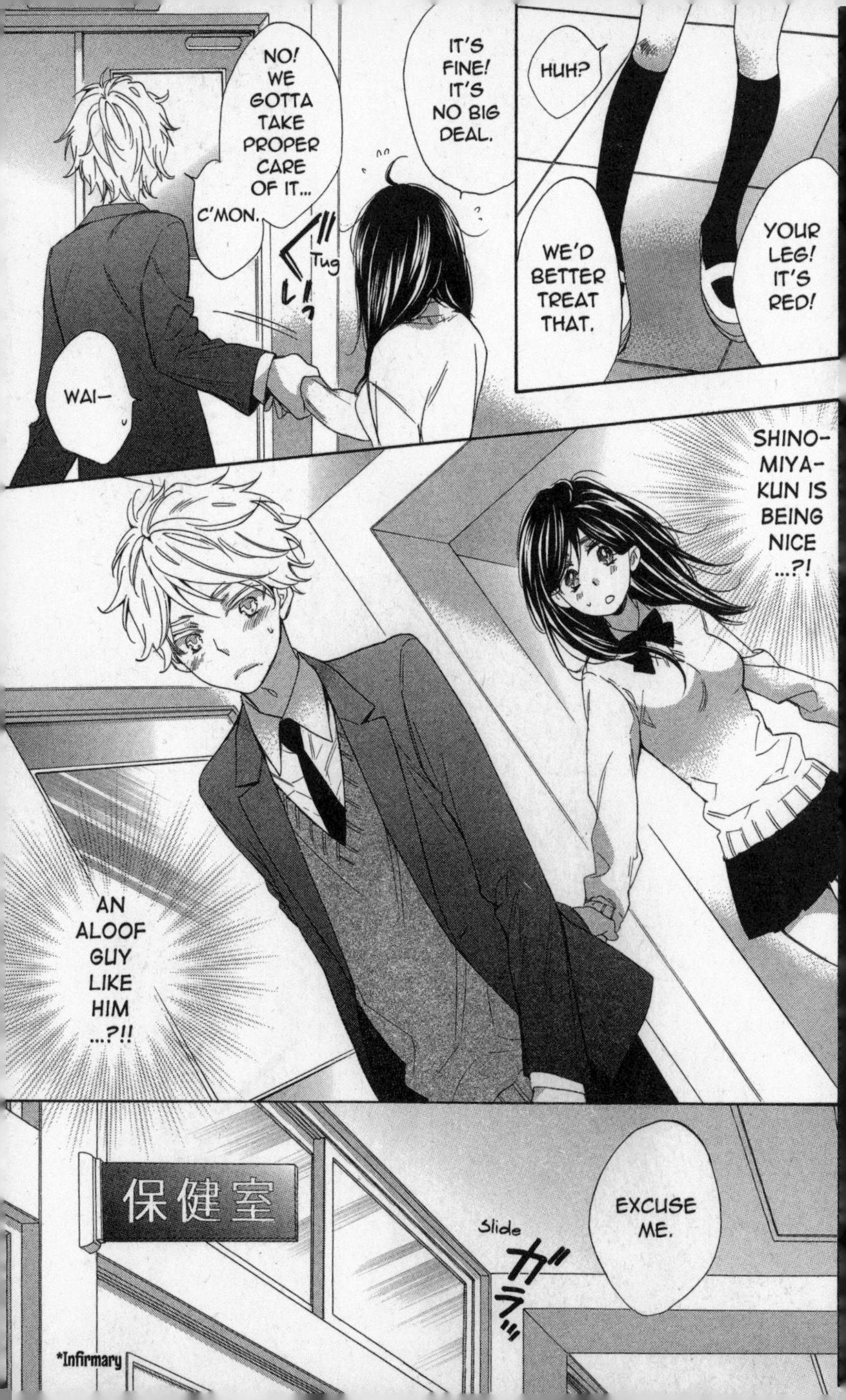
HUH?
YOUR LEG! IT'S RED!
WE'D BETTER TREAT THAT.
IT'S FINE! IT'S NO BIG DEAL.
NO! WE GOTTA TAKE PROPER CARE OF IT...
C'MON.
Tug
WAI—
SHINO-MIYA-KUN IS BEING NICE ...?!
AN ALOOF GUY LIKE HIM ...?!!
EXCUSE ME.
Slide
保健室
*Infirmary

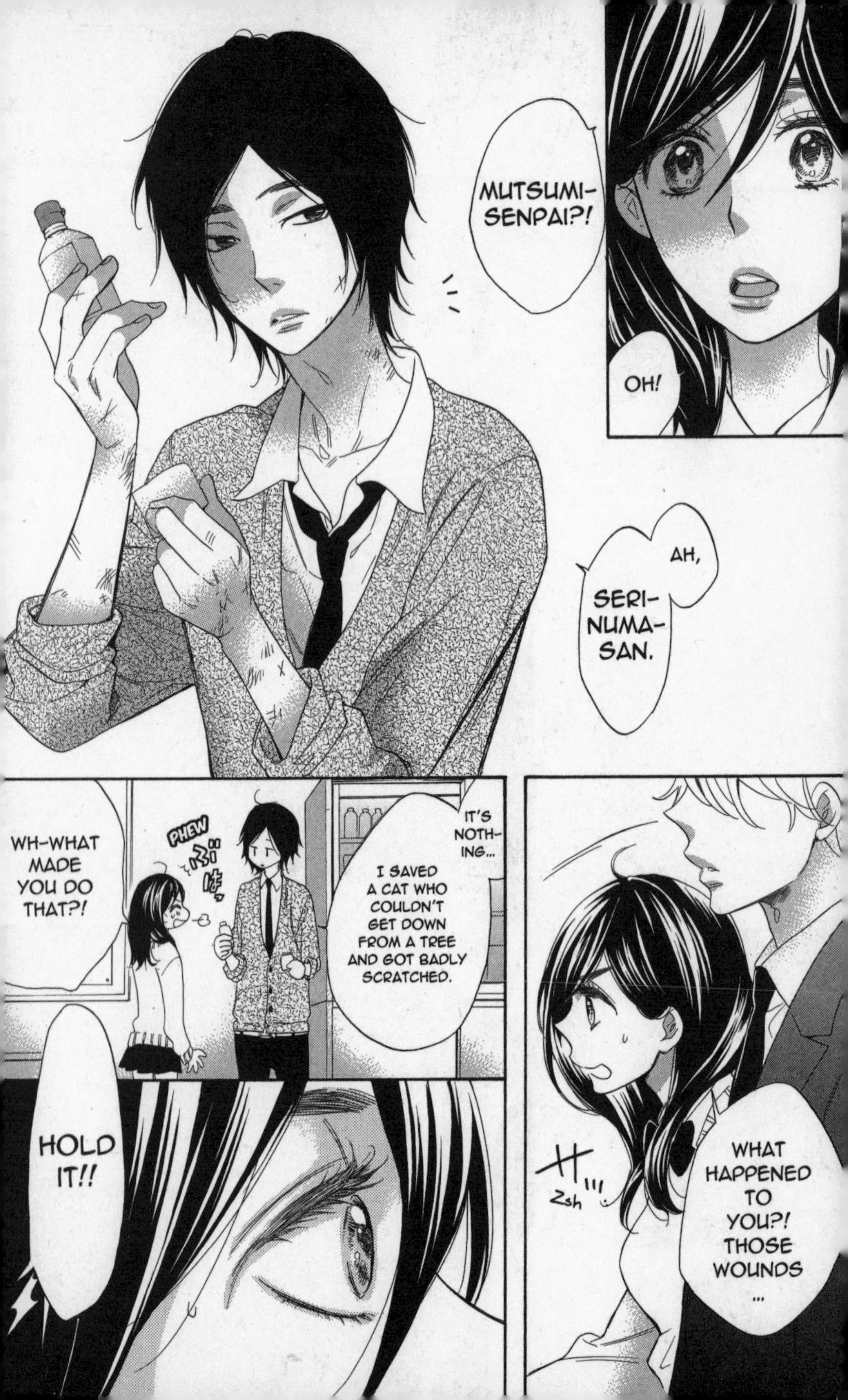
OH!
MUTSUMI-SENPAI?!
AH, SERI-NUMA-SAN.
Zsh
WHAT HAPPENED TO YOU?! THOSE WOUNDS ...
IT'S NOTH-ING...
I SAVED A CAT WHO COULDN'T GET DOWN FROM A TREE AND GOT BADLY SCRATCHED.
PHEW
WH-WHAT MADE YOU DO THAT?!
HOLD IT!!

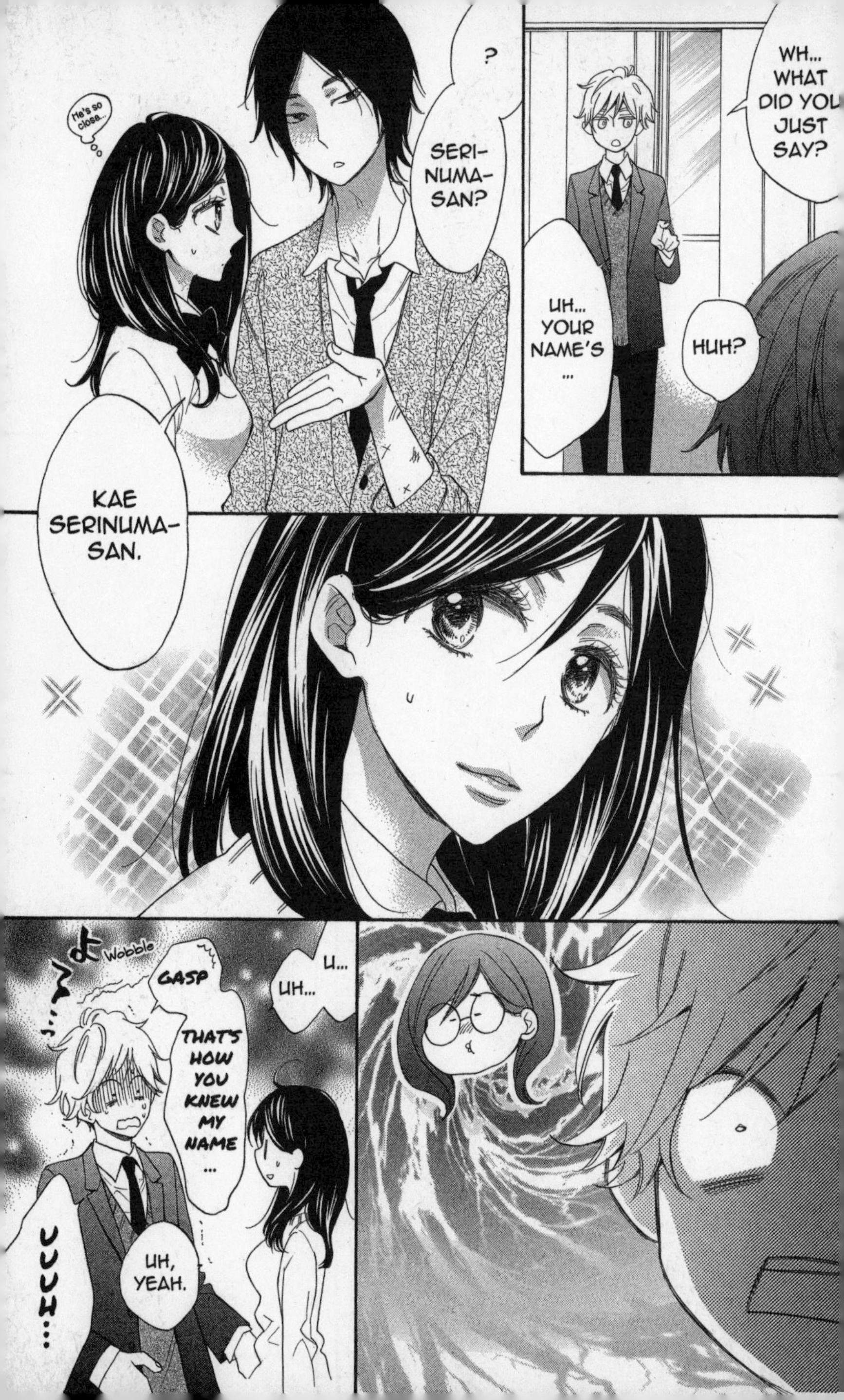
WH... WHAT DID YOU JUST SAY?
HUH?
UH... YOUR NAME'S ...
?
SERI-NUMA-SAN?
He's so close...
KAE SERINUMA-SAN.
U... UH...
Wobble
GASP
THAT'S HOW YOU KNEW MY NAME ...
UH, YEAH.
UUUH...

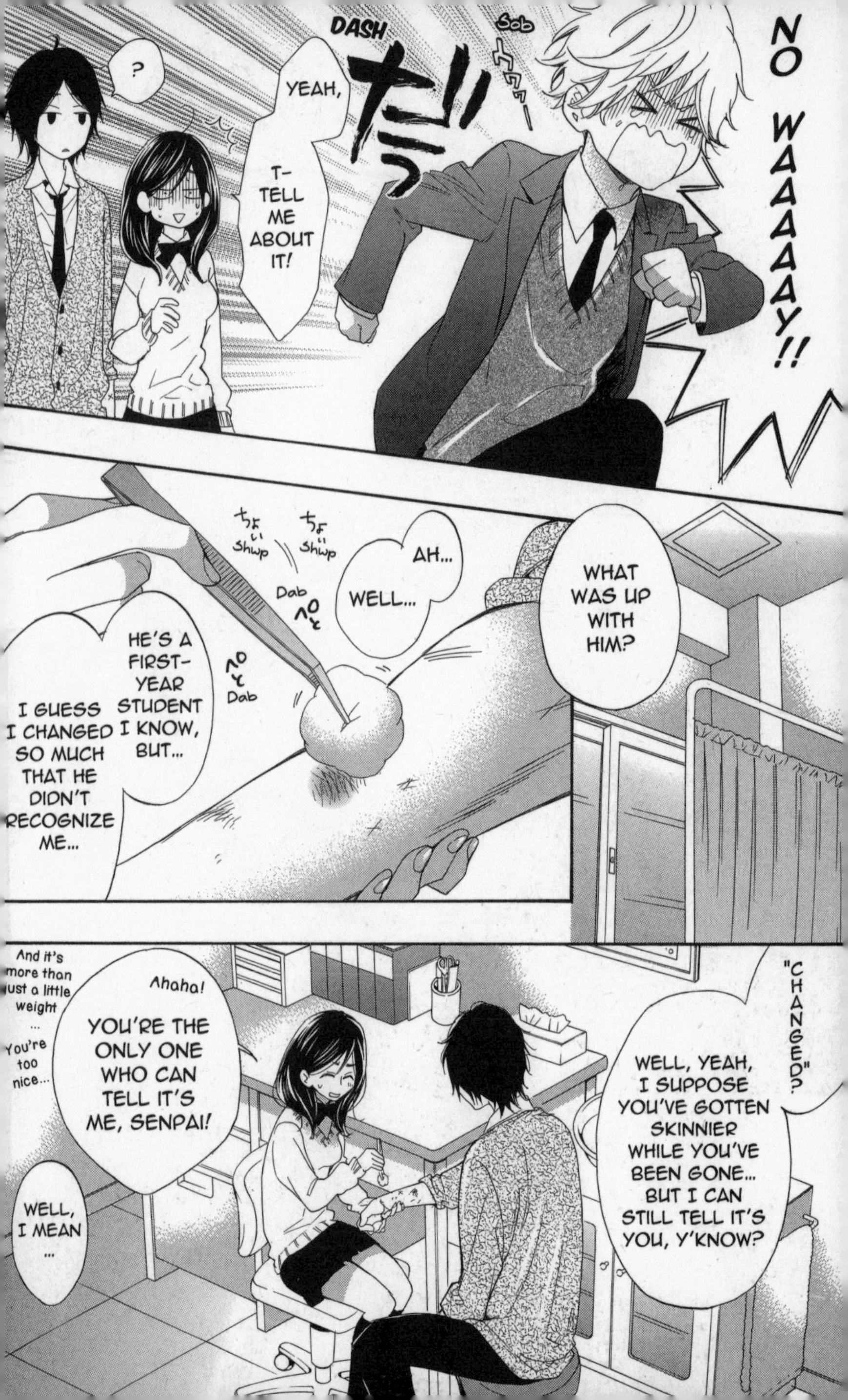
NO WAAAAAY!!
Sob
DASH
YEAH,
T-TELL ME ABOUT IT!
?
WHAT WAS UP WITH HIM?
AH... WELL...
Shwp
Shwp
Dab
Dab
HE'S A FIRST-YEAR STUDENT I KNOW, BUT...
I GUESS I CHANGED SO MUCH THAT HE DIDN'T RECOGNIZE ME...
"CHANGED"?
WELL, YEAH, I SUPPOSE YOU'VE GOTTEN SKINNIER WHILE YOU'VE BEEN GONE... BUT I CAN STILL TELL IT'S YOU, Y'KNOW?
Ahaha!
YOU'RE THE ONLY ONE WHO CAN TELL IT'S ME, SENPAI!
And it's more than just a little weight ... You're too nice...
WELL, I MEAN ...

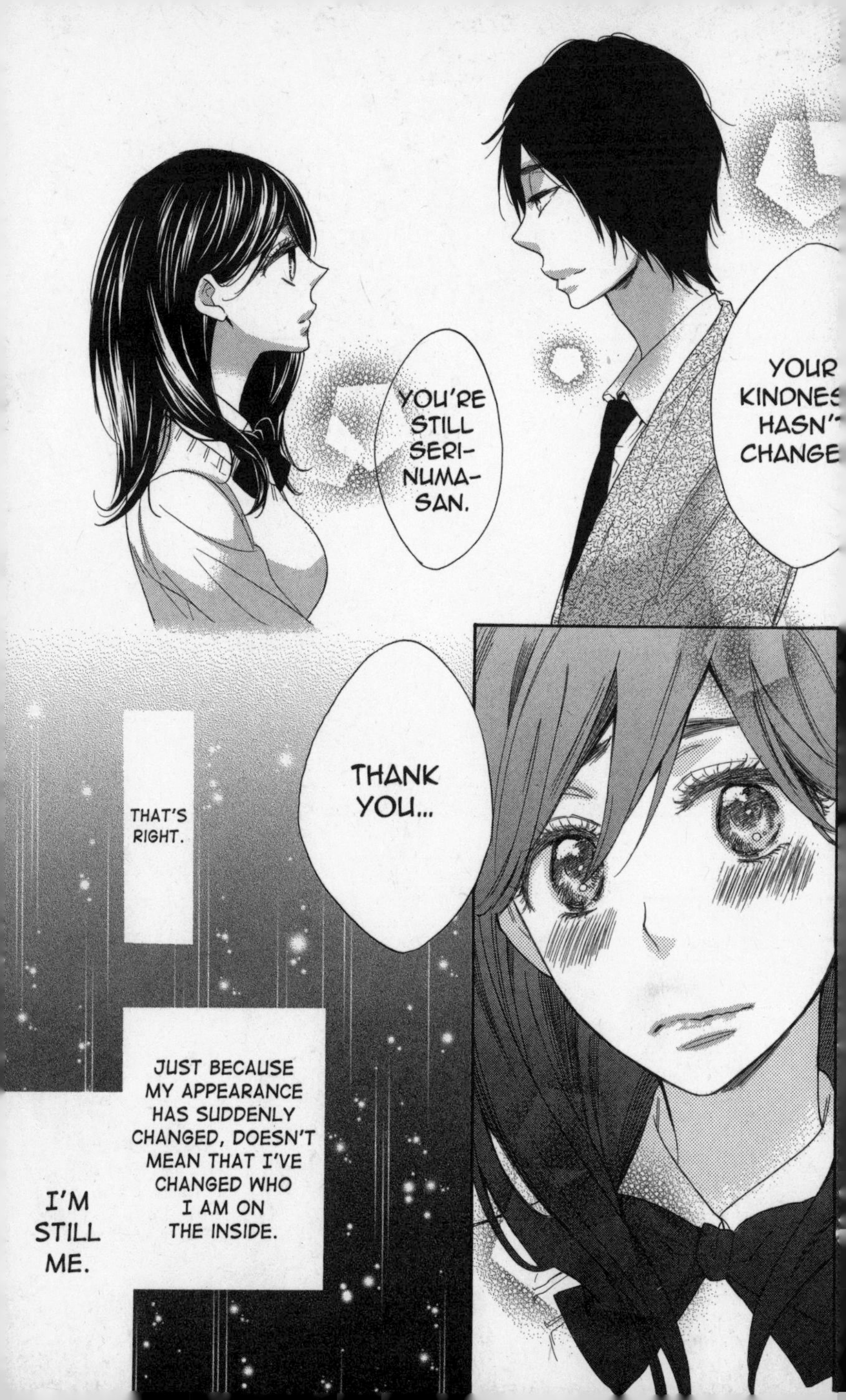
YOUR KINDNES HASN'T CHANGE
YOU'RE STILL SERI-NUMA-SAN.
THANK YOU...
THAT'S RIGHT.
JUST BECAUSE MY APPEARANCE HAS SUDDENLY CHANGED, DOESN'T MEAN THAT I'VE CHANGED WHO I AM ON THE INSIDE.
I'M STILL ME.

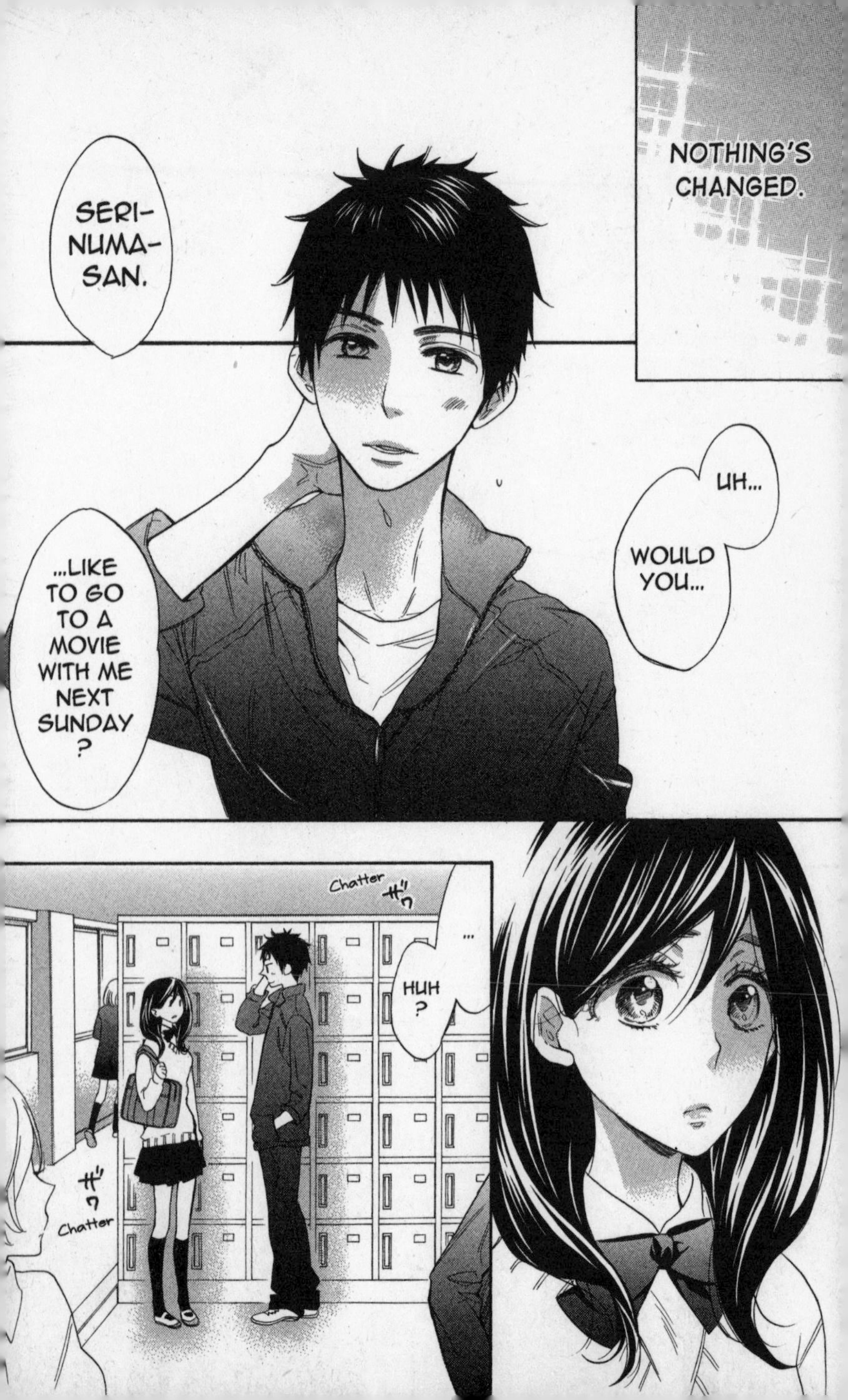
NOTHING'S CHANGED.
SERI-NUMA-SAN.
UH...
WOULD YOU...
...LIKE TO GO TO A MOVIE WITH ME NEXT SUNDAY?
...
HUH?
Chatter ザワ
ザワ Chatter

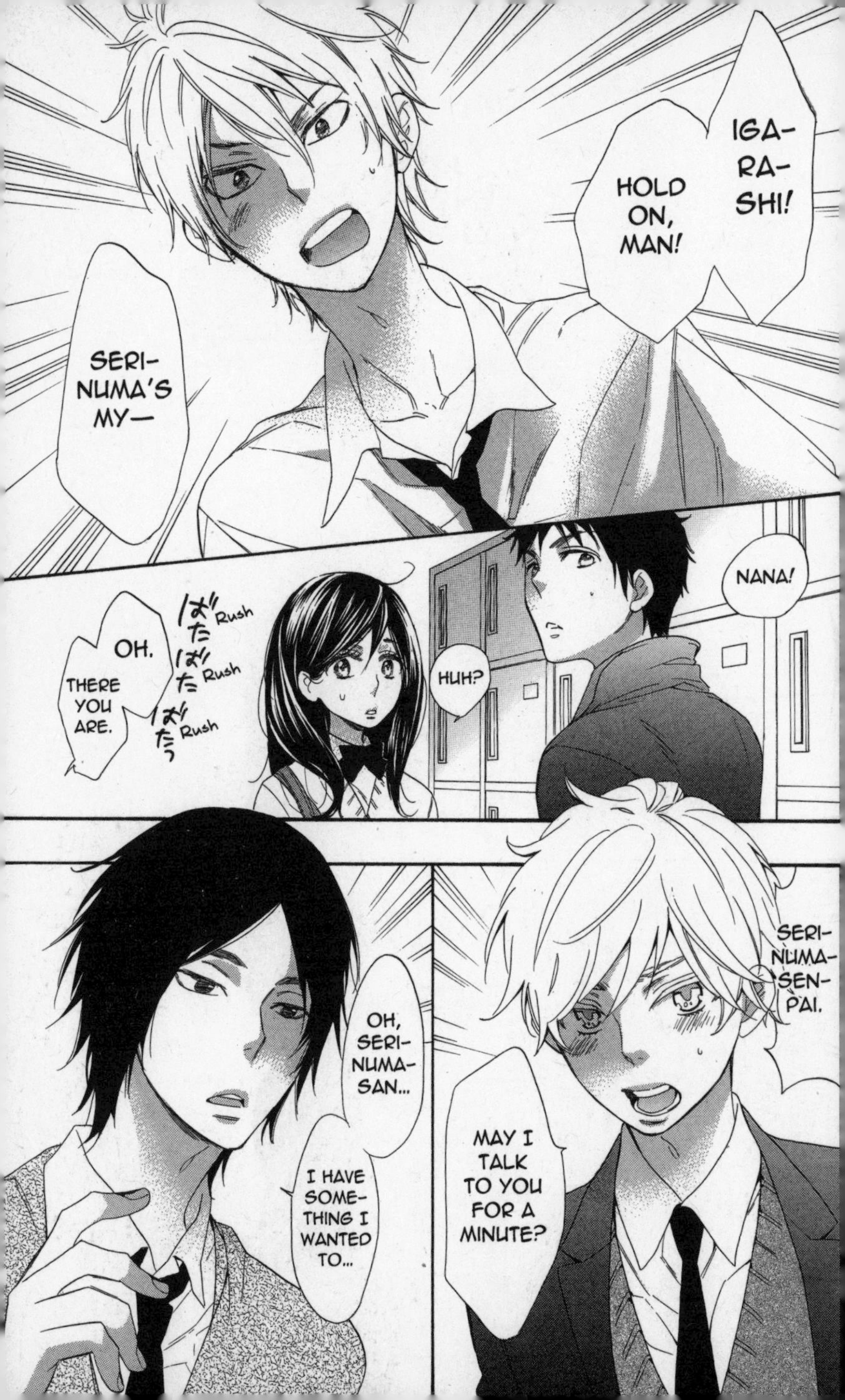
IGA-RA-SHI!
HOLD ON, MAN!
SERI-NUMA'S MY—
NANA!
HUH?
ばた Rush
ばた Rush
ばたっ Rush
OH.
THERE YOU ARE.
SERI-NUMA-SEN-PAI.
MAY I TALK TO YOU FOR A MINUTE?
OH, SERI-NUMA-SAN...
I HAVE SOME-THING I WANTED TO...

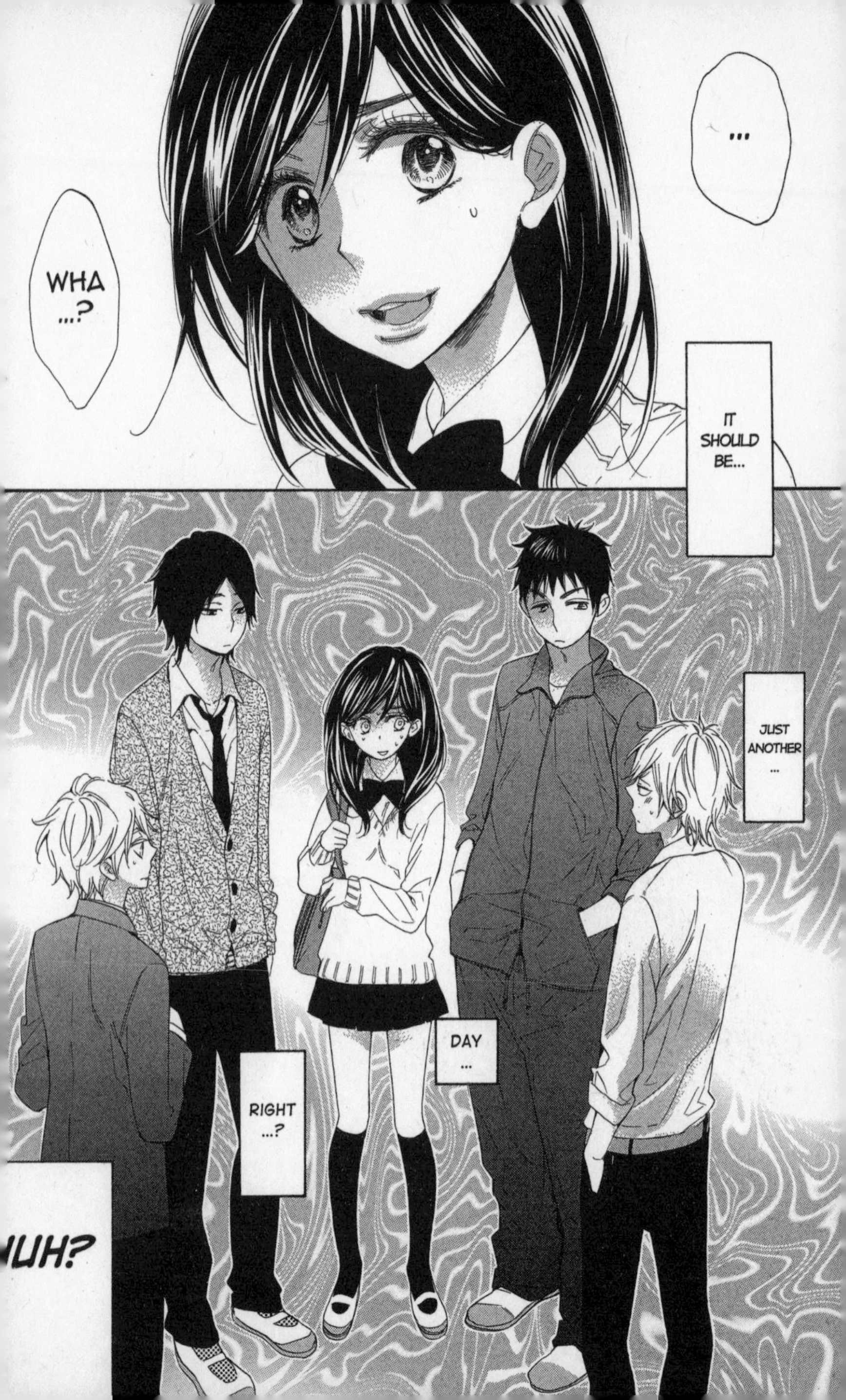
...
WHA ...?
IT SHOULD BE...
JUST ANOTHER ...
DAY ...
RIGHT ...?
HUH?

KiSS HiM, NOT ME!

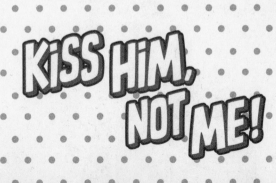

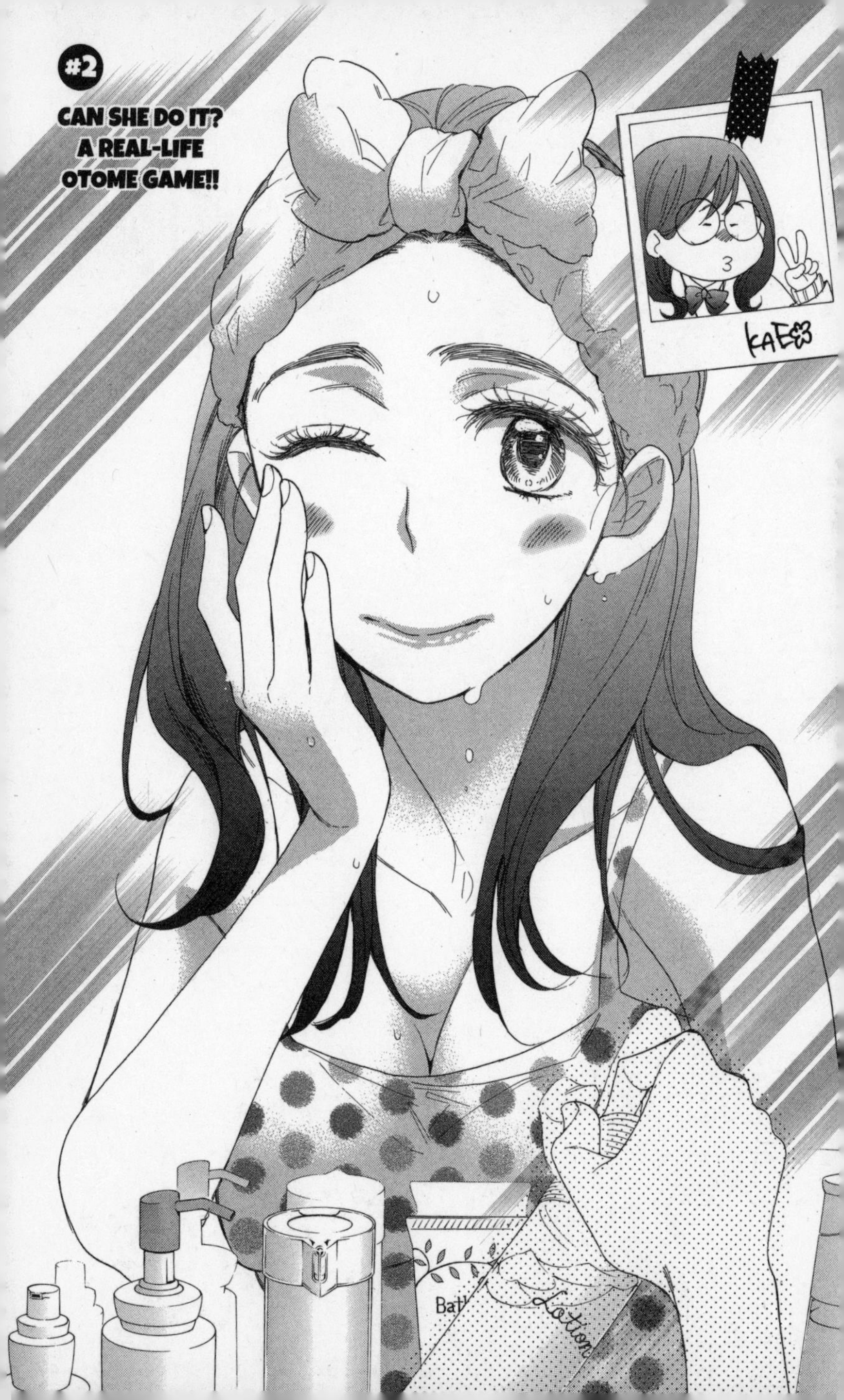
#2
CAN SHE DO IT? A REAL-LIFE OTOME GAME!!
KAE
Lotion

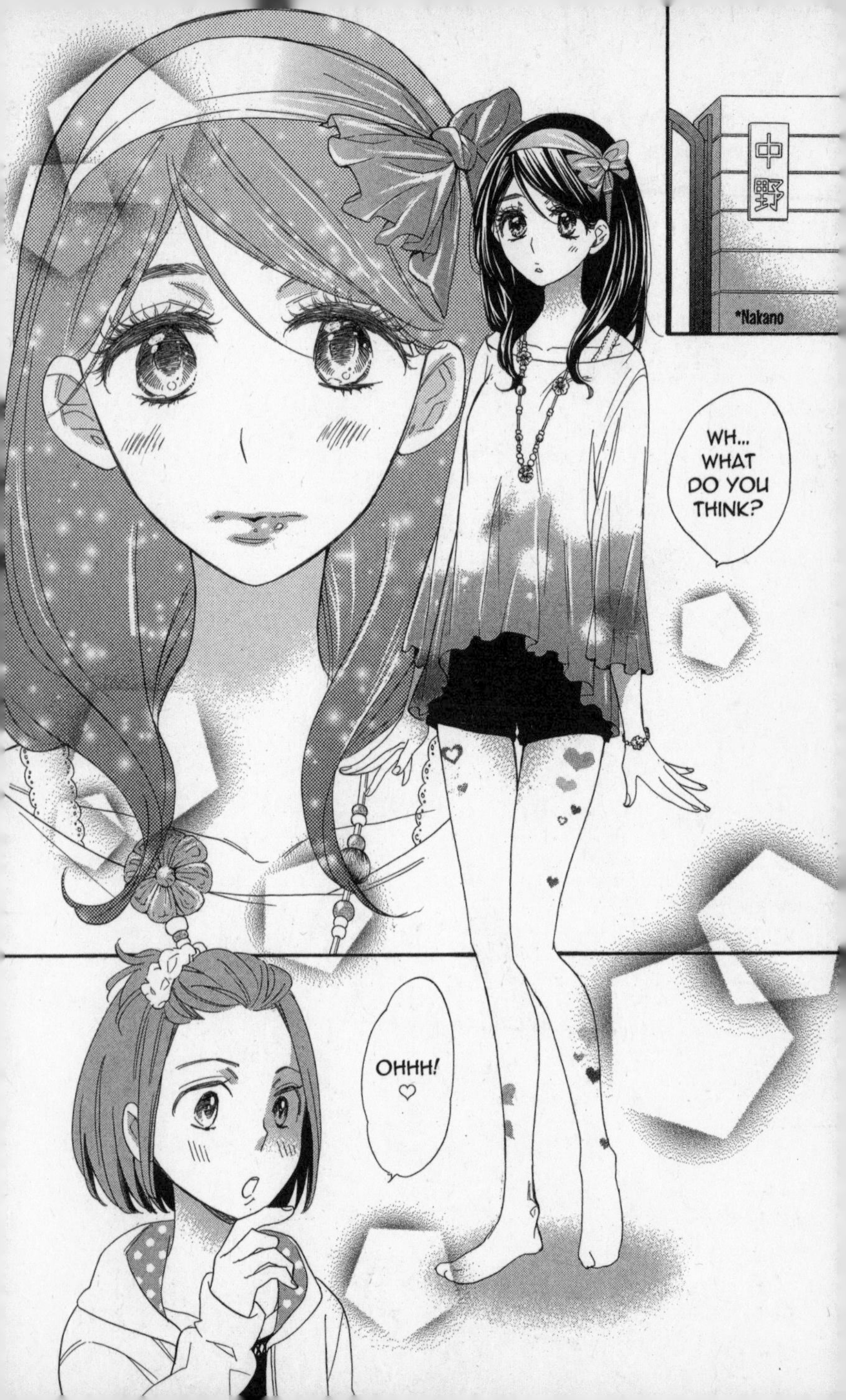
中野
*Nakano
WH... WHAT DO YOU THINK?
OHHH! ♡

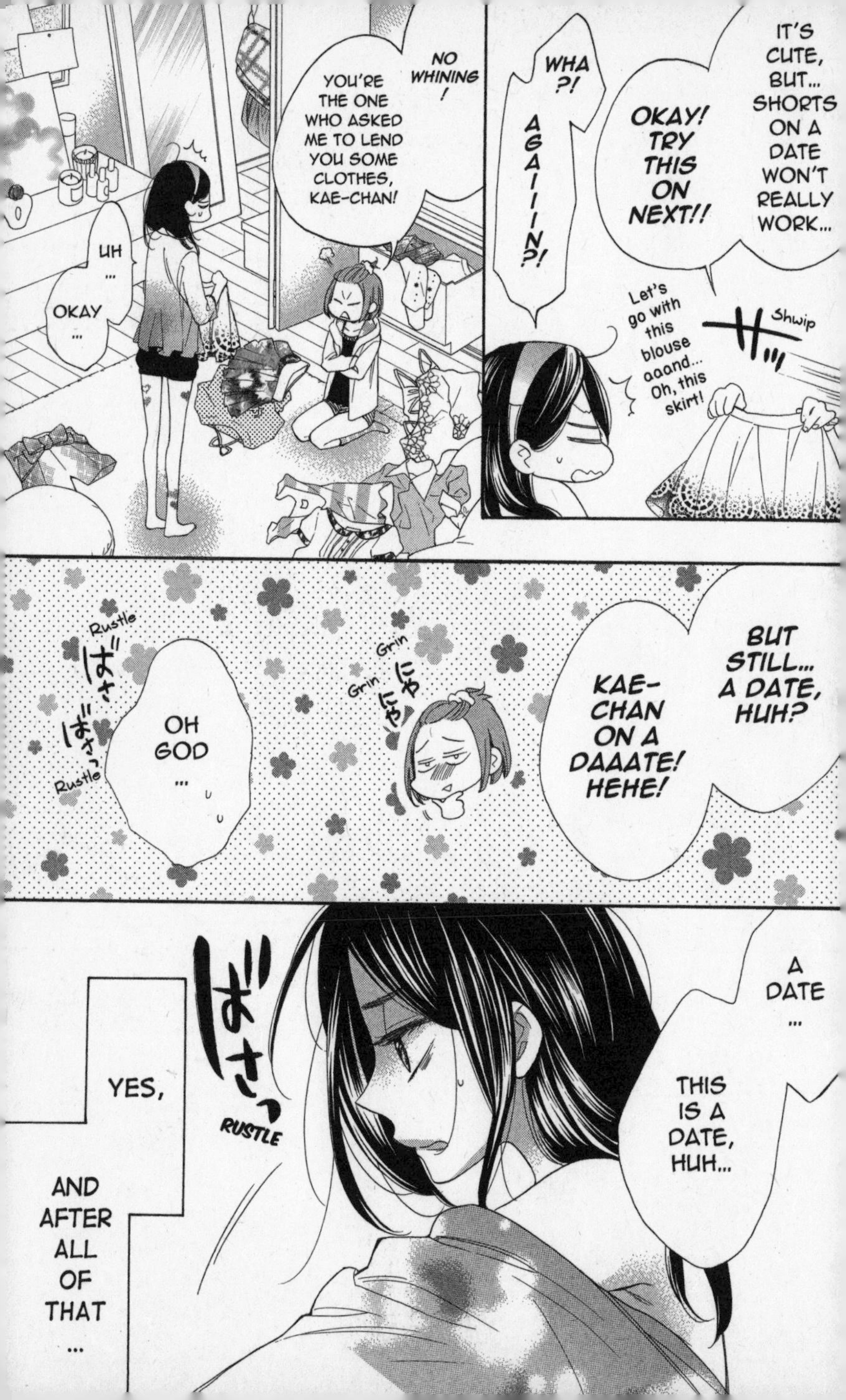
IT'S CUTE, BUT... SHORTS ON A DATE WON'T REALLY WORK...
OKAY! TRY THIS ON NEXT!!
Let's go with this blouse aaand... Oh, this skirt!
Shwip
WHA?!
AGAIIIN?!
NO WHINING!
YOU'RE THE ONE WHO ASKED ME TO LEND YOU SOME CLOTHES, KAE-CHAN!
UH... OKAY...
BUT STILL... A DATE, HUH?
KAE-CHAN ON A DAAATE! HEHE!
にやにや
Grin Grin
OH GOD...
ばさばさっ
Rustle Rustle
A DATE...
THIS IS A DATE, HUH...
ばさっ
RUSTLE
YES,
AND AFTER ALL OF THAT...

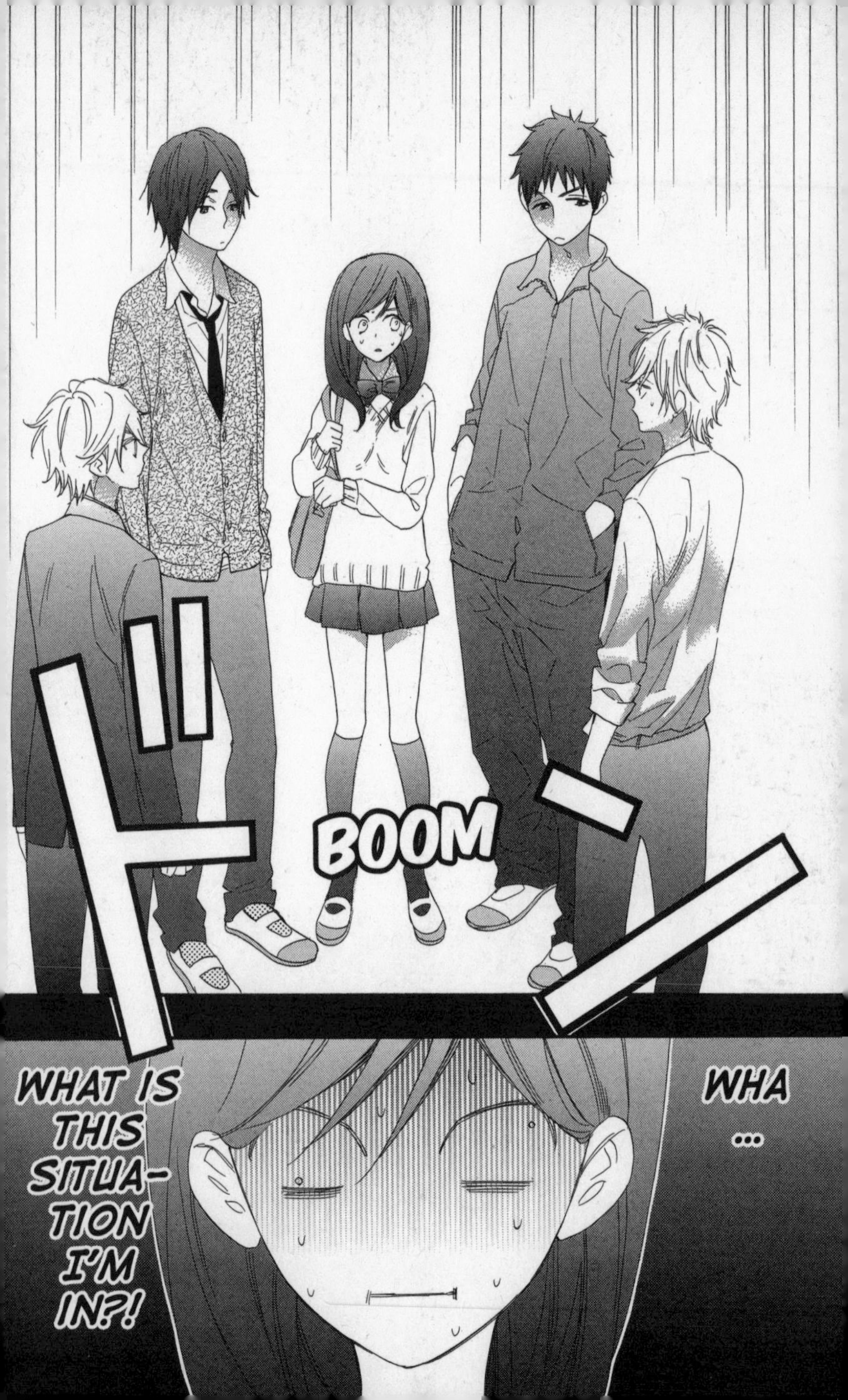
BOOM
WHA ...
WHAT IS THIS SITUATION I'M IN?!

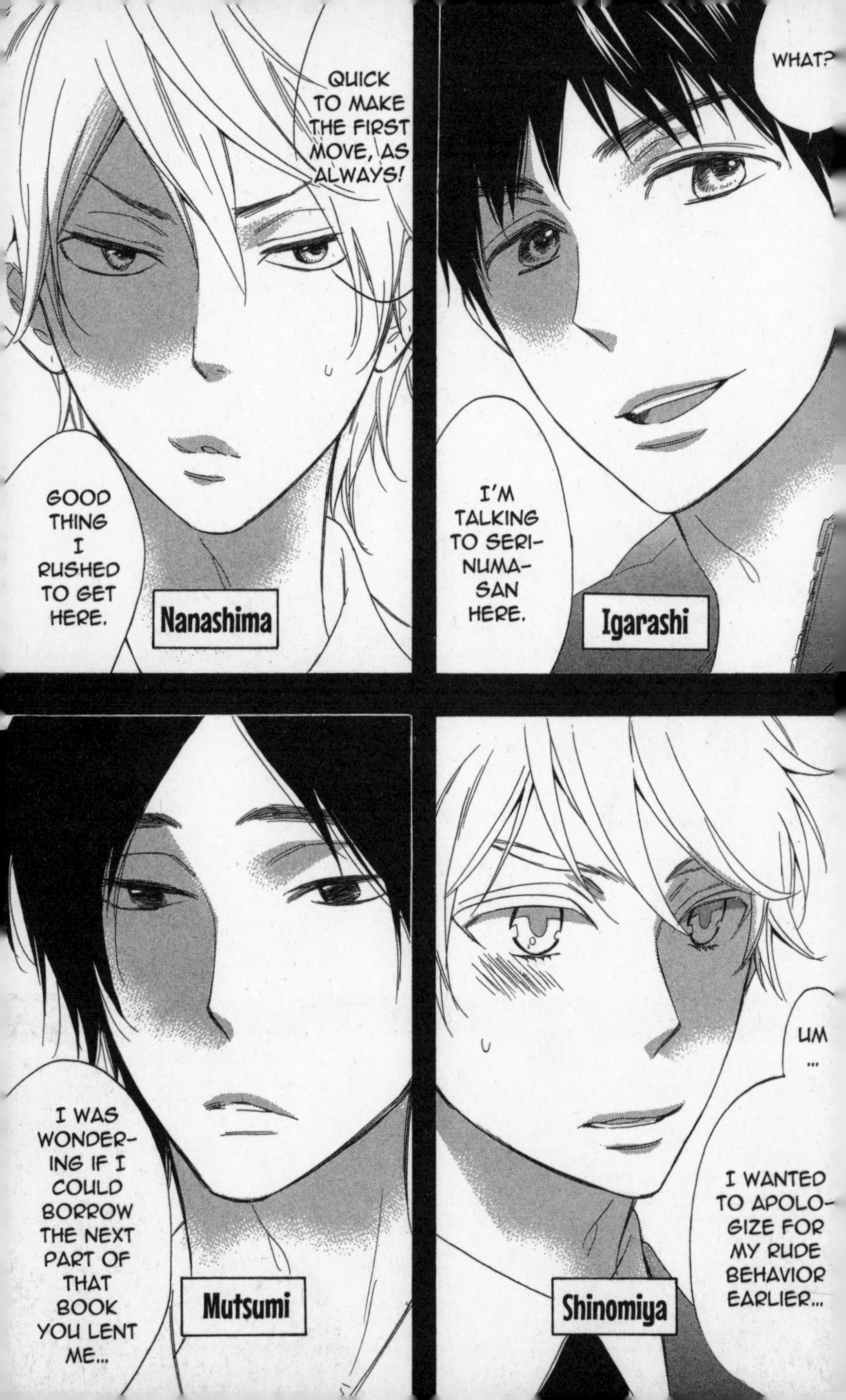
WHAT?
I'M TALKING TO SERI-NUMA-SAN HERE.
Igarashi
QUICK TO MAKE THE FIRST MOVE, AS ALWAYS!
GOOD THING I RUSHED TO GET HERE.
Nanashima
UM ...
I WANTED TO APOLOGIZE FOR MY RUDE BEHAVIOR EARLIER...
Shinomiya
I WAS WONDERING IF I COULD BORROW THE NEXT PART OF THAT BOOK YOU LENT ME...
Mutsumi

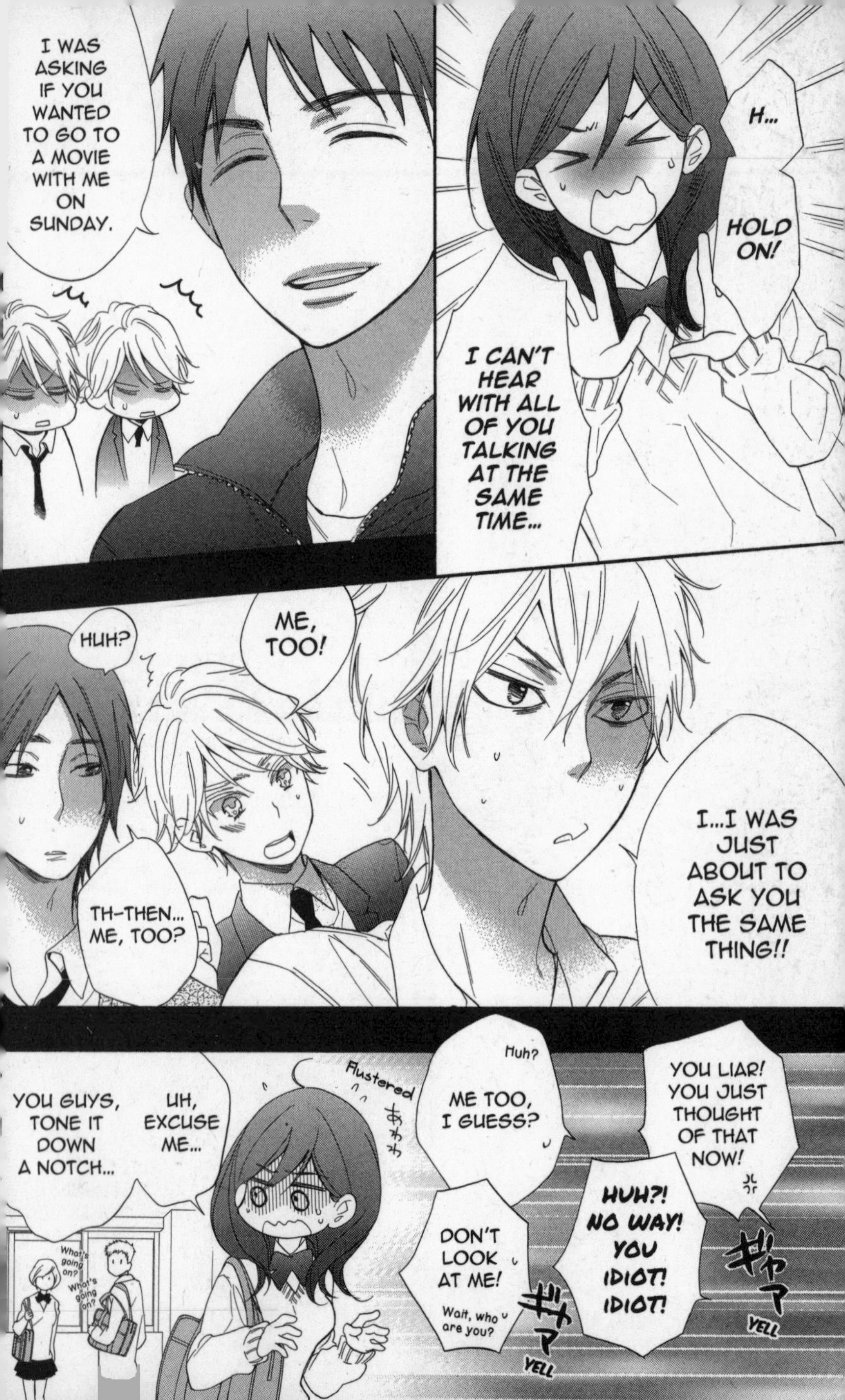
H... HOLD ON!
I CAN'T HEAR WITH ALL OF YOU TALKING AT THE SAME TIME...
I WAS ASKING IF YOU WANTED TO GO TO A MOVIE WITH ME ON SUNDAY.
I...I WAS JUST ABOUT TO ASK YOU THE SAME THING!!
ME, TOO!
HUH?
TH-THEN... ME, TOO?
YOU LIAR! YOU JUST THOUGHT OF THAT NOW!
ギャア
YELL
HUH?! NO WAY! YOU IDIOT! IDIOT!
ギャア
YELL
Huh?
ME TOO, I GUESS?
DON'T LOOK AT ME!
Wait, who are you?
Flustered
あわわ
UH, EXCUSE ME...
YOU GUYS, TONE IT DOWN A NOTCH...
What's going on?
What's going on?

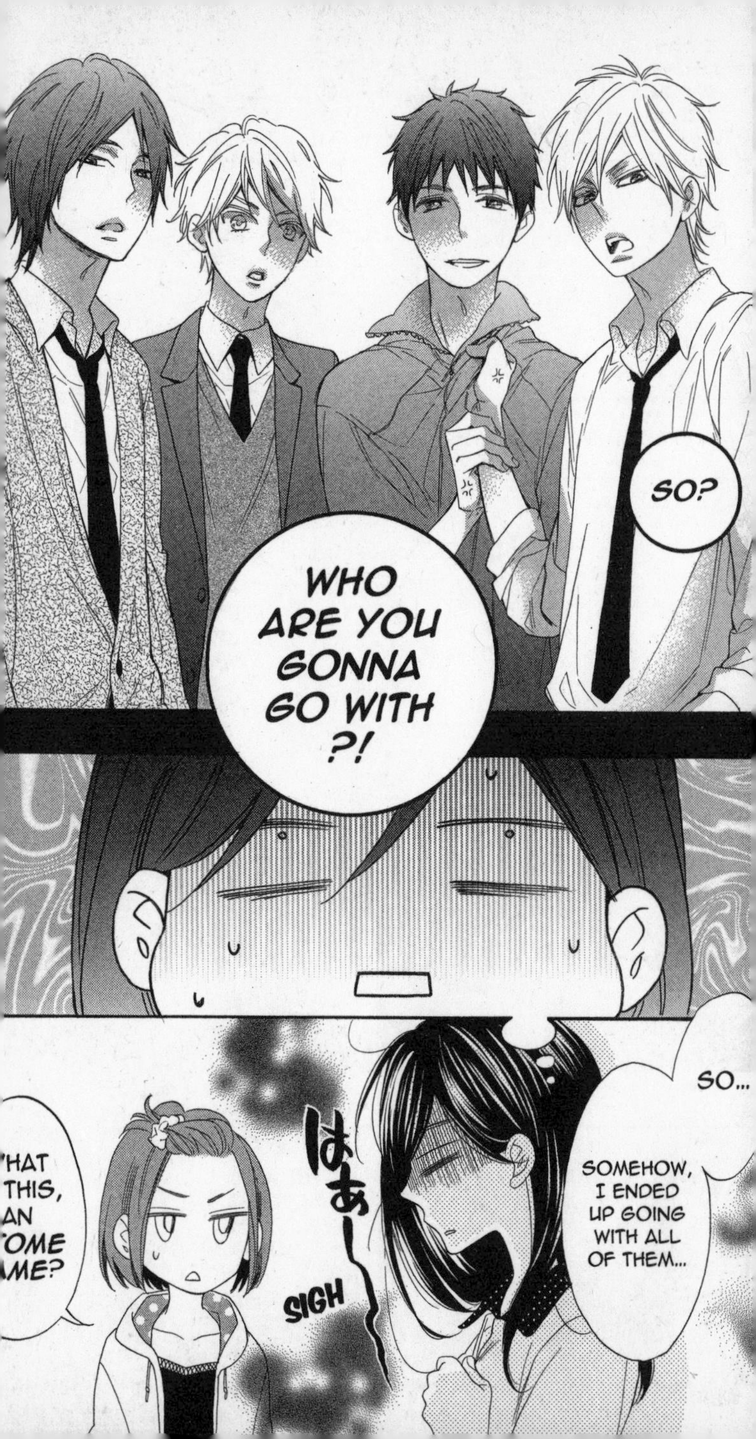
SO?
WHO ARE YOU GONNA GO WITH ?!
SO...
SOMEHOW, I ENDED UP GOING WITH ALL OF THEM...
はあー
SIGH
HAT THIS, AN OME ME?

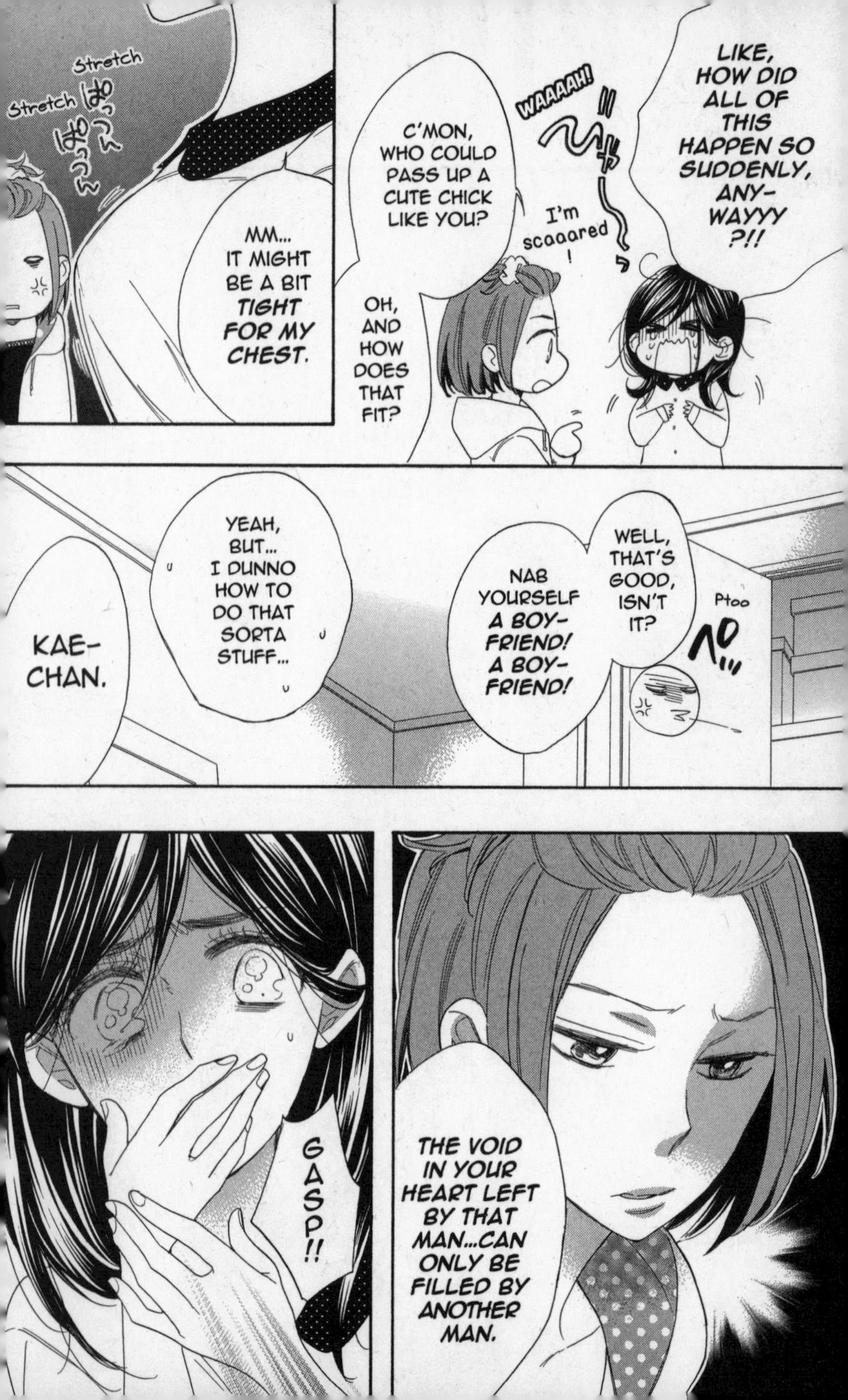
LIKE, HOW DID ALL OF THIS HAPPEN SO SUDDENLY, ANY-WAYYY?!!
WAAAAH!
I'm scaaared!
C'MON, WHO COULD PASS UP A CUTE CHICK LIKE YOU?
OH, AND HOW DOES THAT FIT?
MM... IT MIGHT BE A BIT TIGHT FOR MY CHEST.
Stretch
Stretch
Ptoo
WELL, THAT'S GOOD, ISN'T IT?
NAB YOURSELF A BOY-FRIEND! A BOY-FRIEND!
YEAH, BUT... I DUNNO HOW TO DO THAT SORTA STUFF...
KAE-CHAN.
THE VOID IN YOUR HEART LEFT BY THAT MAN...CAN ONLY BE FILLED BY ANOTHER MAN.
GASP!!

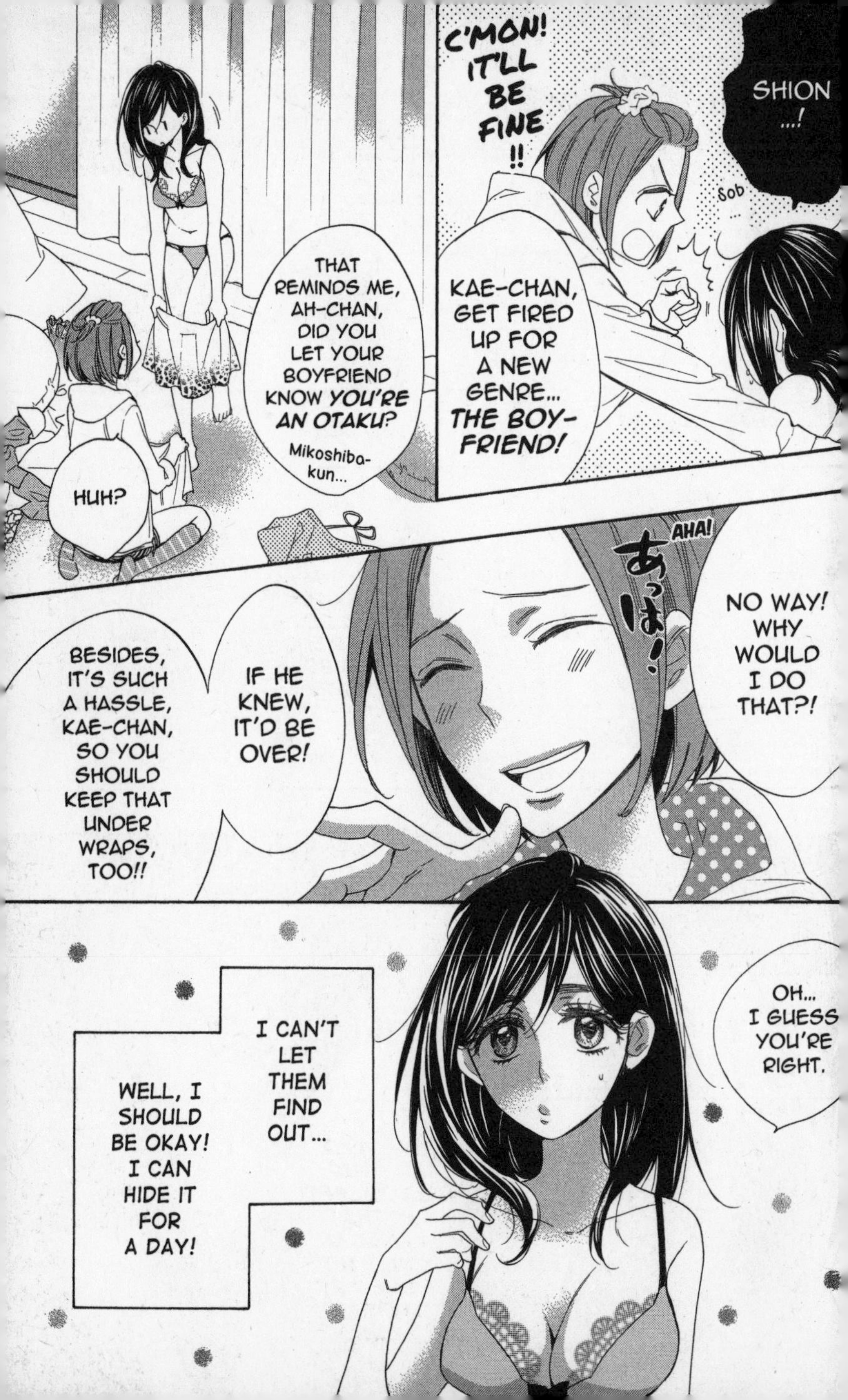
SHION ...!
C'MON! IT'LL BE FINE!!
Sob
KAE-CHAN, GET FIRED UP FOR A NEW GENRE... THE BOY-FRIEND!
THAT REMINDS ME, AH-CHAN, DID YOU LET YOUR BOYFRIEND KNOW YOU'RE AN OTAKU?
Mikoshiba-kun...
HUH?
NO WAY! WHY WOULD I DO THAT?!
あっは! AHA!
IF HE KNEW, IT'D BE OVER!
BESIDES, IT'S SUCH A HASSLE, KAE-CHAN, SO YOU SHOULD KEEP THAT UNDER WRAPS, TOO!!
OH... I GUESS YOU'RE RIGHT.
I CAN'T LET THEM FIND OUT...
WELL, I SHOULD BE OKAY! I CAN HIDE IT FOR A DAY!

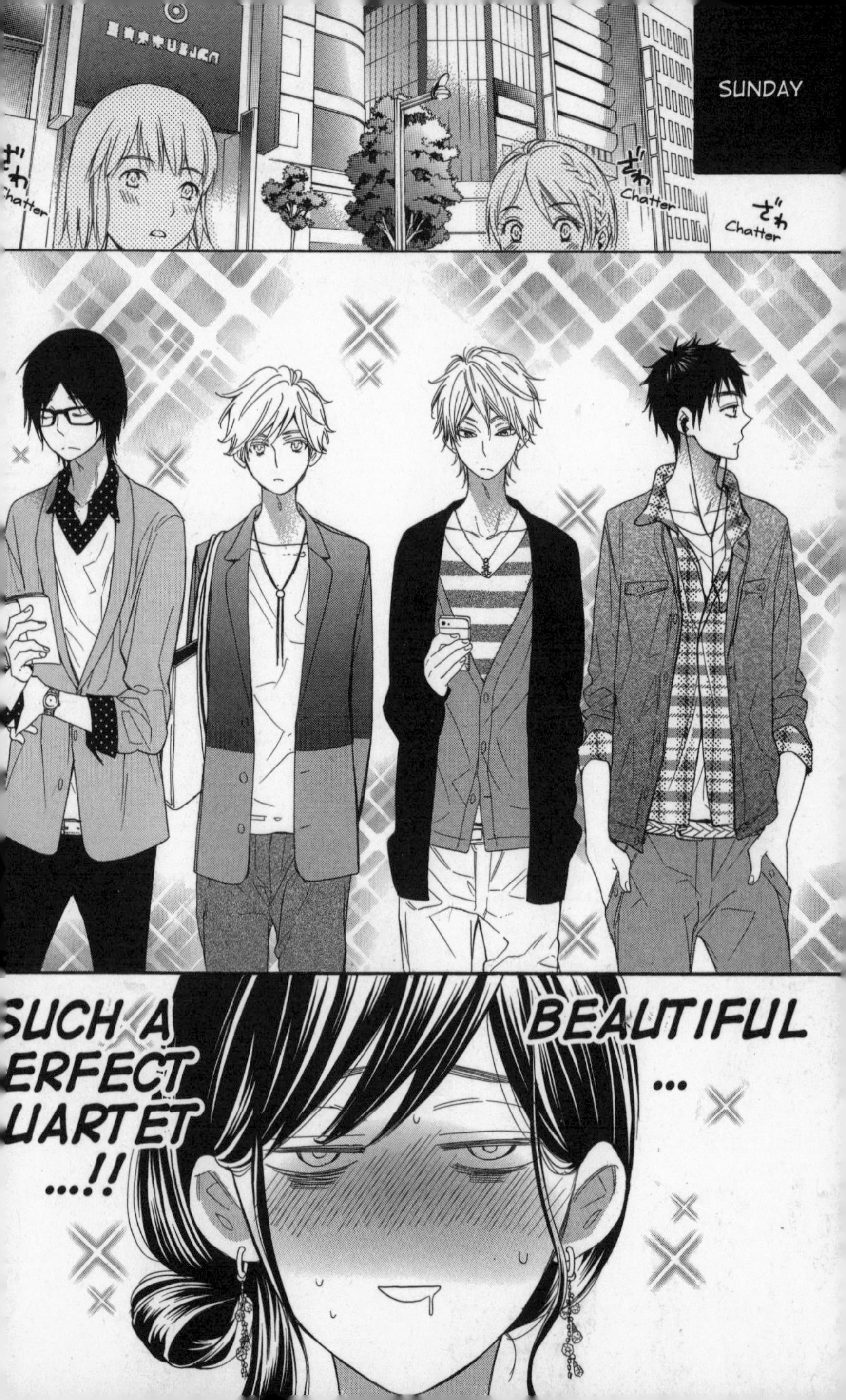
SUNDAY
ざわ Chatter
ざわ Chatter
ざわ Chatter
BEAUTIFUL ...
SUCH A ERFECT UARTET ....!!

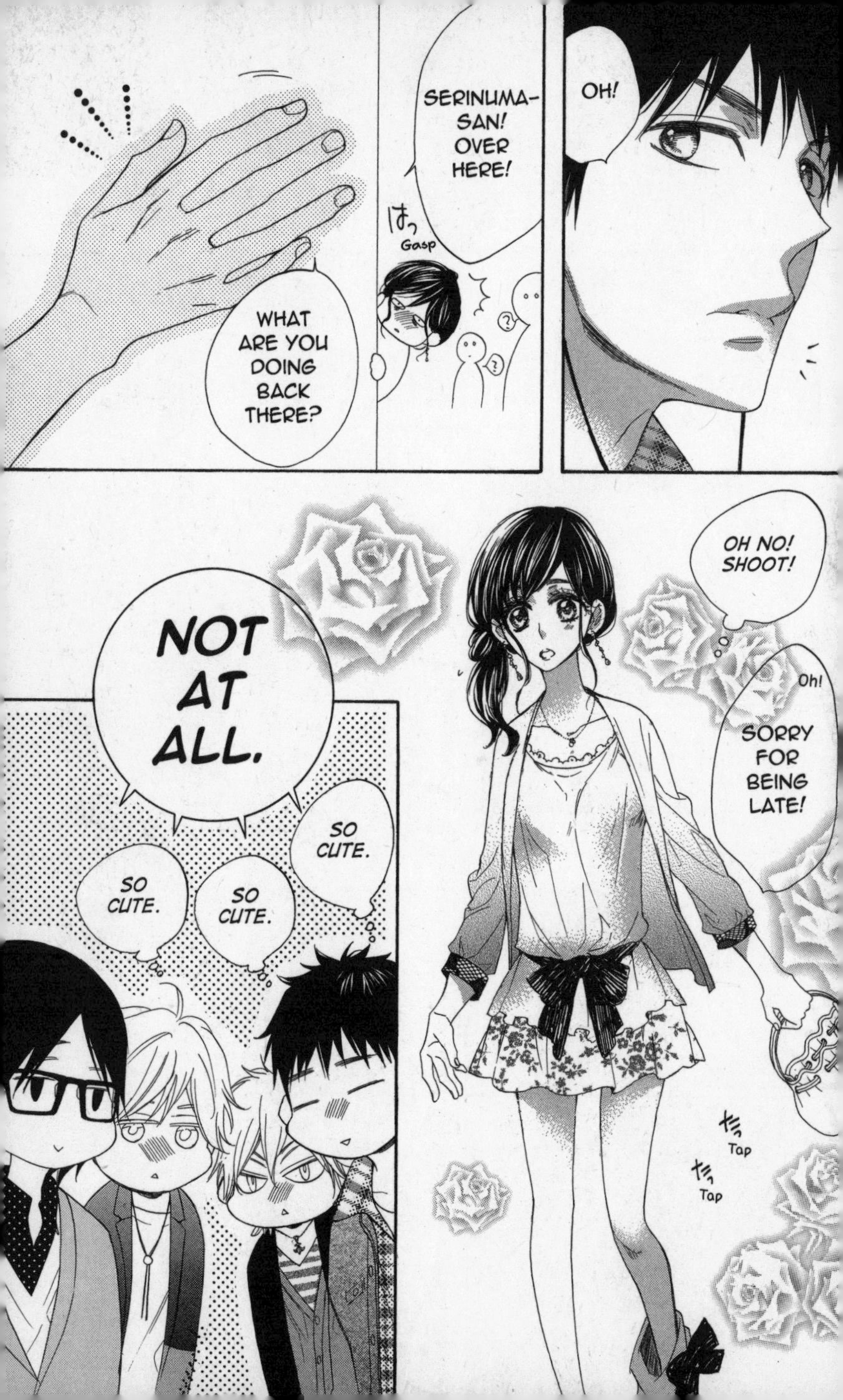
OH!
SERINUMA-SAN! OVER HERE!
はっ
Gasp
WHAT ARE YOU DOING BACK THERE?
OH NO! SHOOT!
Oh!
SORRY FOR BEING LATE!
Tap
Tap
NOT AT ALL.
SO CUTE.
SO CUTE.
SO CUTE.

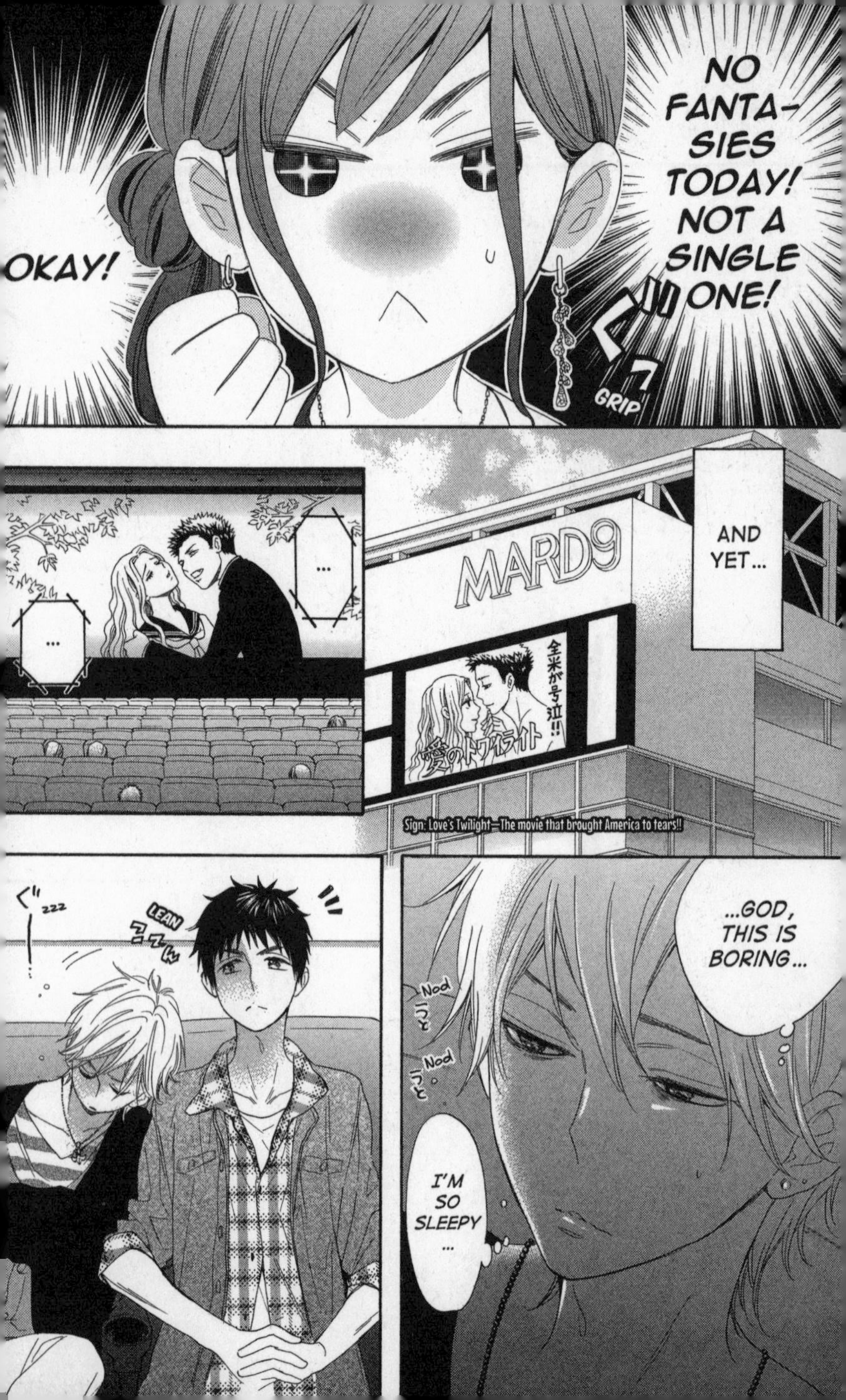
NO FANTA-
SIES
TODAY!
NOT A
SINGLE
ONE!
OKAY!
GRIP
AND YET...
全米が号泣!!
愛のトワイライト
Sign: Love's Twilight—The movie that brought America to tears!!
...
...
...GOD, THIS IS BORING...
Nod
Nod
I'M SO SLEEPY ...
LEAN
zzz

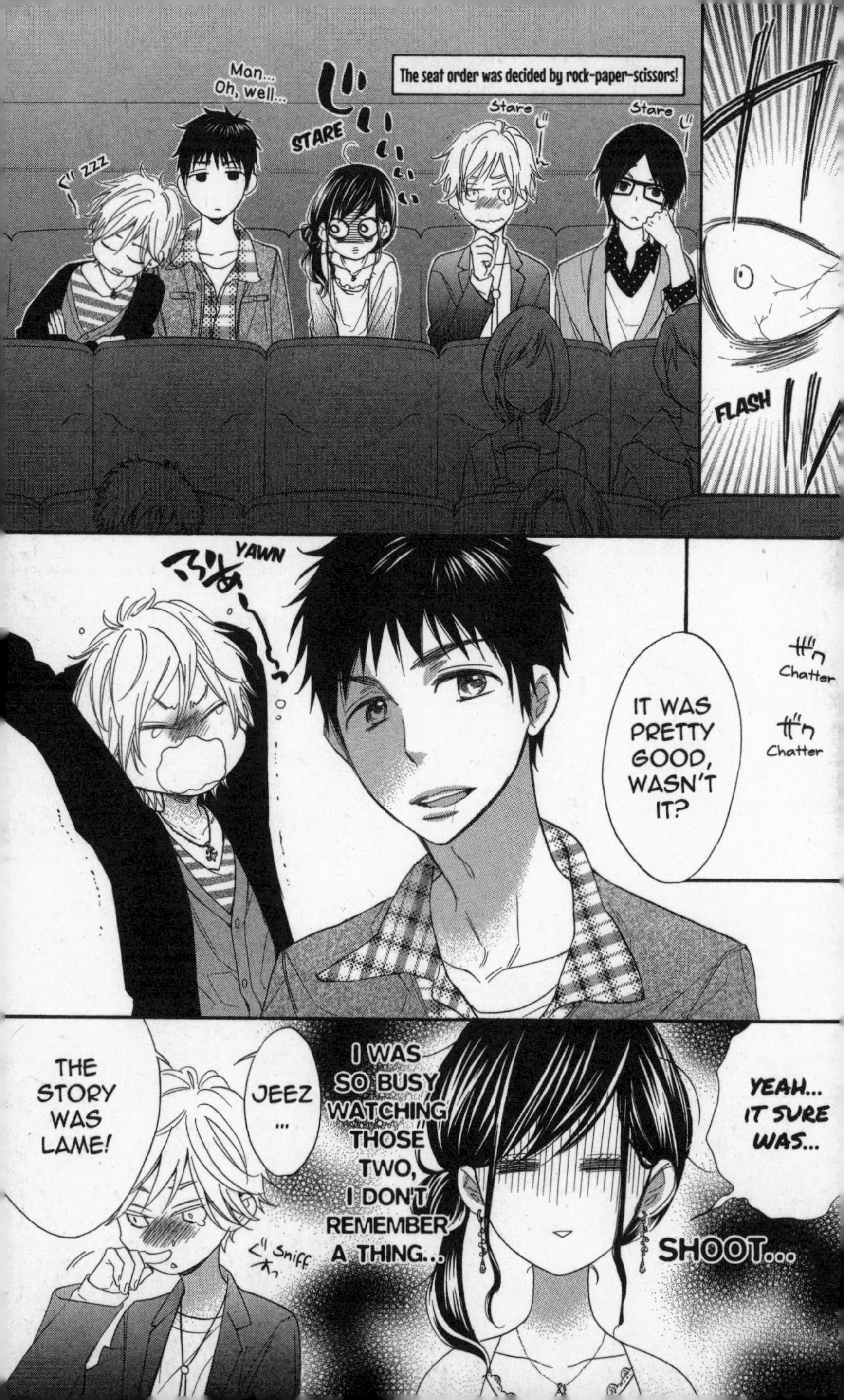

FLASH
The seat order was decided by rock-paper-scissors!
Stare
Stare
STARE
Man... Oh, well...
ZZZ
Chatter
Chatter
IT WAS PRETTY GOOD, WASN'T IT?
YAWN
YEAH... IT SURE WAS...
SHOOT...
I WAS SO BUSY WATCHING THOSE TWO, I DON'T REMEMBER A THING...
JEEZ...
THE STORY WAS LAME!
Sniff

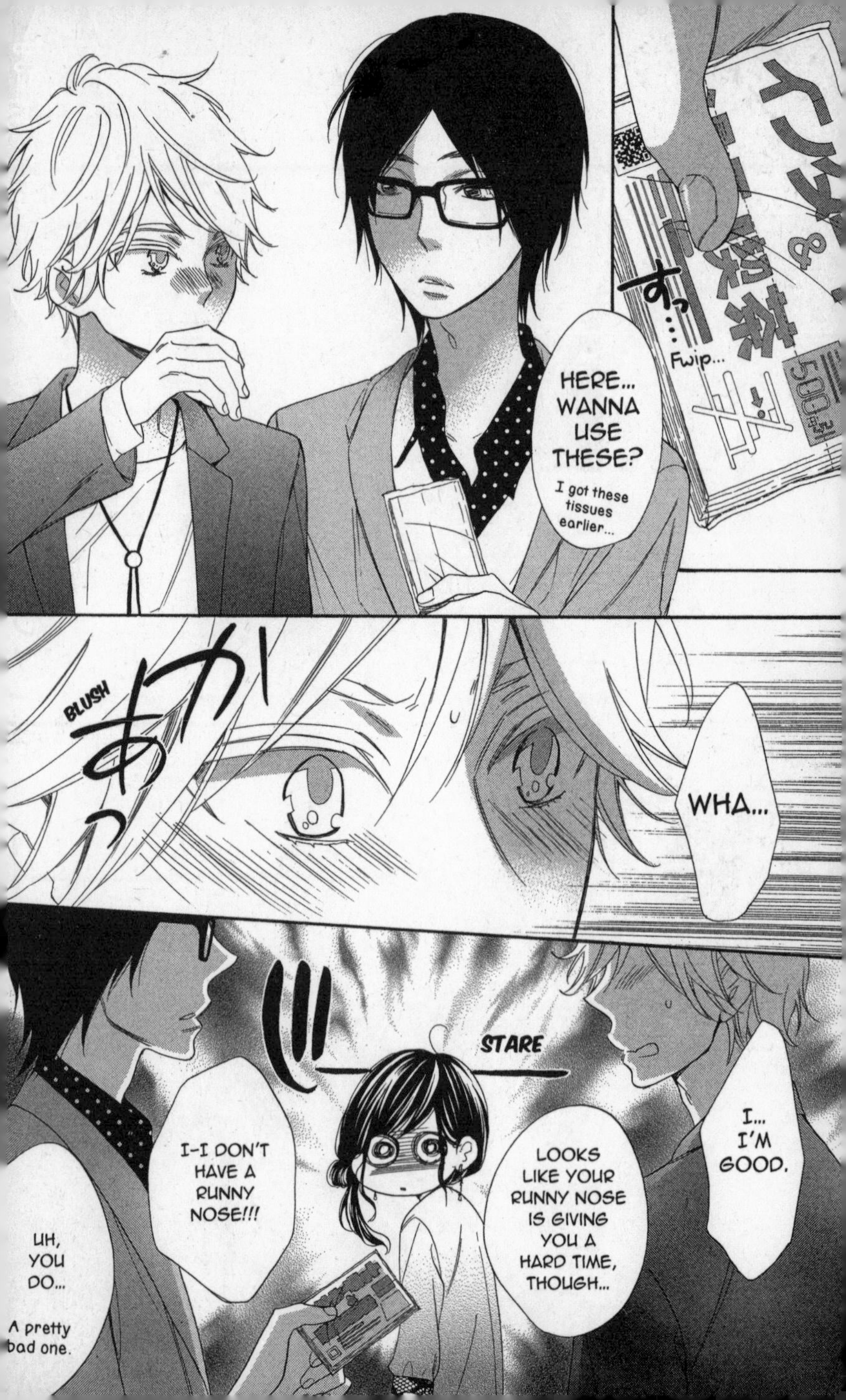

すっ…
Fwip...
HERE... WANNA USE THESE?
I got these tissues earlier...
WHA...
あかっ
BLUSH
I... I'M GOOD.
STARE
LOOKS LIKE YOUR RUNNY NOSE IS GIVING YOU A HARD TIME, THOUGH...
I-I DON'T HAVE A RUNNY NOSE!!!
UH, YOU DO...
A pretty bad one.

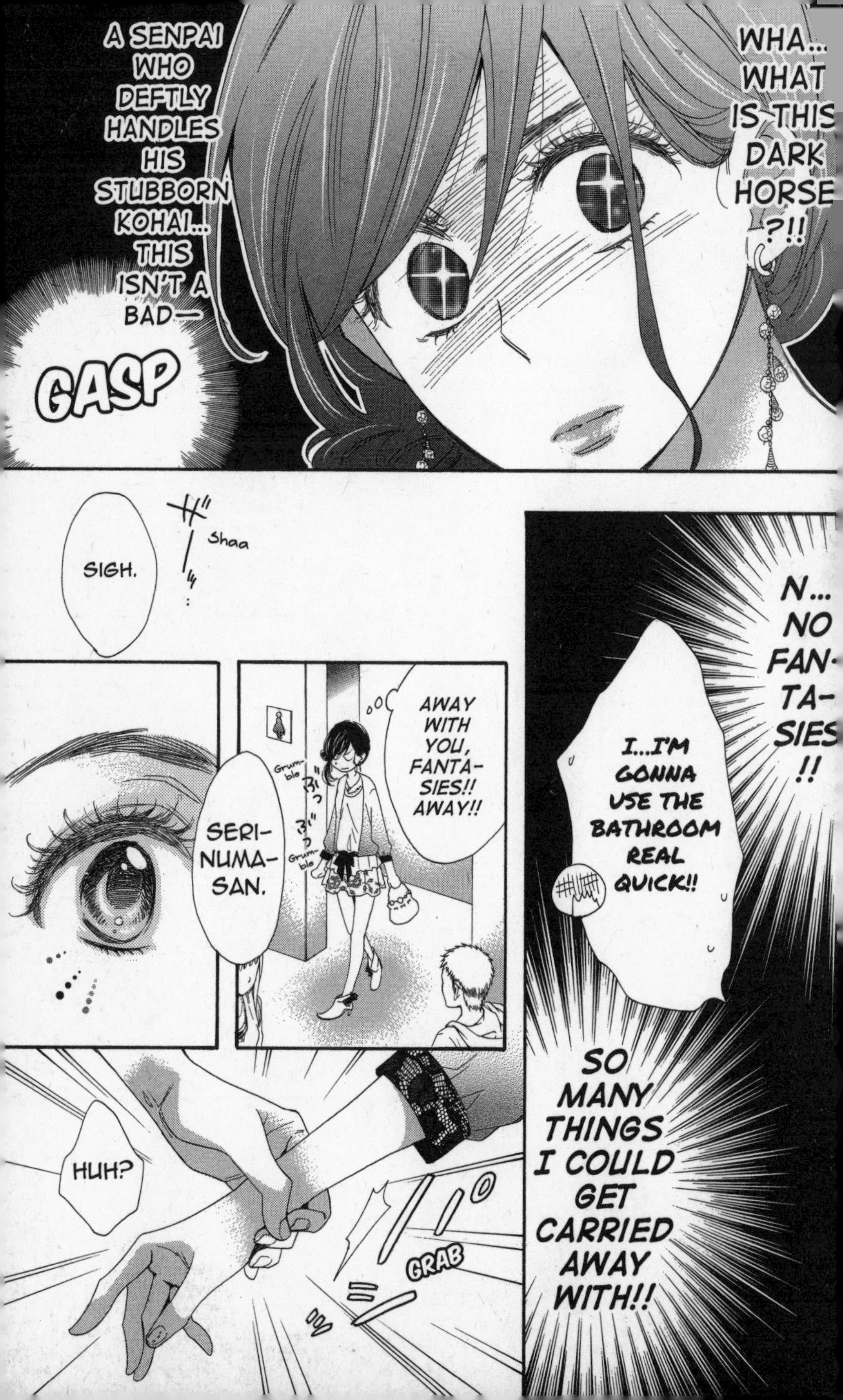
WHA... WHAT IS THIS DARK HORSE?!!
A SENPAI WHO DEFTLY HANDLES HIS STUBBORN KOHAI... THIS ISN'T A BAD—
GASP
N... NO FANTASIES!!
I...I'M GONNA USE THE BATHROOM REAL QUICK!!
SO MANY THINGS I COULD GET CARRIED AWAY WITH!!
SIGH.
Shaa
AWAY WITH YOU, FANTASIES!! AWAY!!
Grumble
Grumble
SERI-NUMA-SAN.
HUH?
GRAB

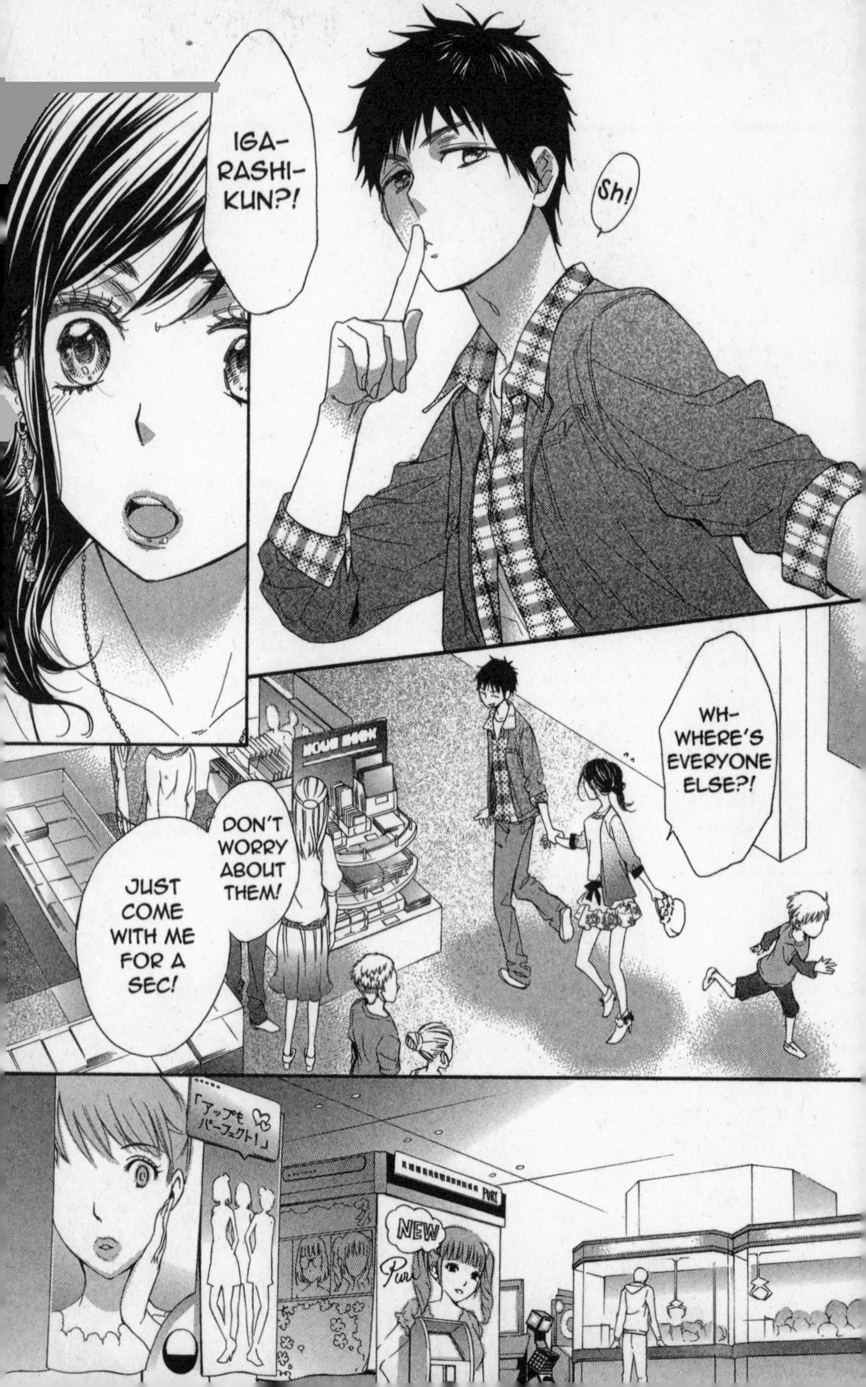
IGA-RASHI-KUN?!
Sh!
WH-WHERE'S EVERYONE ELSE?!
DON'T WORRY ABOUT THEM!
JUST COME WITH ME FOR A SEC!
「アップもパーフェクト!」
NEW
Puri

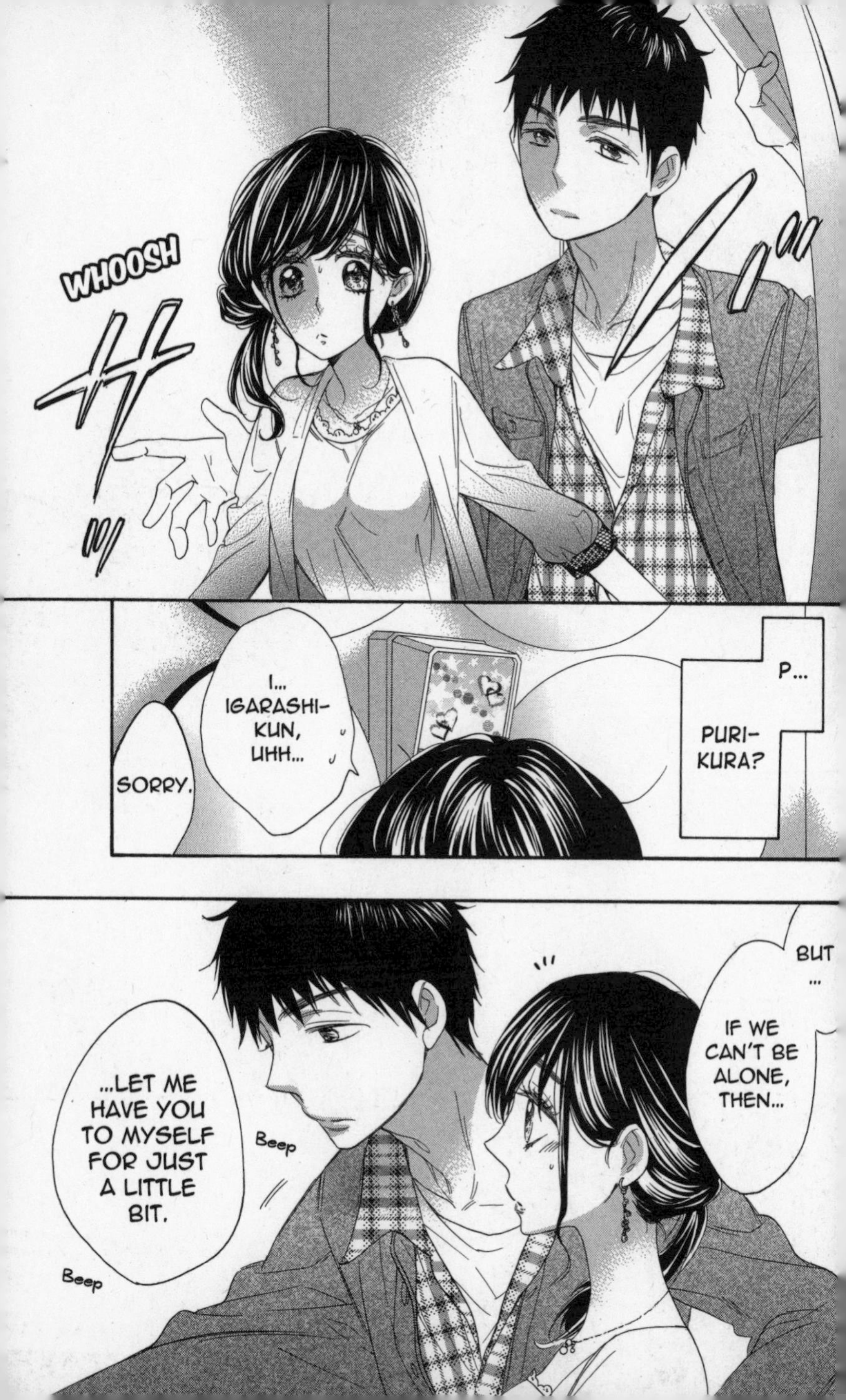
WHOOSH
P... PURI-KURA?
I... IGARASHI-KUN, UHH...
SORRY.
BUT ...
IF WE CAN'T BE ALONE, THEN...
...LET ME HAVE YOU TO MYSELF FOR JUST A LITTLE BIT.
Beep
Beep

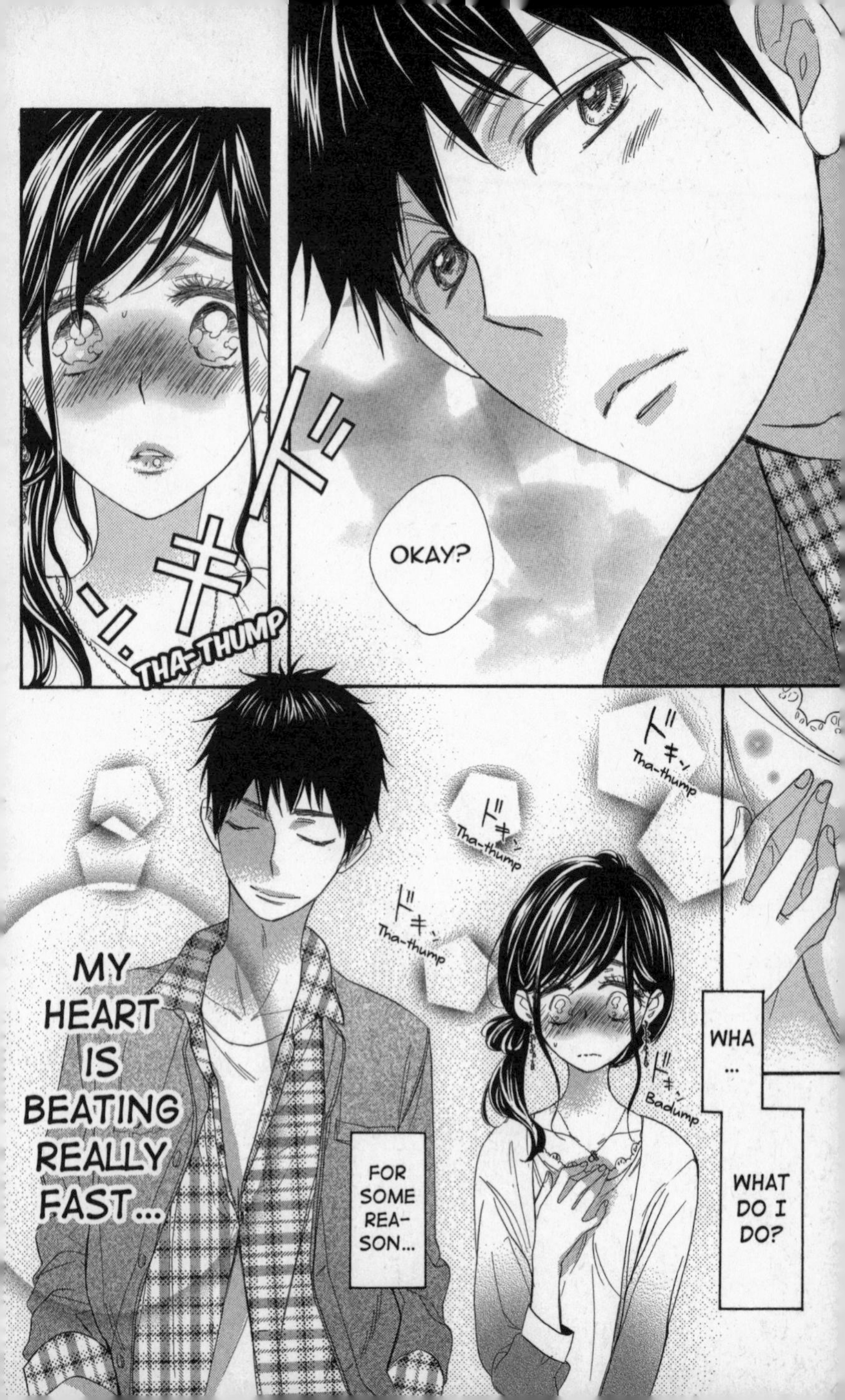
OKAY?
ドキッ
THA-THUMP
WHA...
WHAT DO I DO?
ドキッ
Tha-thump
ドキッ
Tha-thump
ドキッ
Tha-thump
ドキッ
Badump
FOR SOME REA-SON...
MY HEART IS BEATING REALLY FAST...

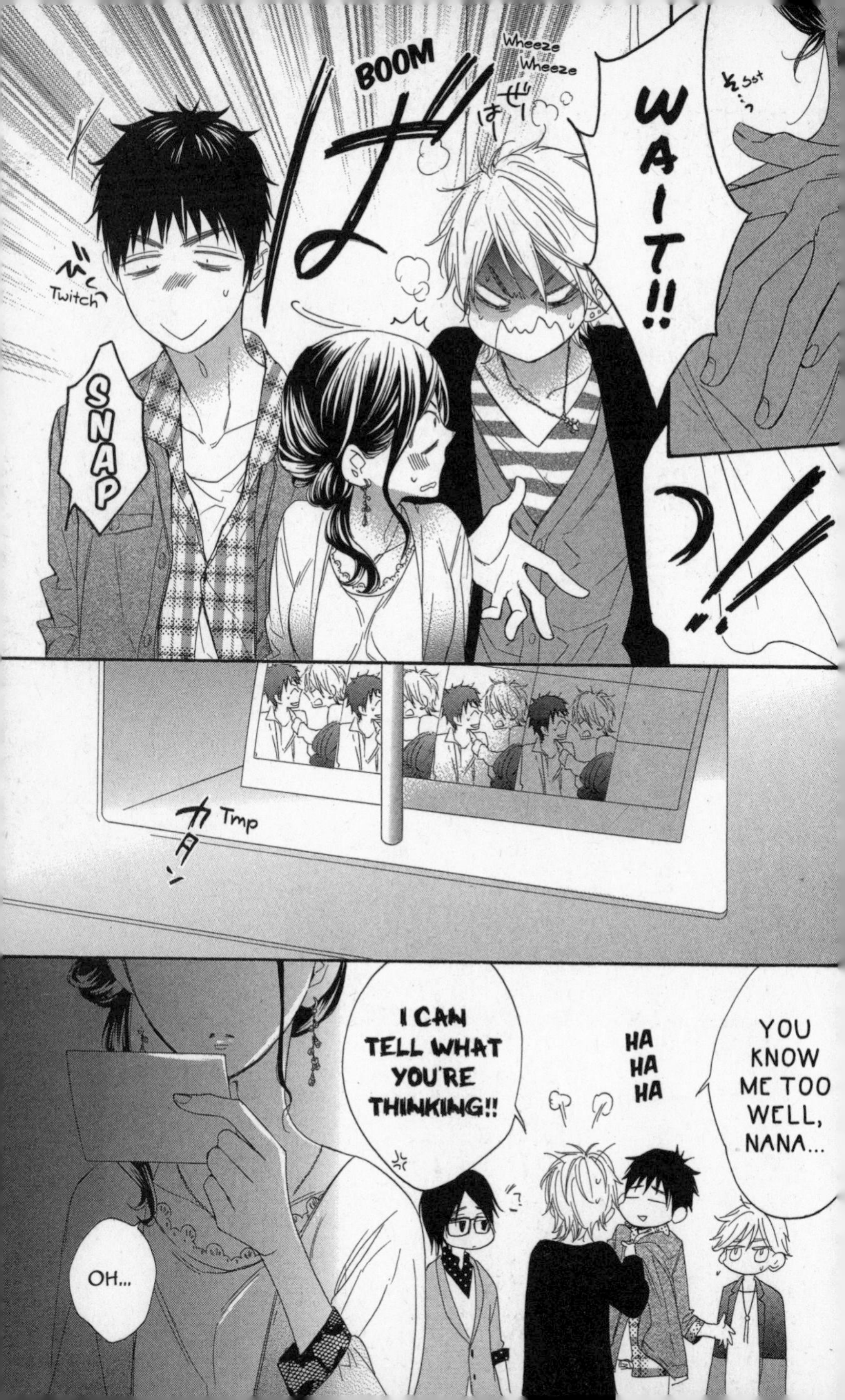
Sst
WAIT!!
Wheeze Wheeze
BOOM
Twitch
SNAP
Tmp
YOU KNOW ME TOO WELL, NANA...
HA HA HA
I CAN TELL WHAT YOU'RE THINKING!!
OH...

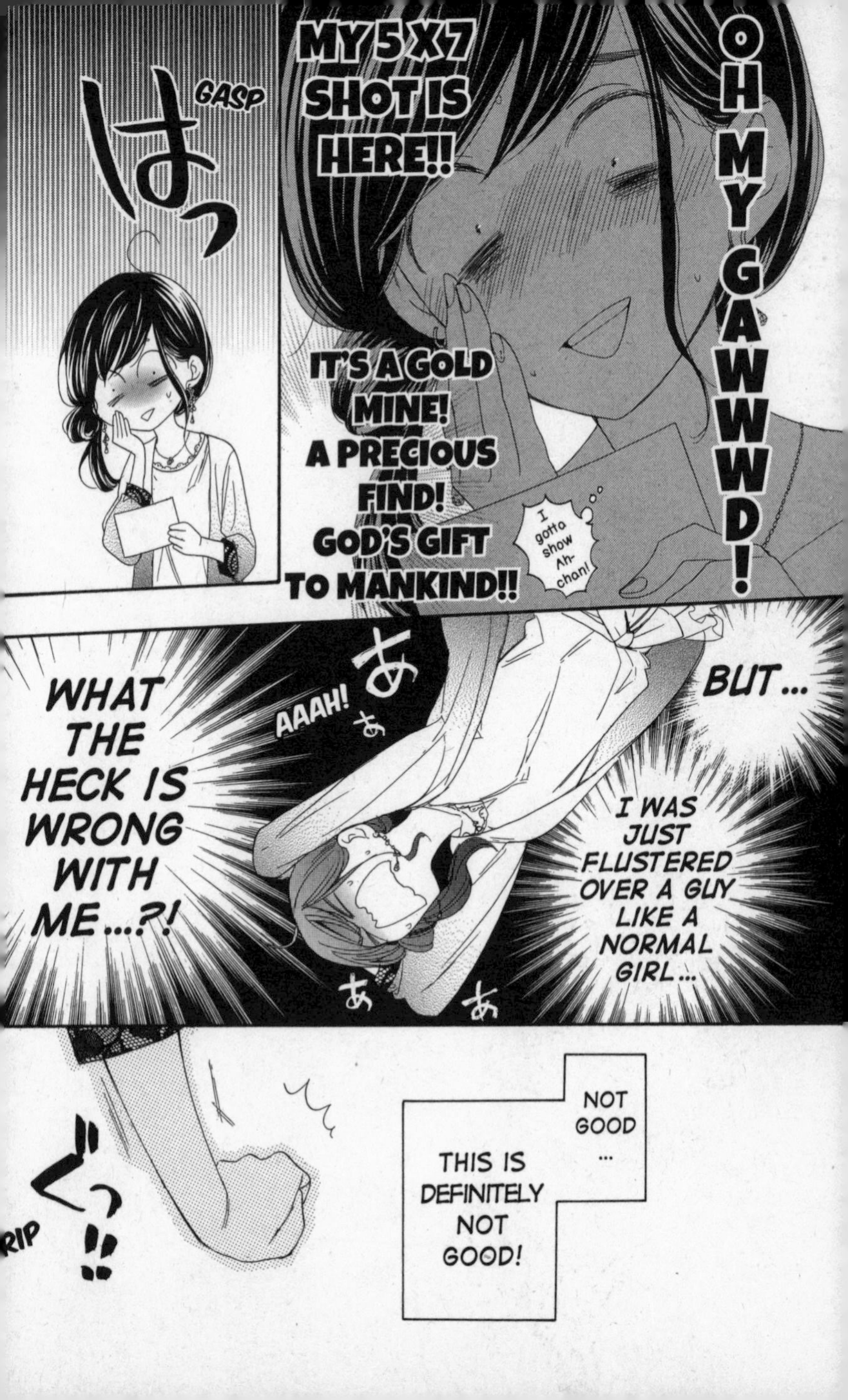
OH MY GAWWWD!
MY 5 X 7 SHOT IS HERE!!
IT'S A GOLD MINE! A PRECIOUS FIND! GOD'S GIFT TO MANKIND!!
I gotta show Ah-chan!
はっ
GASP
BUT...
I WAS JUST FLUSTERED OVER A GUY LIKE A NORMAL GIRL...
あ
AAAH!
あ
あ
あ
WHAT THE HECK IS WRONG WITH ME...?!
NOT GOOD...
THIS IS DEFINITELY NOT GOOD!
ぐっ!!
RIP

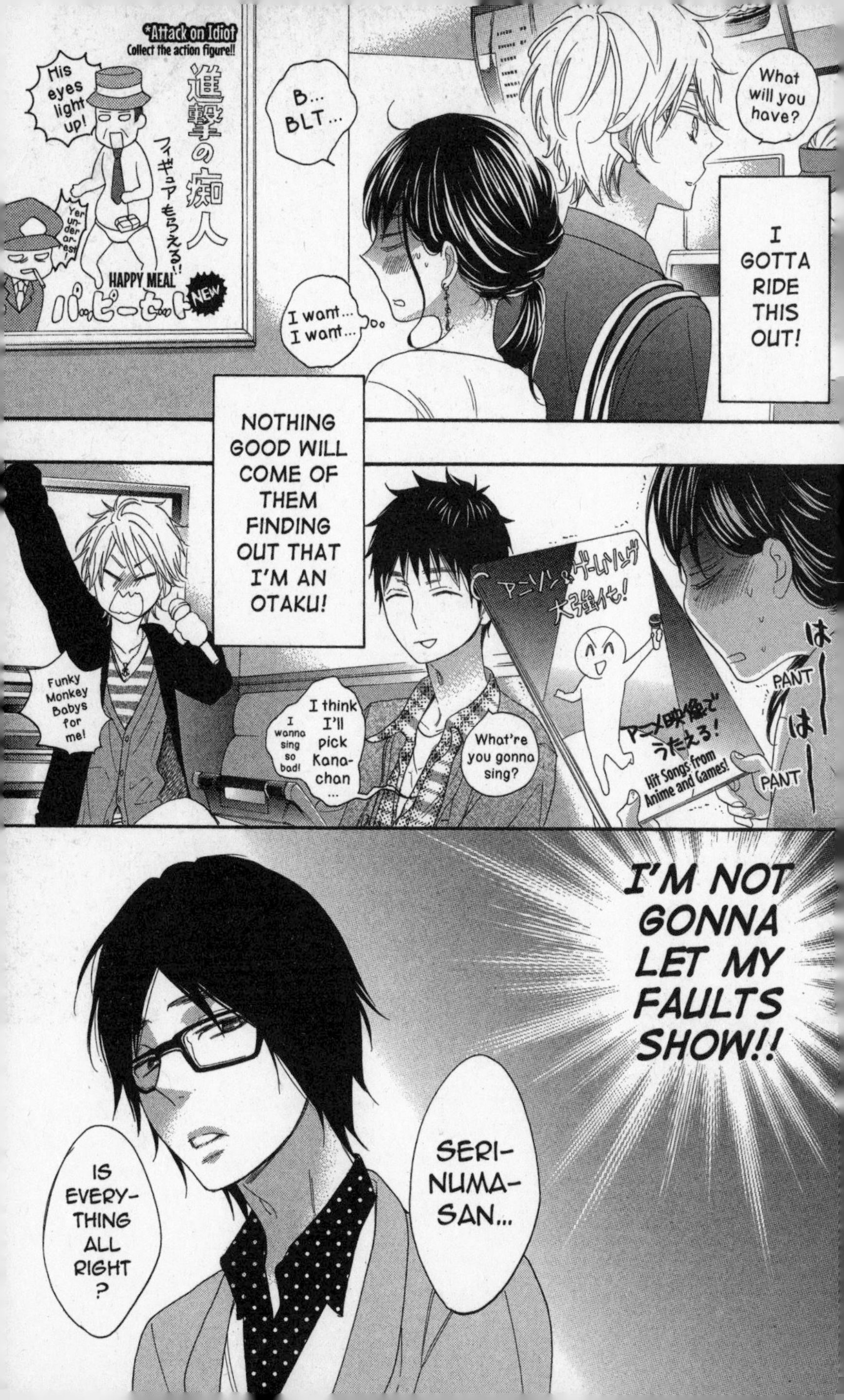
What will you have?
B... BLT...
I GOTTA RIDE THIS OUT!
*Attack on Idiot
Collect the action figure!!
進撃の痴人
フィギュアもらえる!!
His eyes light up!
Yer under arrest!
HAPPY MEAL
NEW
I want... I want...
NOTHING GOOD WILL COME OF THEM FINDING OUT THAT I'M AN OTAKU!
PANT
PANT
アニメ映像でうたえる!
Hit Songs from Anime and Games!
What're you gonna sing?
I think I'll pick Kana-chan...
I wanna sing so bad!
Funky Monkey Babys for me!
I'M NOT GONNA LET MY FAULTS SHOW!!
SERI-NUMA-SAN...
IS EVERYTHING ALL RIGHT?

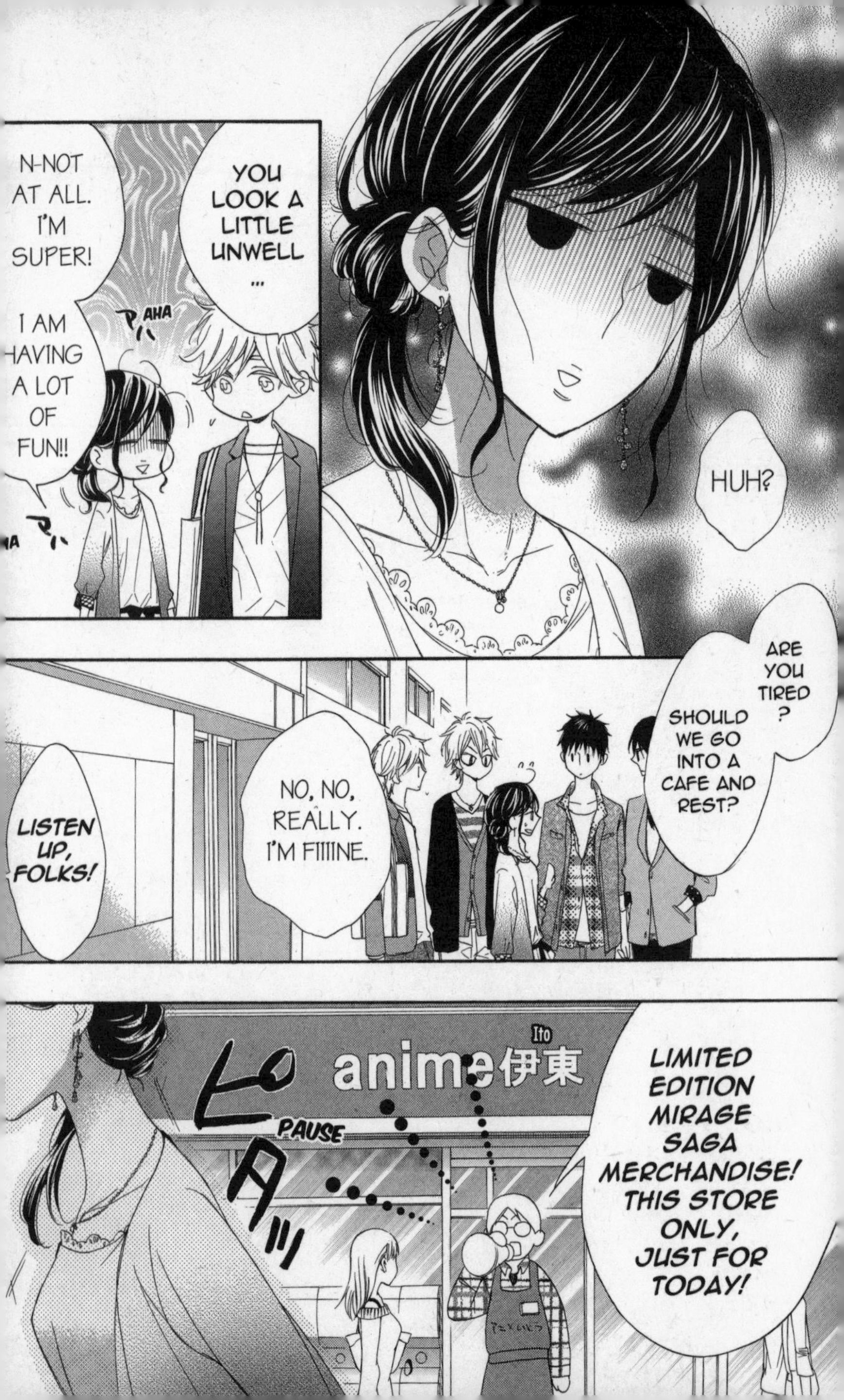
HUH?
YOU LOOK A LITTLE UNWELL ...
AHA
N-NOT AT ALL. I'M SUPER!
I AM HAVING A LOT OF FUN!!
HA
ARE YOU TIRED?
SHOULD WE GO INTO A CAFE AND REST?
NO, NO, REALLY. I'M FIIIINE.
LISTEN UP, FOLKS!
LIMITED EDITION MIRAGE SAGA MERCHANDISE! THIS STORE ONLY, JUST FOR TODAY!
Ito
anime 伊東
PAUSE

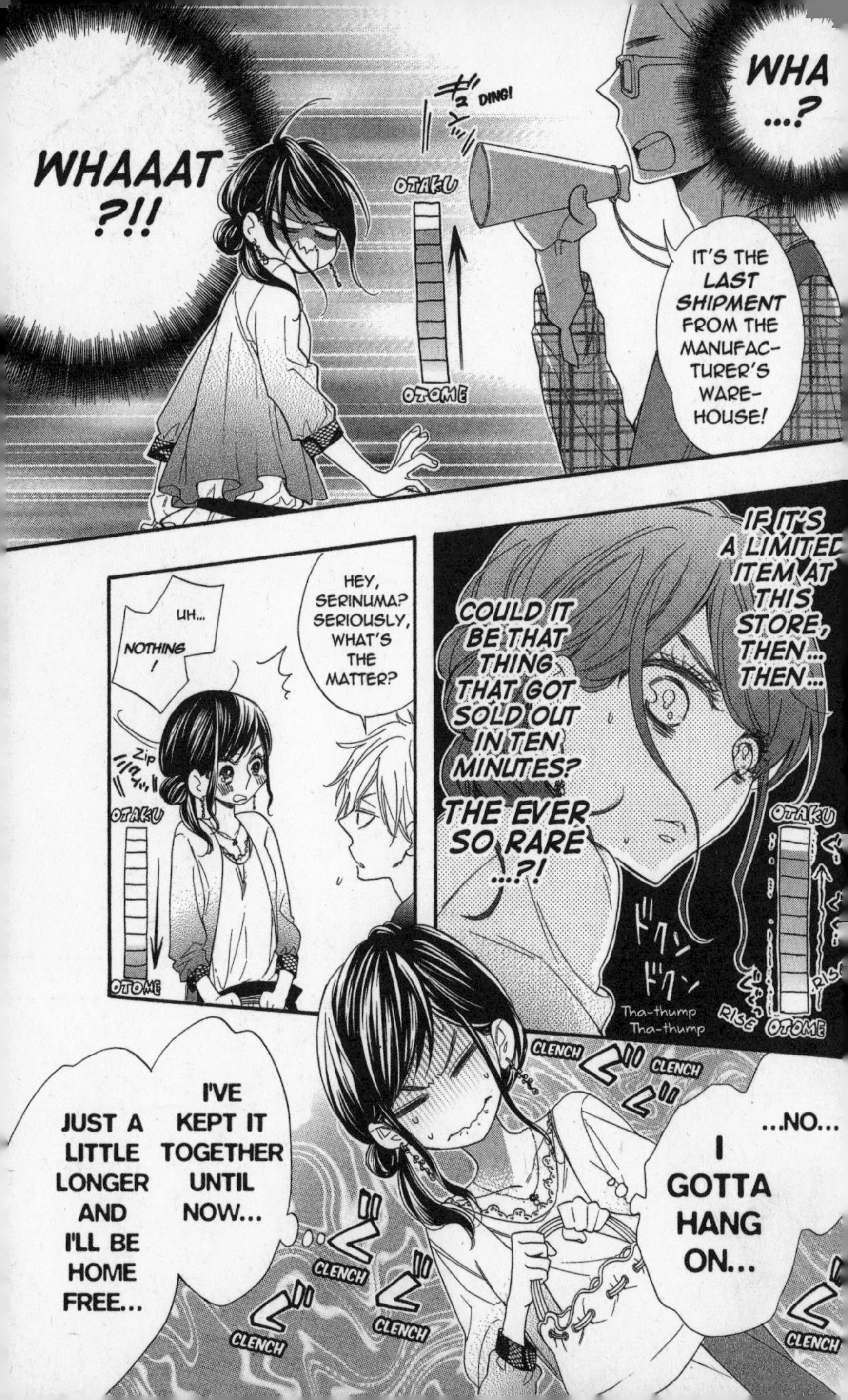
WHA ...?
IT'S THE LAST SHIPMENT FROM THE MANUFACTURER'S WAREHOUSE!
DING!
OTAKU
OTOME
WHAAAT ?!!
IF IT'S A LIMITED ITEM AT THIS STORE, THEN... THEN...
COULD IT BE THAT THING THAT GOT SOLD OUT IN TEN MINUTES?
THE EVER SO RARE ...?!
Tha-thump Tha-thump
OTAKU
RISE
RISE
OTOME
HEY, SERINUMA? SERIOUSLY, WHAT'S THE MATTER?
UH... NOTHING!
Zip
OTAKU
OTOME
...NO... I GOTTA HANG ON...
CLENCH
CLENCH
CLENCH
I'VE KEPT IT TOGETHER UNTIL NOW...
JUST A LITTLE LONGER AND I'LL BE HOME FREE...
CLENCH
CLENCH
CLENCH

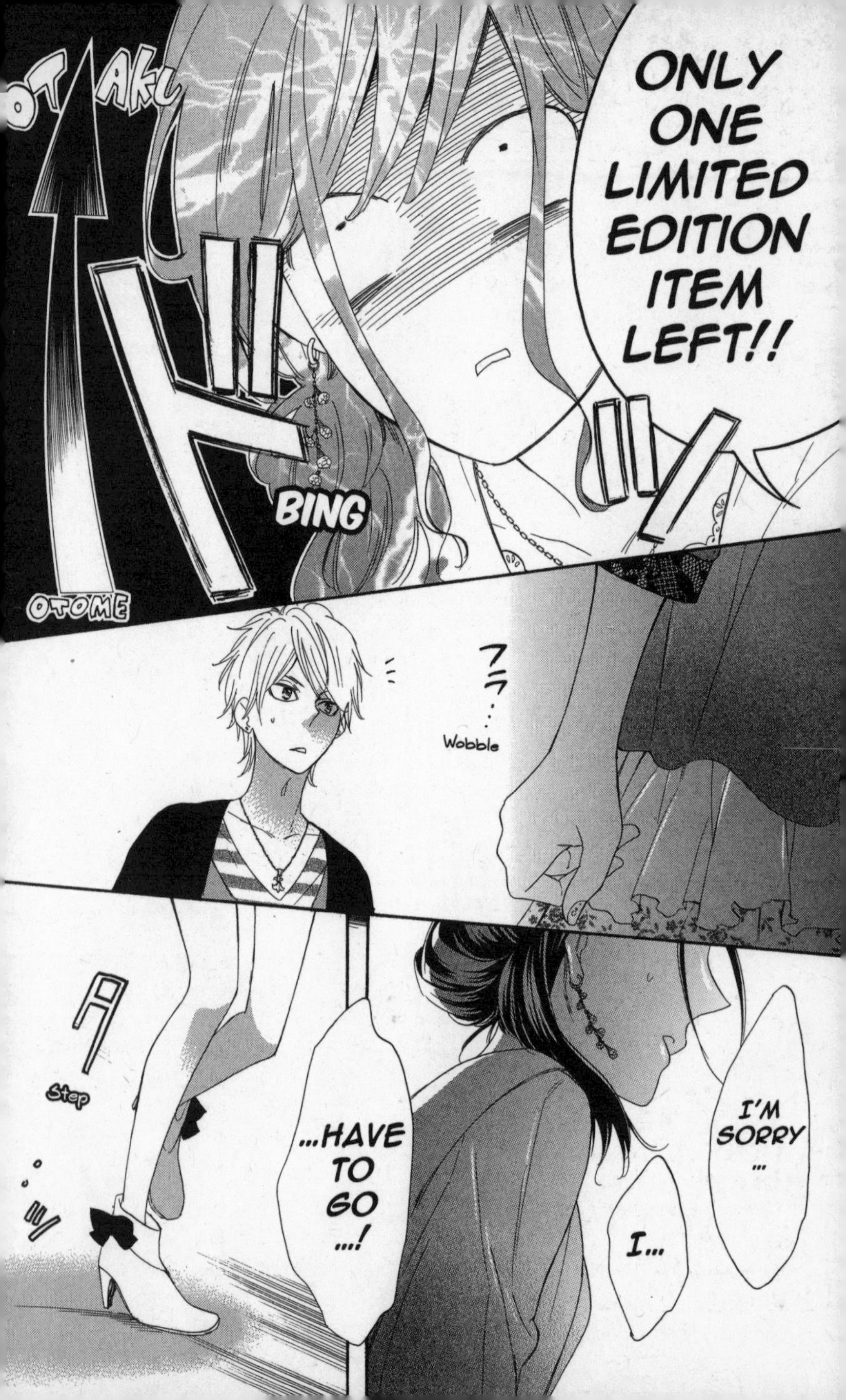
ONLY ONE LIMITED EDITION ITEM LEFT!!
BING
OTAKU
OTOME
Wobble
I'M SORRY...
I...
...HAVE TO GO...!
Step

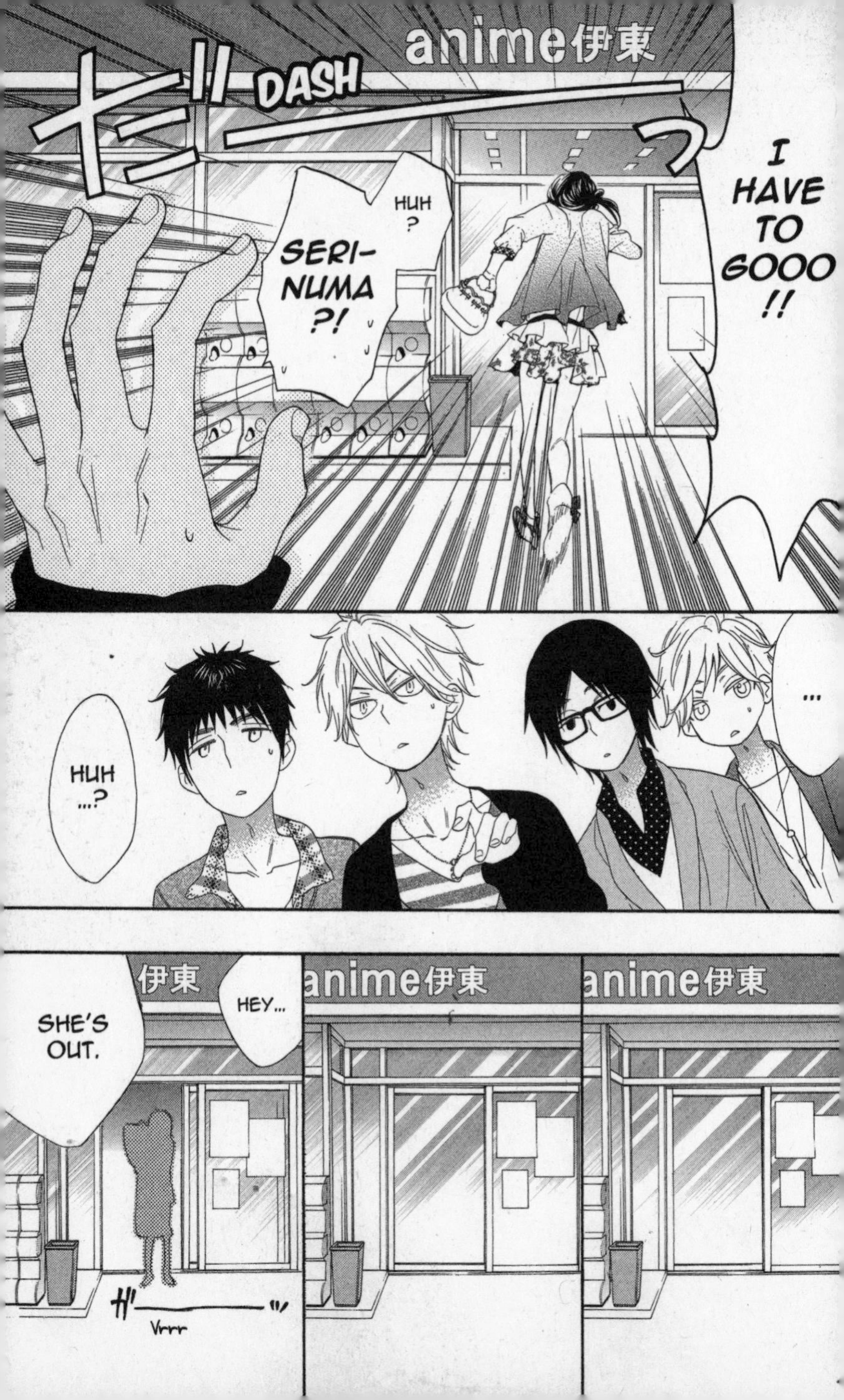
anime伊東
DASH
I HAVE TO GOOO!!
HUH?
SERI-NUMA?!
...
HUH...?
anime伊東
anime伊東
伊東
HEY...
SHE'S OUT.
Vrrr

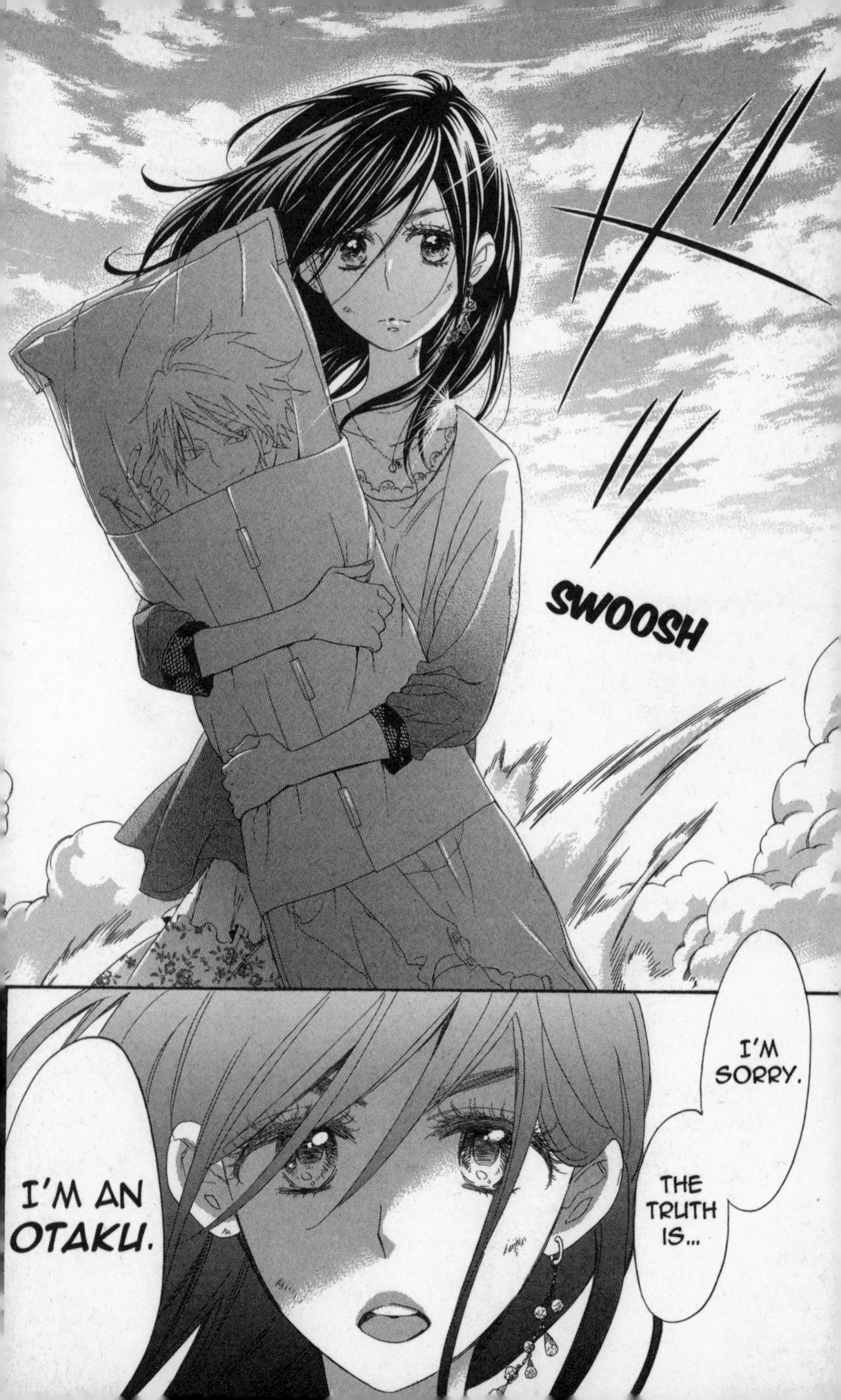
SWOOSH
I'M SORRY.
THE TRUTH IS...
I'M AN OTAKU.

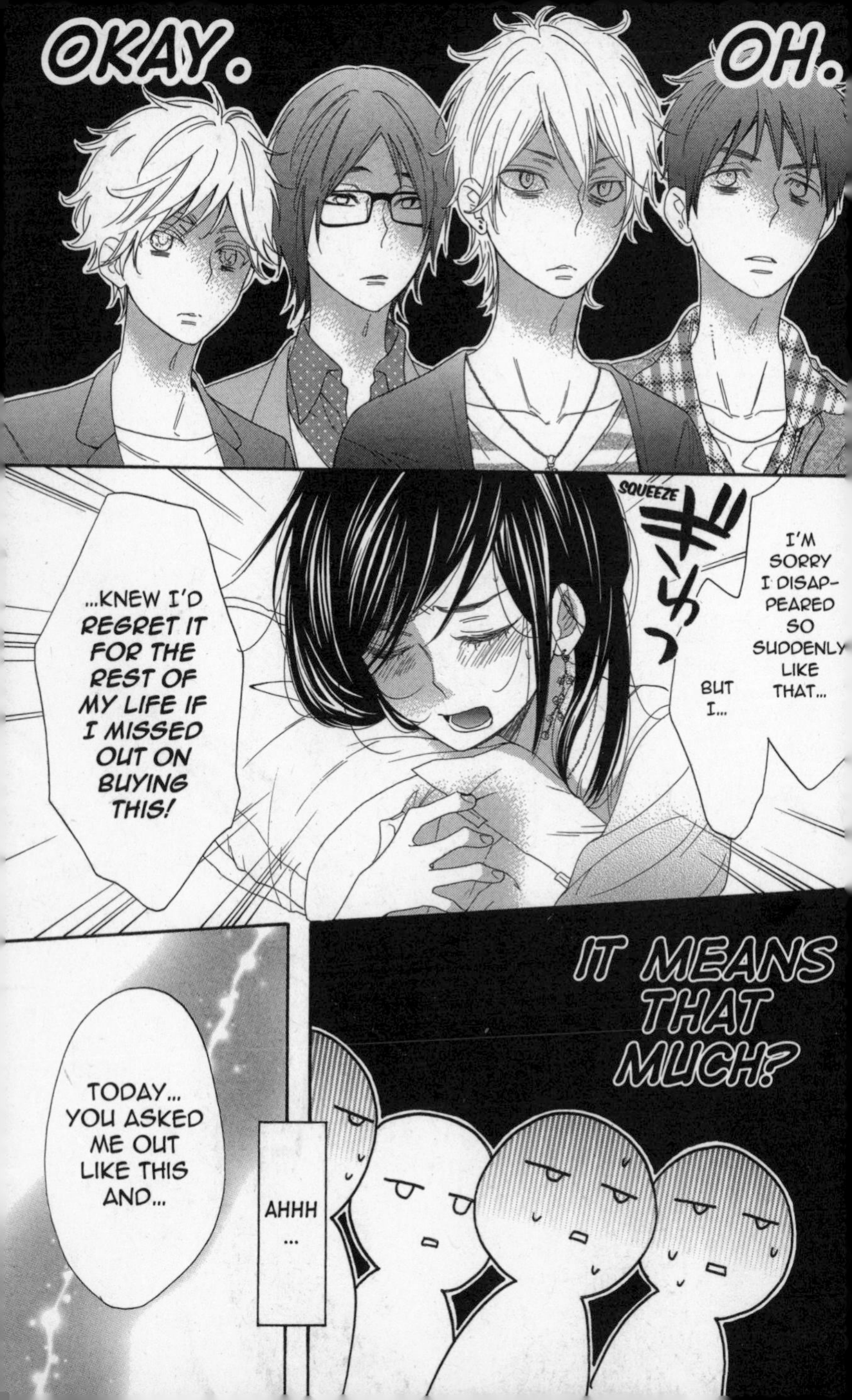
OH.
OKAY.
I'M SORRY I DISAPPEARED SO SUDDENLY LIKE THAT...
BUT I...
SQUEEZE
...KNEW I'D REGRET IT FOR THE REST OF MY LIFE IF I MISSED OUT ON BUYING THIS!
IT MEANS THAT MUCH?
AHHH...
TODAY... YOU ASKED ME OUT LIKE THIS AND...

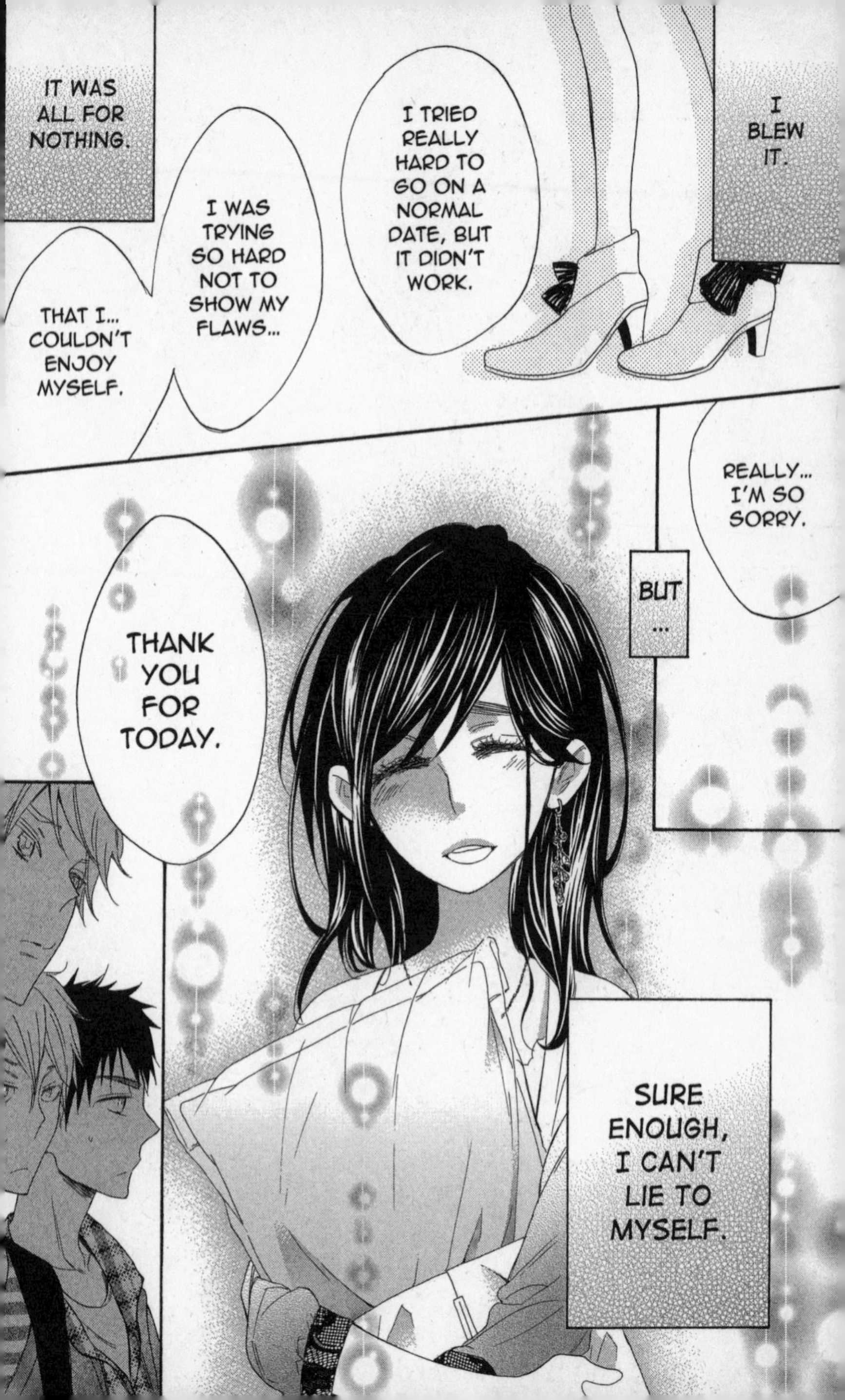
I BLEW IT.
I TRIED REALLY HARD TO GO ON A NORMAL DATE, BUT IT DIDN'T WORK.
IT WAS ALL FOR NOTHING.
I WAS TRYING SO HARD NOT TO SHOW MY FLAWS...
THAT I... COULDN'T ENJOY MYSELF.
REALLY... I'M SO SORRY.
BUT ...
THANK YOU FOR TODAY.
SURE ENOUGH, I CAN'T LIE TO MYSELF.

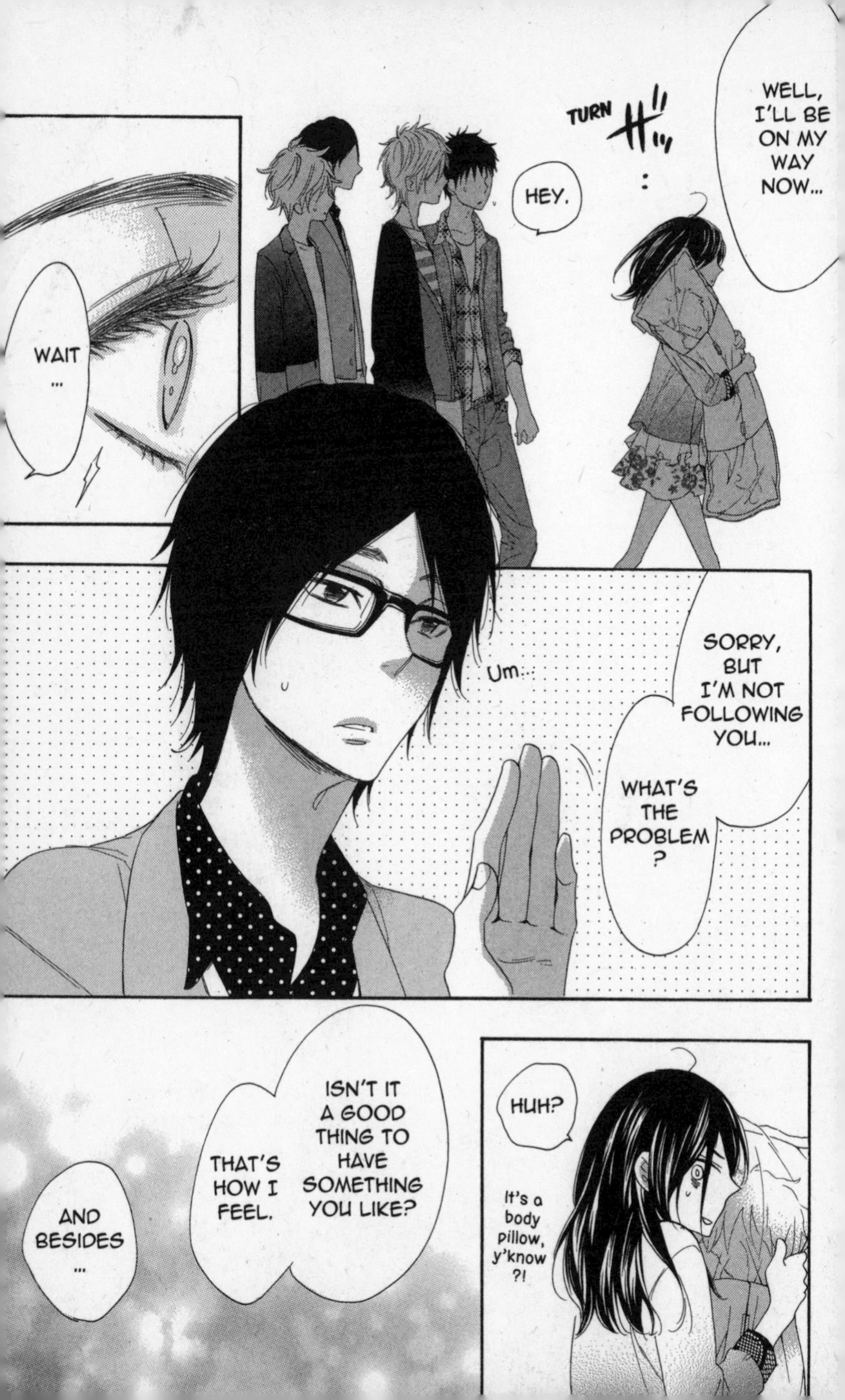
WELL, I'LL BE ON MY WAY NOW...
TURN
HEY.
WAIT ...
SORRY, BUT I'M NOT FOLLOWING YOU...
WHAT'S THE PROBLEM ?
Um...
HUH?
It's a body pillow, y'know ?!
ISN'T IT A GOOD THING TO HAVE SOMETHING YOU LIKE?
THAT'S HOW I FEEL.
AND BESIDES ...

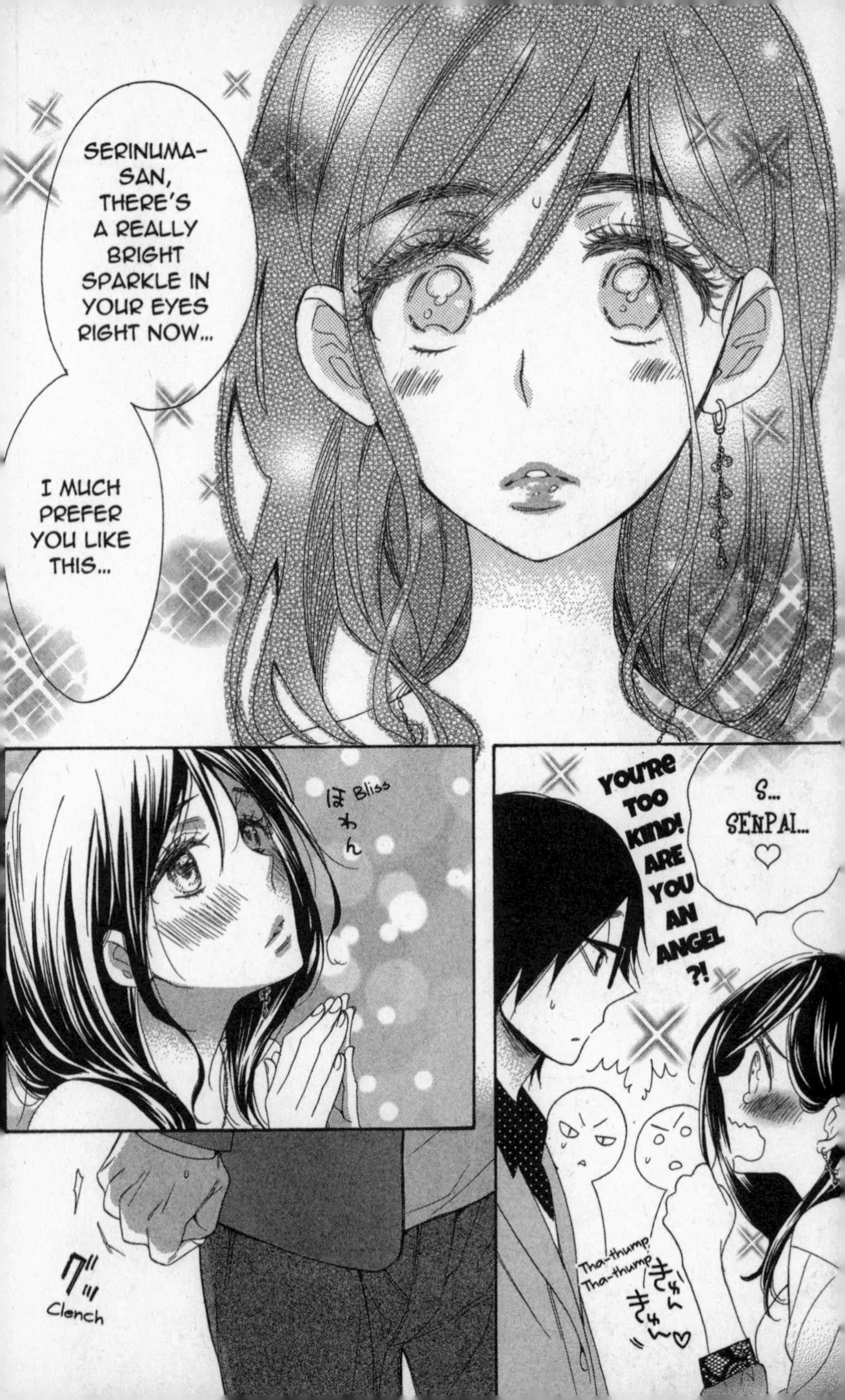
SERINUMA-SAN, THERE'S A REALLY BRIGHT SPARKLE IN YOUR EYES RIGHT NOW...
I MUCH PREFER YOU LIKE THIS...
S... SENPAI... ♡
YOU'RE TOO KIND! ARE YOU AN ANGEL?!
Tha-thump Tha-thump
きゅん きゅん♡
ほわん
Bliss
グッ
Clench

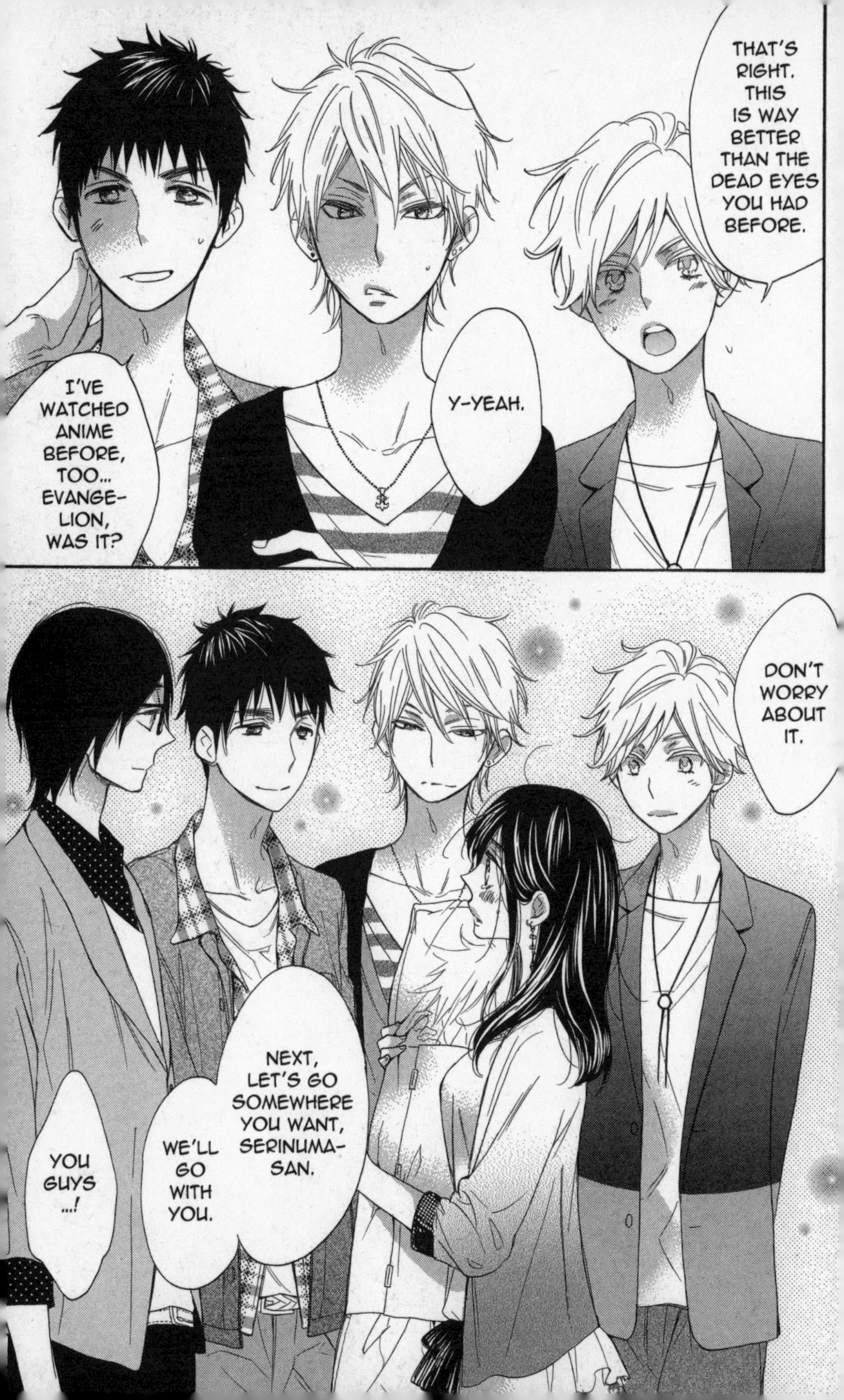
THAT'S RIGHT. THIS IS WAY BETTER THAN THE DEAD EYES YOU HAD BEFORE.
Y-YEAH.
I'VE WATCHED ANIME BEFORE, TOO... EVANGE-LION, WAS IT?
DON'T WORRY ABOUT IT.
NEXT, LET'S GO SOMEWHERE YOU WANT, SERINUMA-SAN.
WE'LL GO WITH YOU.
YOU GUYS ...!

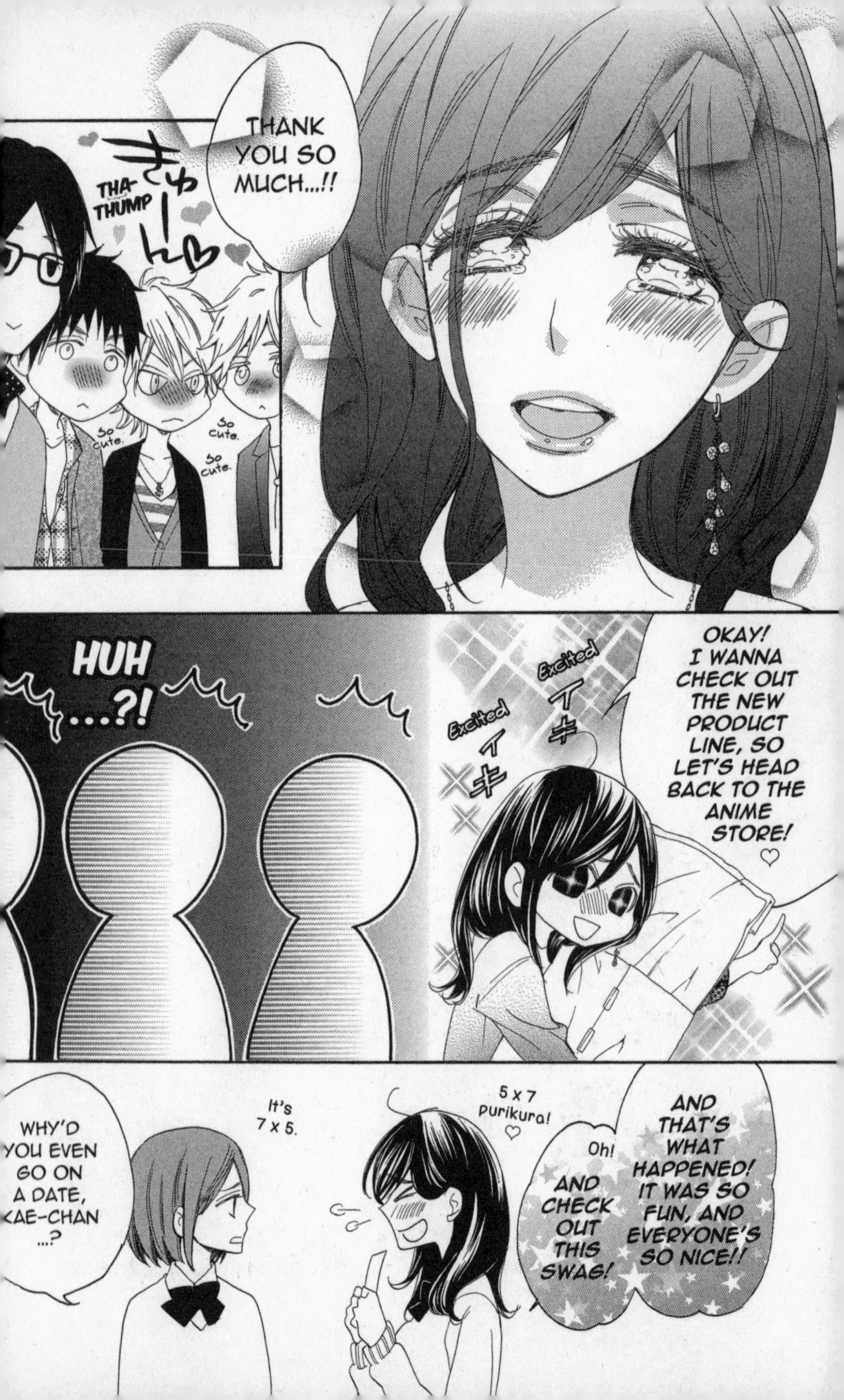
THANK YOU SO MUCH...!!
きゅーん♥
THA-THUMP
So cute.
So cute.
So cute.
OKAY! I WANNA CHECK OUT THE NEW PRODUCT LINE, SO LET'S HEAD BACK TO THE ANIME STORE! ♡
Excited イキ
Excited イキ
HUH ...?!
AND THAT'S WHAT HAPPENED! IT WAS SO FUN, AND EVERYONE'S SO NICE!!
Oh! AND CHECK OUT THIS SWAG!
5 x 7 purikura! ♡
It's 7 x 5.
WHY'D YOU EVEN GO ON A DATE, KAE-CHAN ...?

ROCK, PAPER ...
AH!
I DON'T TRUST THIS GUY...
Hah !!
DON'T TRY HOLDING MY HANDS OR ANY-THING LIKE THAT JUST 'CAUSE YOU'RE NEXT TO ME!
I WON'T! I WON'T!
I GOT IT! I'LL BIND YOUR HANDS LIKE THIS UNTIL WE'RE FINISHED!
SQUEEZE
HUH ...?
THATHUMP
Good idea!

KiSS HiM, NOT ME!

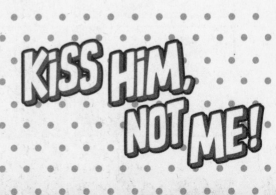

#3 CAN SHE GET ALONG WITH THE BALL?

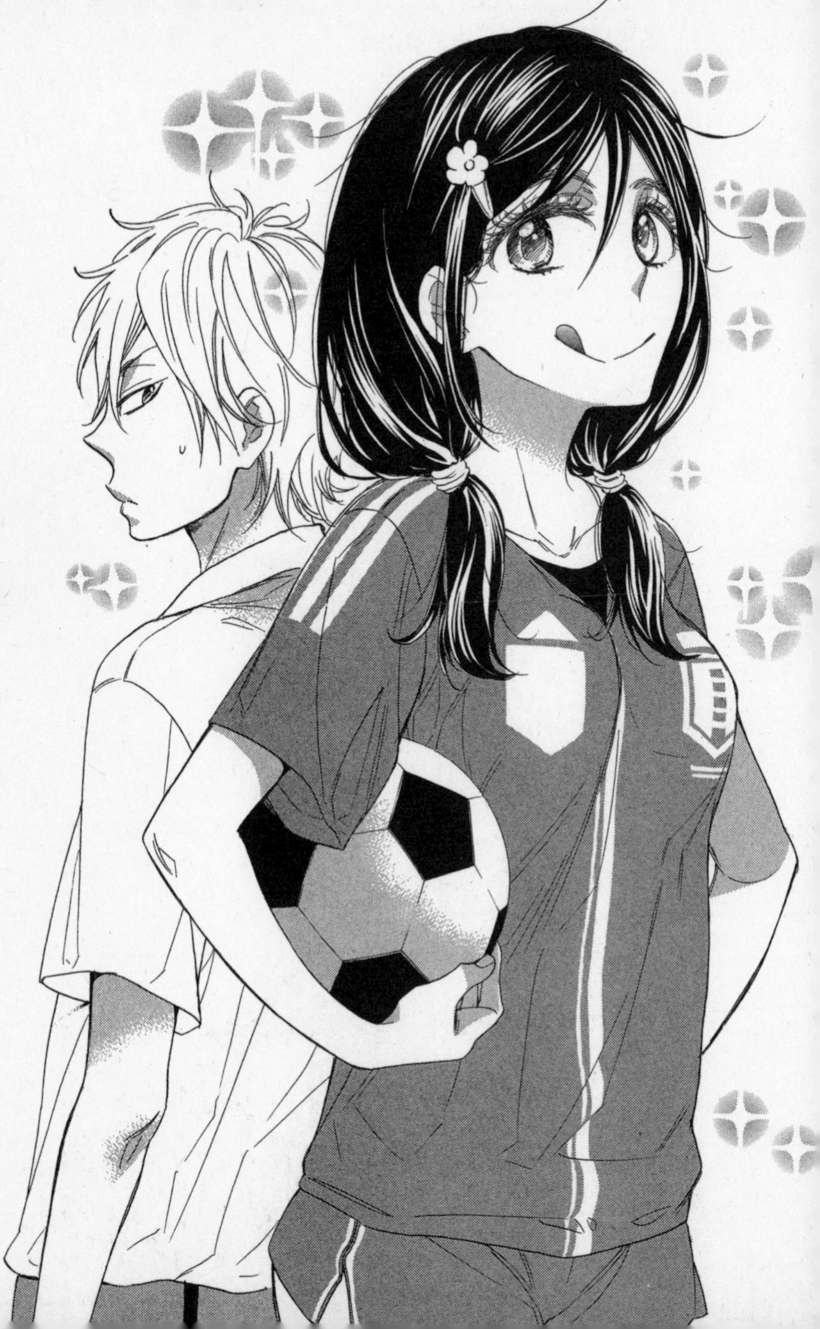

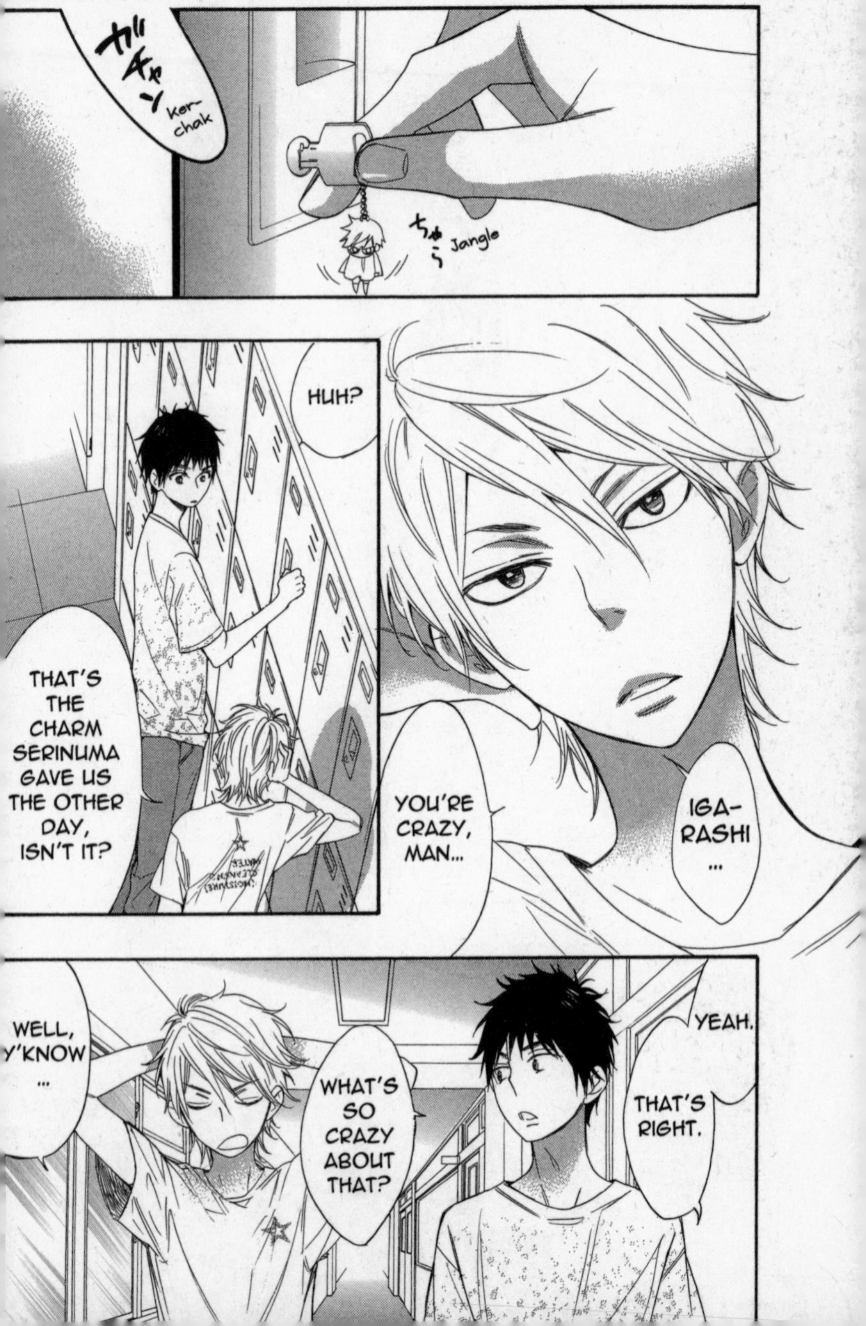
ガチャン
ker-chak
Jangle
IGA-RASHI ...
YOU'RE CRAZY, MAN...
HUH?
THAT'S THE CHARM SERINUMA GAVE US THE OTHER DAY, ISN'T IT?
YEAH.
THAT'S RIGHT.
WHAT'S SO CRAZY ABOUT THAT?
WELL, Y'KNOW ...

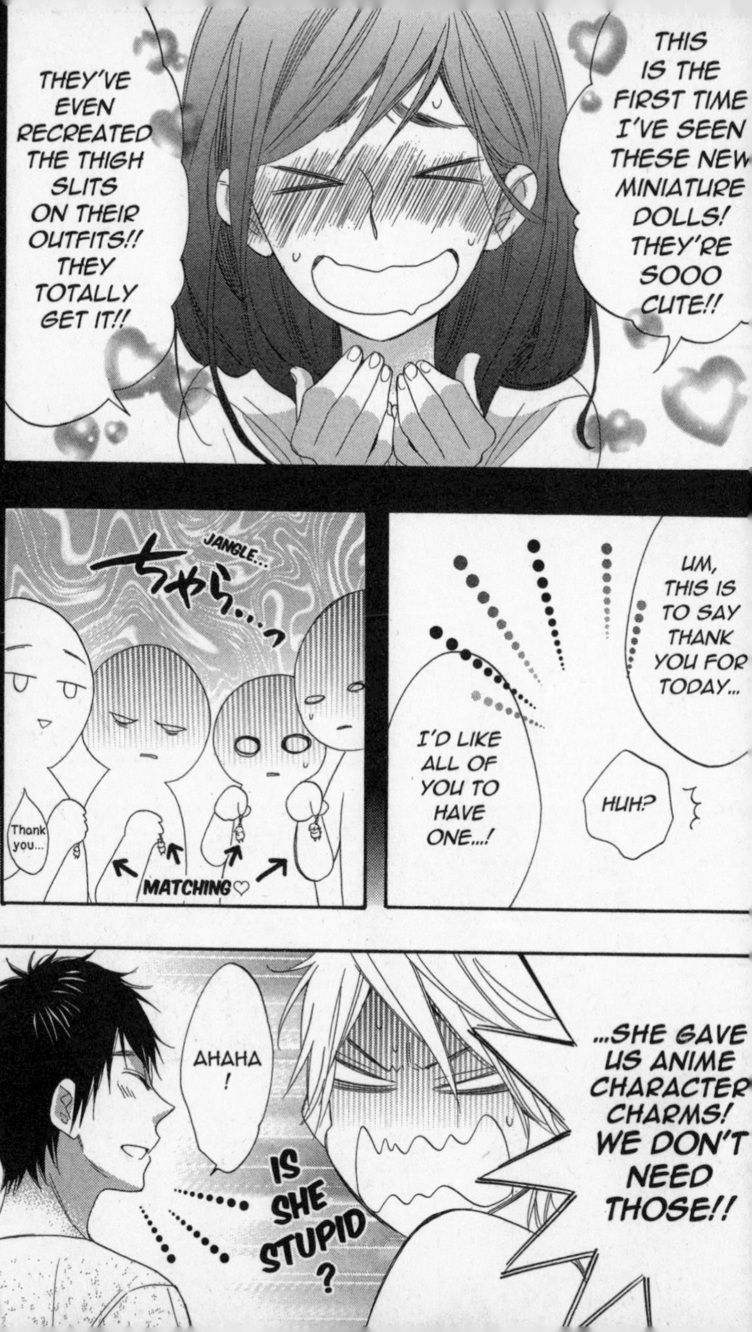
THIS IS THE FIRST TIME I'VE SEEN THESE NEW MINIATURE DOLLS! THEY'RE SOOO CUTE!!
THEY'VE EVEN RECREATED THE THIGH SLITS ON THEIR OUTFITS!! THEY TOTALLY GET IT!!
UM, THIS IS TO SAY THANK YOU FOR TODAY...
HUH?
I'D LIKE ALL OF YOU TO HAVE ONE...!
JANGLE...
ちゃら…っ
Thank you...
MATCHING♡
...SHE GAVE US ANIME CHARACTER CHARMS! WE DON'T NEED THOSE!!
AHAHA!
IS SHE STUPID?

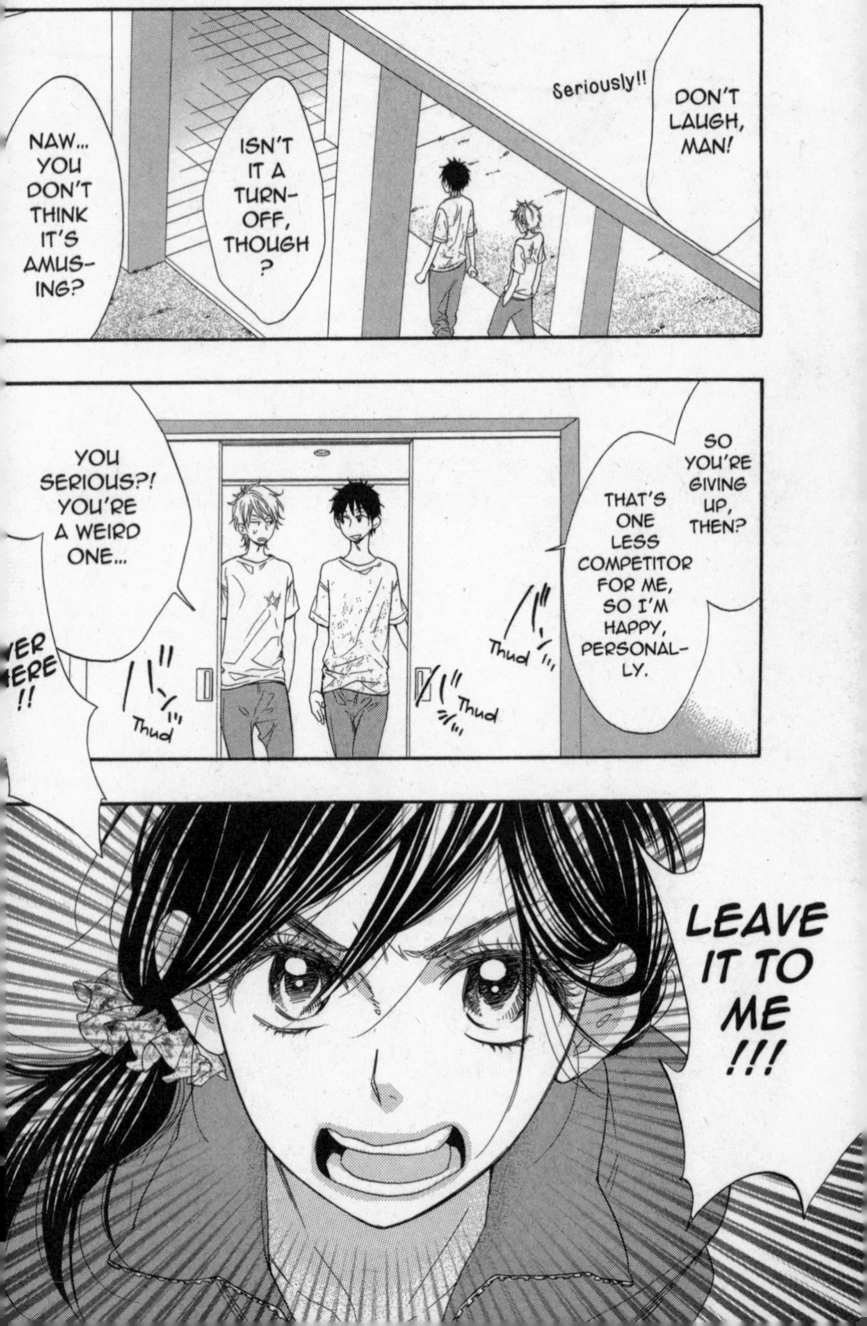
DON'T LAUGH, MAN!
Seriously!!
ISN'T IT A TURN-OFF, THOUGH?
NAW... YOU DON'T THINK IT'S AMUSING?
SO YOU'RE GIVING UP, THEN?
THAT'S ONE LESS COMPETITOR FOR ME, SO I'M HAPPY, PERSONALLY.
Thud
Thud
YOU SERIOUS?! YOU'RE A WEIRD ONE...
Thud
LEAVE IT TO ME!!!

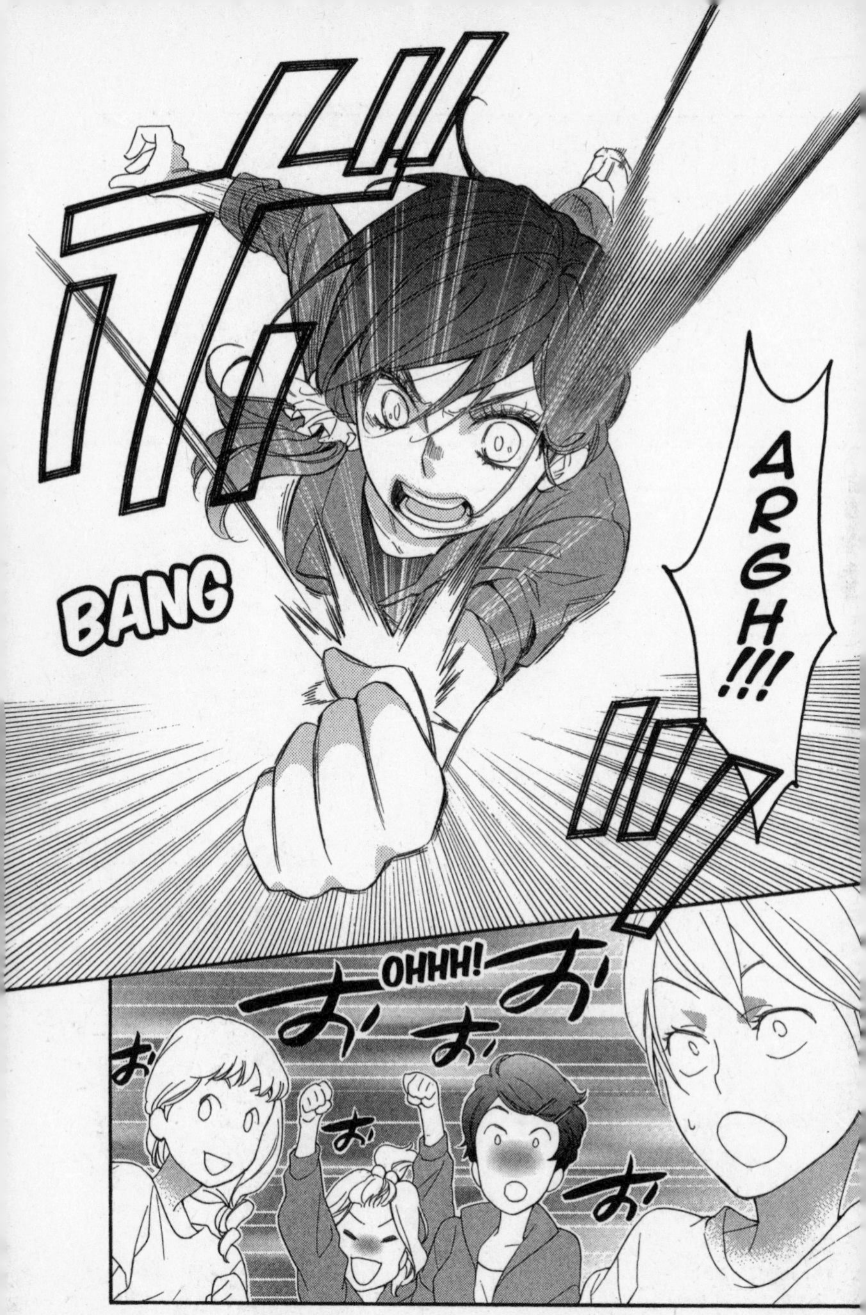
ARGH!!!
BANG
OHHH!

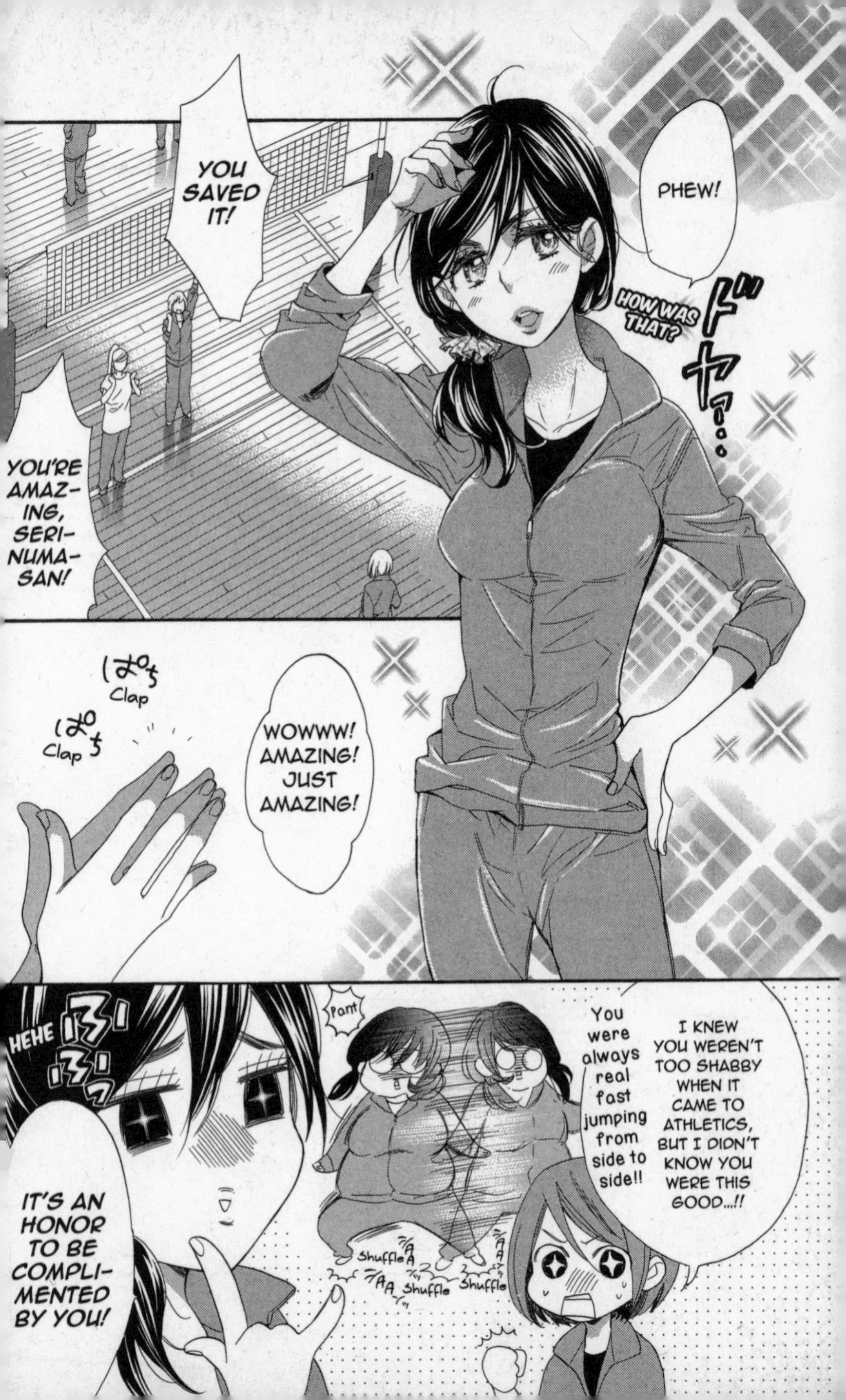
PHEW!
HOW WAS THAT?
YOU SAVED IT!
YOU'RE AMAZING, SERINUMA-SAN!
WOWWW! AMAZING! JUST AMAZING!
ぱち Clap
ぱち Clap
I KNEW YOU WEREN'T TOO SHABBY WHEN IT CAME TO ATHLETICS, BUT I DIDN'T KNOW YOU WERE THIS GOOD...!!
You were always real fast jumping from side to side!!
Pant
Shuffle
Shuffle
Shuffle
HEHE
IT'S AN HONOR TO BE COMPLIMENTED BY YOU!

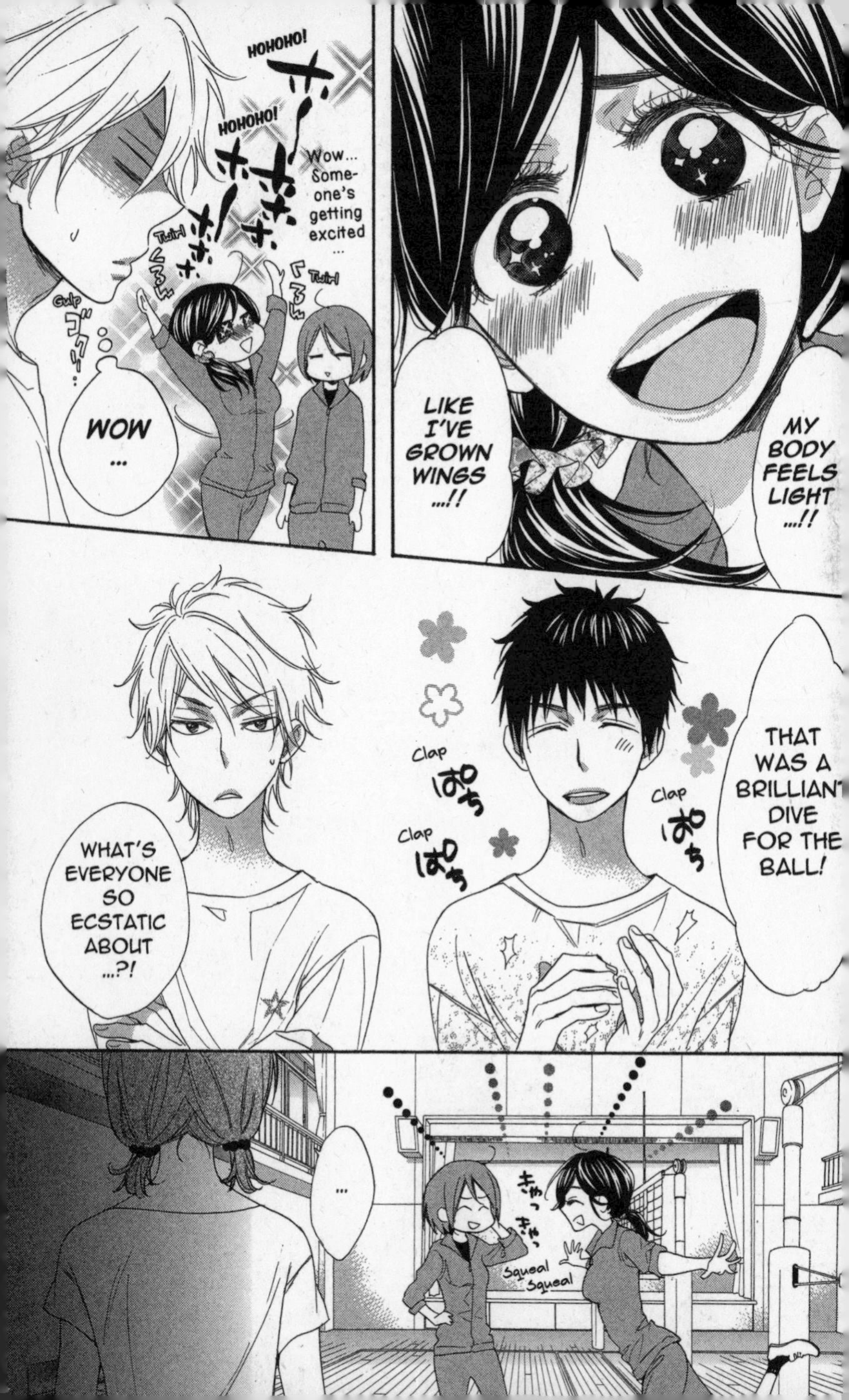
MY BODY FEELS LIGHT ...!!
LIKE I'VE GROWN WINGS ...!!
HOHOHO!
HOHOHO!
Wow... Some-one's getting excited ...
Twirl
Twirl
Gulp
WOW ...
THAT WAS A BRILLIANT DIVE FOR THE BALL!
Clap
Clap
Clap
WHAT'S EVERYONE SO ECSTATIC ABOUT ...?!
Squeal
Squeal
...

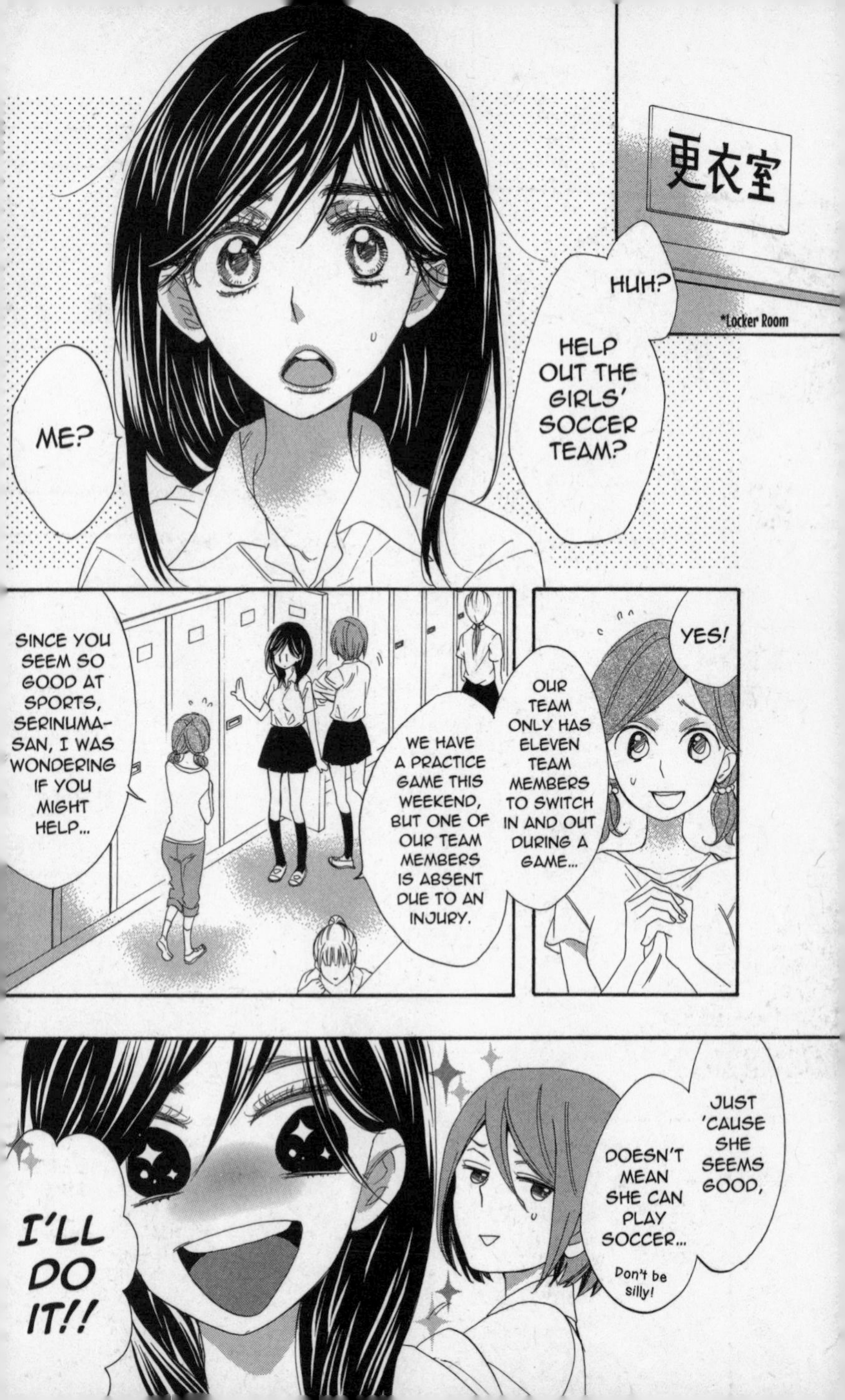
更衣室
*Locker Room
HUH?
HELP OUT THE GIRLS' SOCCER TEAM?
ME?
YES!
OUR TEAM ONLY HAS ELEVEN TEAM MEMBERS TO SWITCH IN AND OUT DURING A GAME...
WE HAVE A PRACTICE GAME THIS WEEKEND, BUT ONE OF OUR TEAM MEMBERS IS ABSENT DUE TO AN INJURY.
SINCE YOU SEEM SO GOOD AT SPORTS, SERINUMA-SAN, I WAS WONDERING IF YOU MIGHT HELP...
JUST 'CAUSE SHE SEEMS GOOD,
DOESN'T MEAN SHE CAN PLAY SOCCER...
Don't be silly!
I'LL DO IT!!

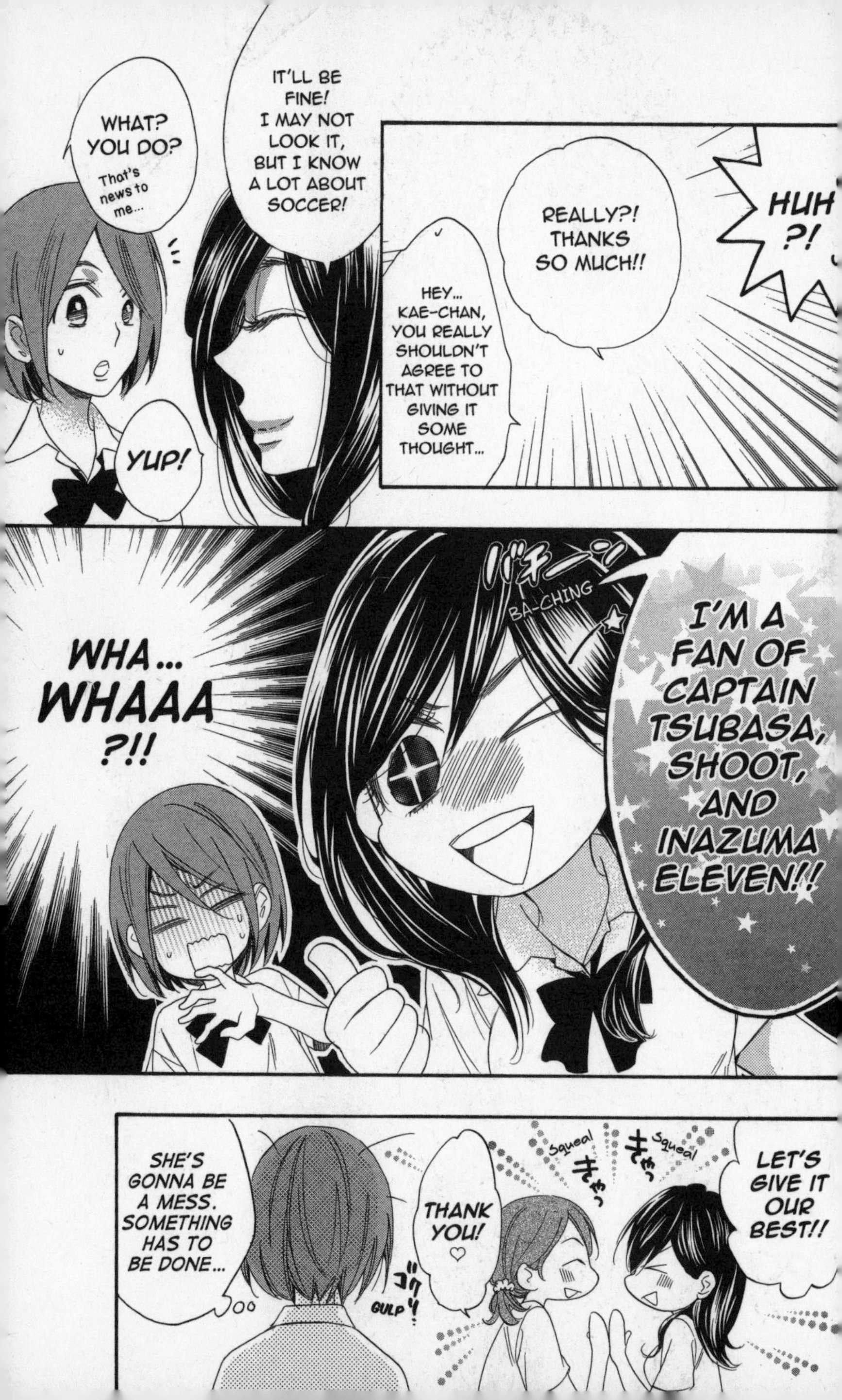
HUH ?!
REALLY?! THANKS SO MUCH!!
HEY... KAE-CHAN, YOU REALLY SHOULDN'T AGREE TO THAT WITHOUT GIVING IT SOME THOUGHT...
IT'LL BE FINE! I MAY NOT LOOK IT, BUT I KNOW A LOT ABOUT SOCCER!
WHAT? YOU DO?
That's news to me...
YUP!
BA-CHING
I'M A FAN OF CAPTAIN TSUBASA, SHOOT, AND INAZUMA ELEVEN!!
WHA... WHAAA ?!!
LET'S GIVE IT OUR BEST!!
Squeal
Squeal
THANK YOU! ♡
GULP
SHE'S GONNA BE A MESS. SOMETHING HAS TO BE DONE...

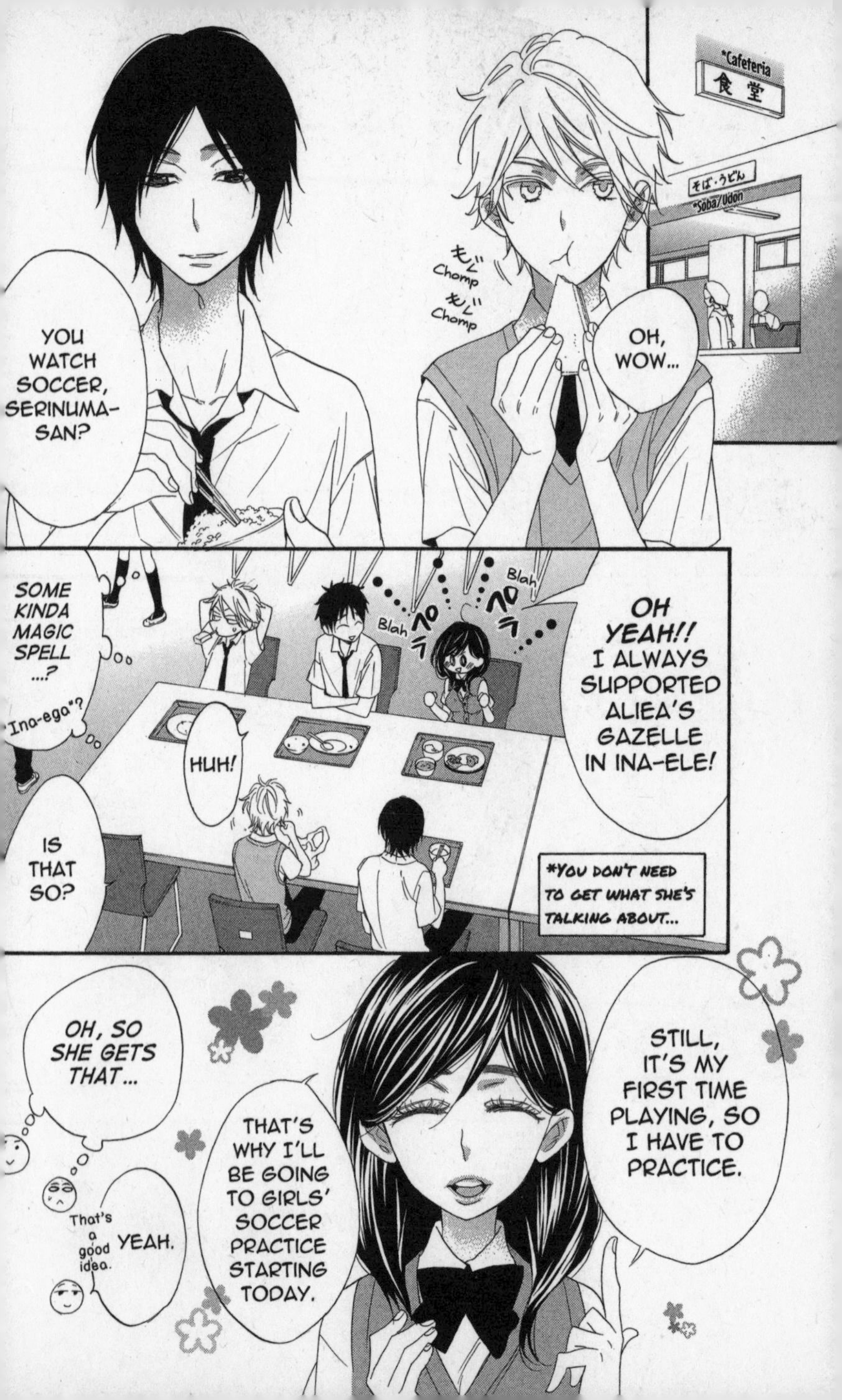
*Cafeteria
食堂
そば・うどん
*Soba/Udon
OH, WOW...
もぐ Chomp
もぐ Chomp
YOU WATCH SOCCER, SERINUMA-SAN?
OH YEAH!! I ALWAYS SUPPORTED ALIEA'S GAZELLE IN INA-ELE!
Blah
Blah
*YOU DON'T NEED TO GET WHAT SHE'S TALKING ABOUT...
HUH!
SOME KINDA MAGIC SPELL ...?
"Ina-ega"?
IS THAT SO?
STILL, IT'S MY FIRST TIME PLAYING, SO I HAVE TO PRACTICE.
THAT'S WHY I'LL BE GOING TO GIRLS' SOCCER PRACTICE STARTING TODAY.
OH, SO SHE GETS THAT...
YEAH.
That's a good idea.

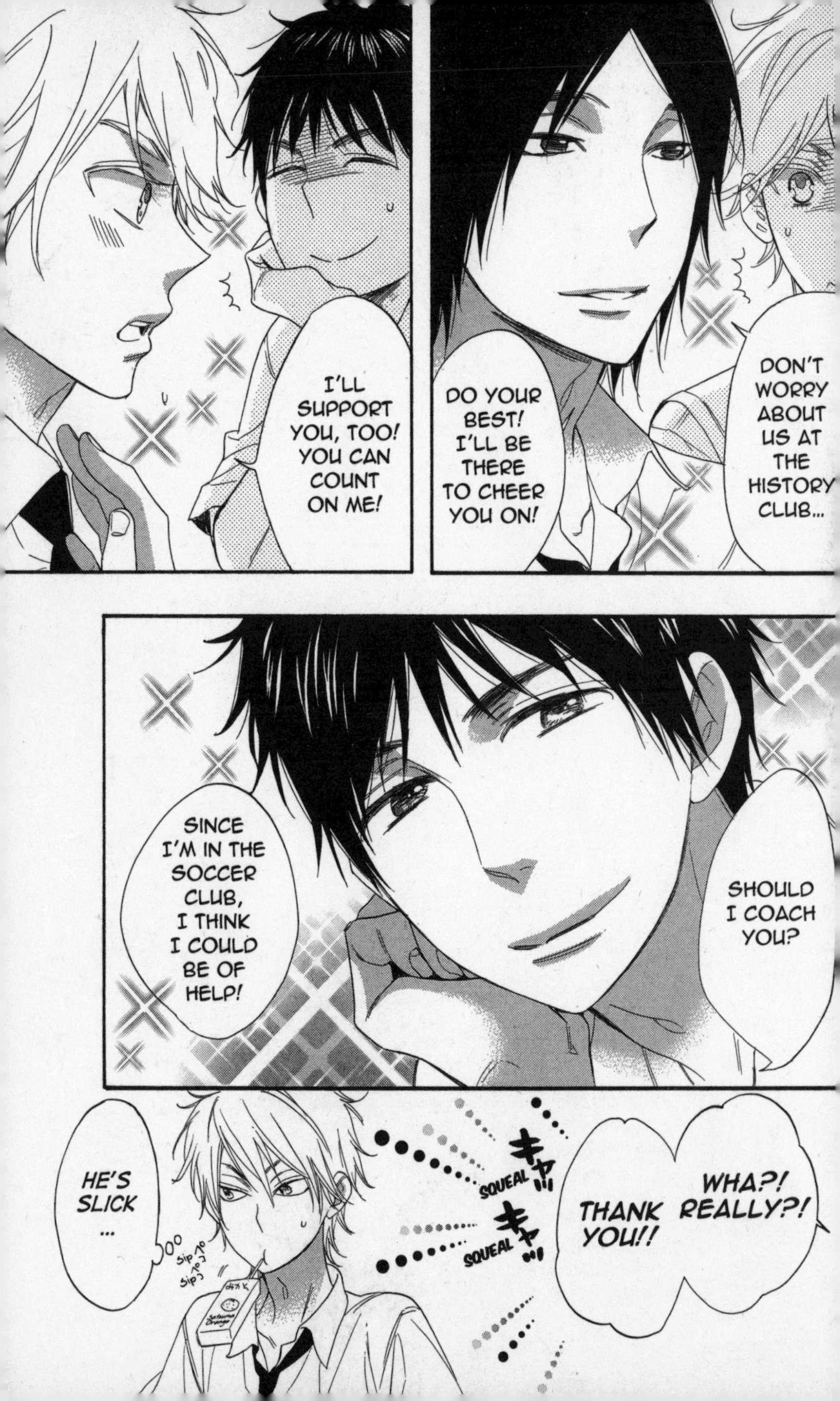
DON'T WORRY ABOUT US AT THE HISTORY CLUB...
DO YOUR BEST! I'LL BE THERE TO CHEER YOU ON!
I'LL SUPPORT YOU, TOO! YOU CAN COUNT ON ME!
SINCE I'M IN THE SOCCER CLUB, I THINK I COULD BE OF HELP!
SHOULD I COACH YOU?
WHA?! REALLY?!
THANK YOU!!
SQUEAL
SQUEAL
HE'S SLICK ...
SIP SIP

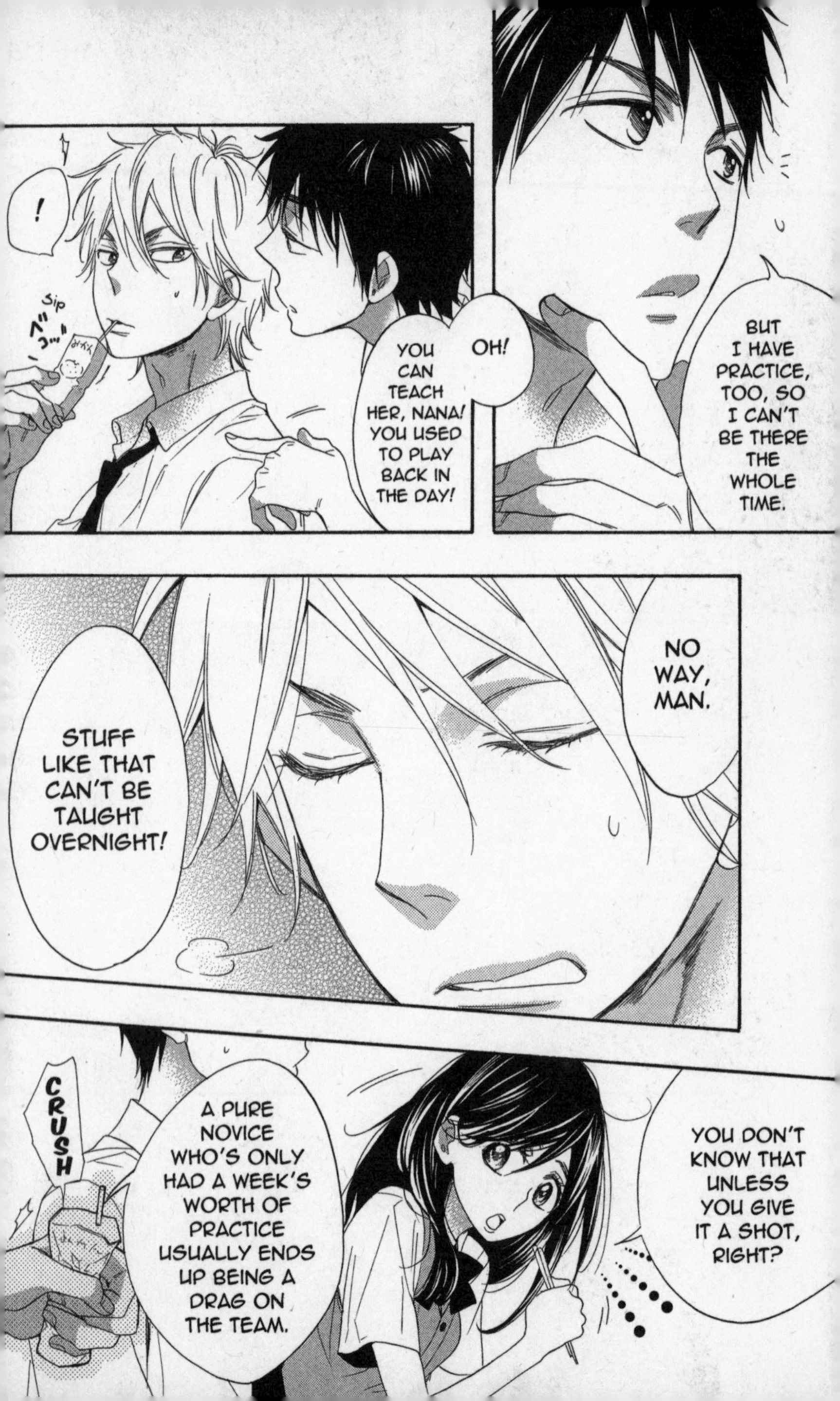
BUT I HAVE PRACTICE, TOO, SO I CAN'T BE THERE THE WHOLE TIME.
OH!
YOU CAN TEACH HER, NANA! YOU USED TO PLAY BACK IN THE DAY!
!
Sip
NO WAY, MAN.
STUFF LIKE THAT CAN'T BE TAUGHT OVERNIGHT!
YOU DON'T KNOW THAT UNLESS YOU GIVE IT A SHOT, RIGHT?
A PURE NOVICE WHO'S ONLY HAD A WEEK'S WORTH OF PRACTICE USUALLY ENDS UP BEING A DRAG ON THE TEAM.
CRUSH

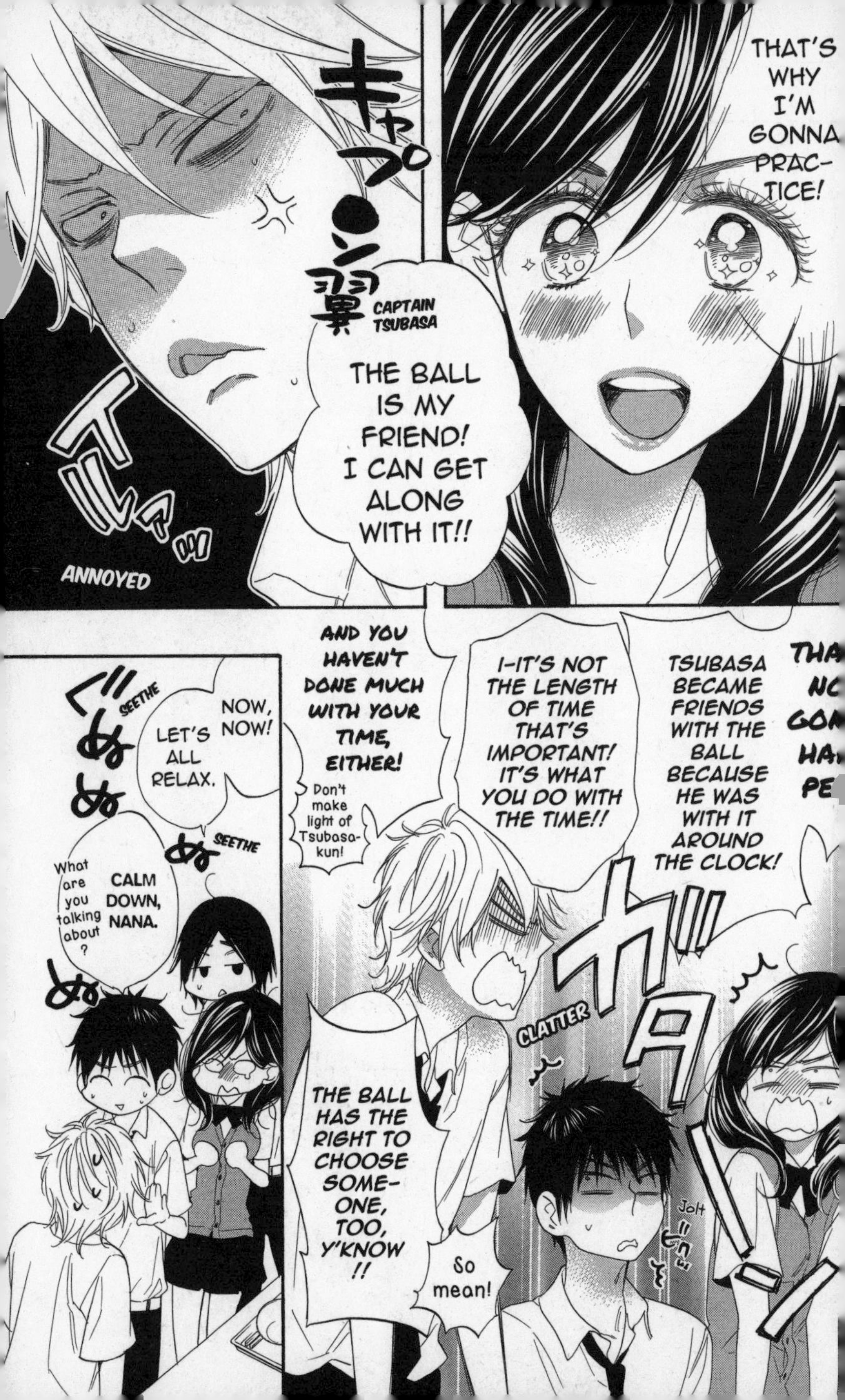
THAT'S WHY I'M GONNA PRAC- TICE!
THE BALL IS MY FRIEND! I CAN GET ALONG WITH IT!!
CAPTAIN TSUBASA
ANNOYED
TSUBASA BECAME FRIENDS WITH THE BALL BECAUSE HE WAS WITH IT AROUND THE CLOCK!
I-IT'S NOT THE LENGTH OF TIME THAT'S IMPORTANT! IT'S WHAT YOU DO WITH THE TIME!!
AND YOU HAVEN'T DONE MUCH WITH YOUR TIME, EITHER!
Don't make light of Tsubasa-kun!
CLATTER
Jolt
THE BALL HAS THE RIGHT TO CHOOSE SOME- ONE, TOO, Y'KNOW !!
So mean!
SEETHE
NOW, NOW! LET'S ALL RELAX.
SEETHE
CALM DOWN, NANA.
What are you talking about ?

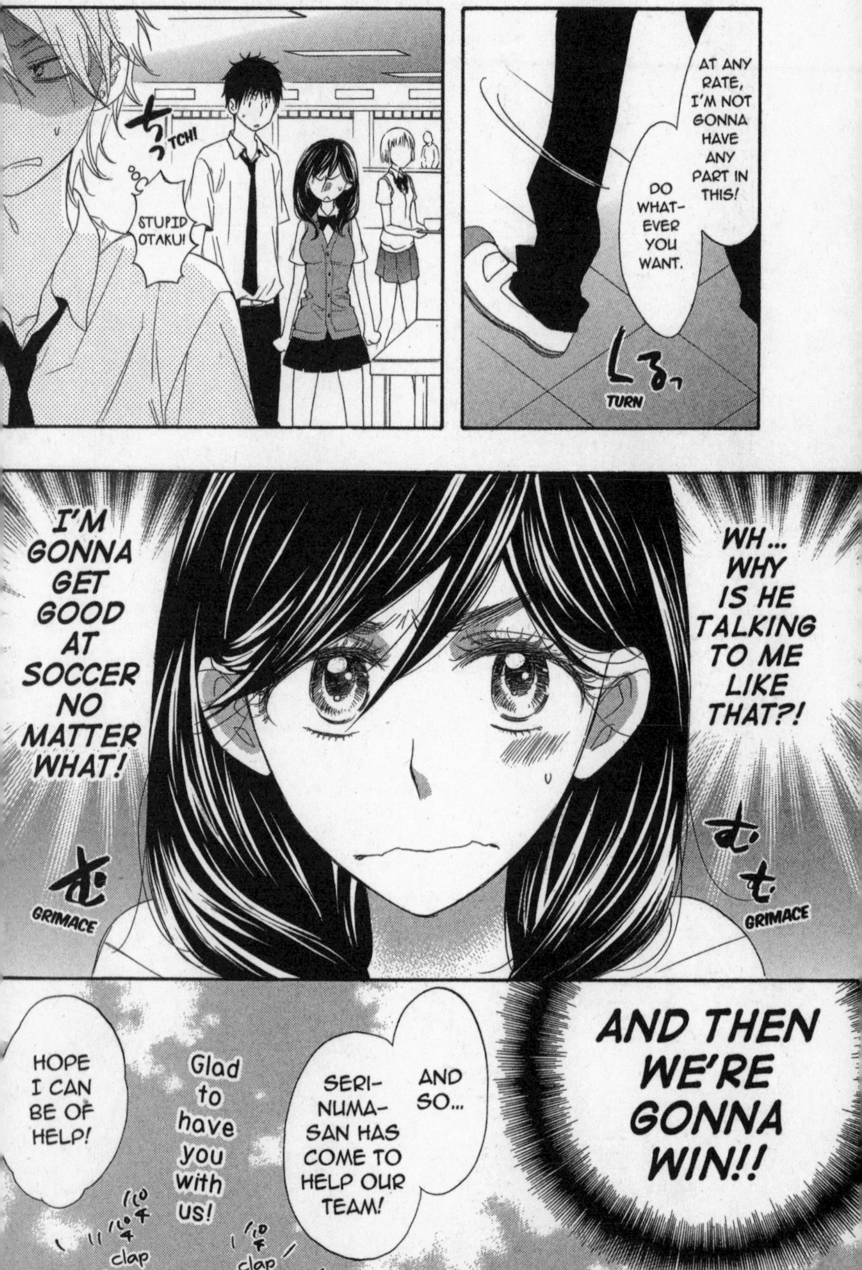
AT ANY RATE, I'M NOT GONNA HAVE ANY PART IN THIS!
DO WHATEVER YOU WANT.
TURN
TCH!
STUPID OTAKU!
WH... WHY IS HE TALKING TO ME LIKE THAT?!
GRIMACE
I'M GONNA GET GOOD AT SOCCER NO MATTER WHAT!
GRIMACE
AND THEN WE'RE GONNA WIN!!
AND SO...
SERINUMA-SAN HAS COME TO HELP OUR TEAM!
clap
Glad to have you with us!
HOPE I CAN BE OF HELP!
clap clap

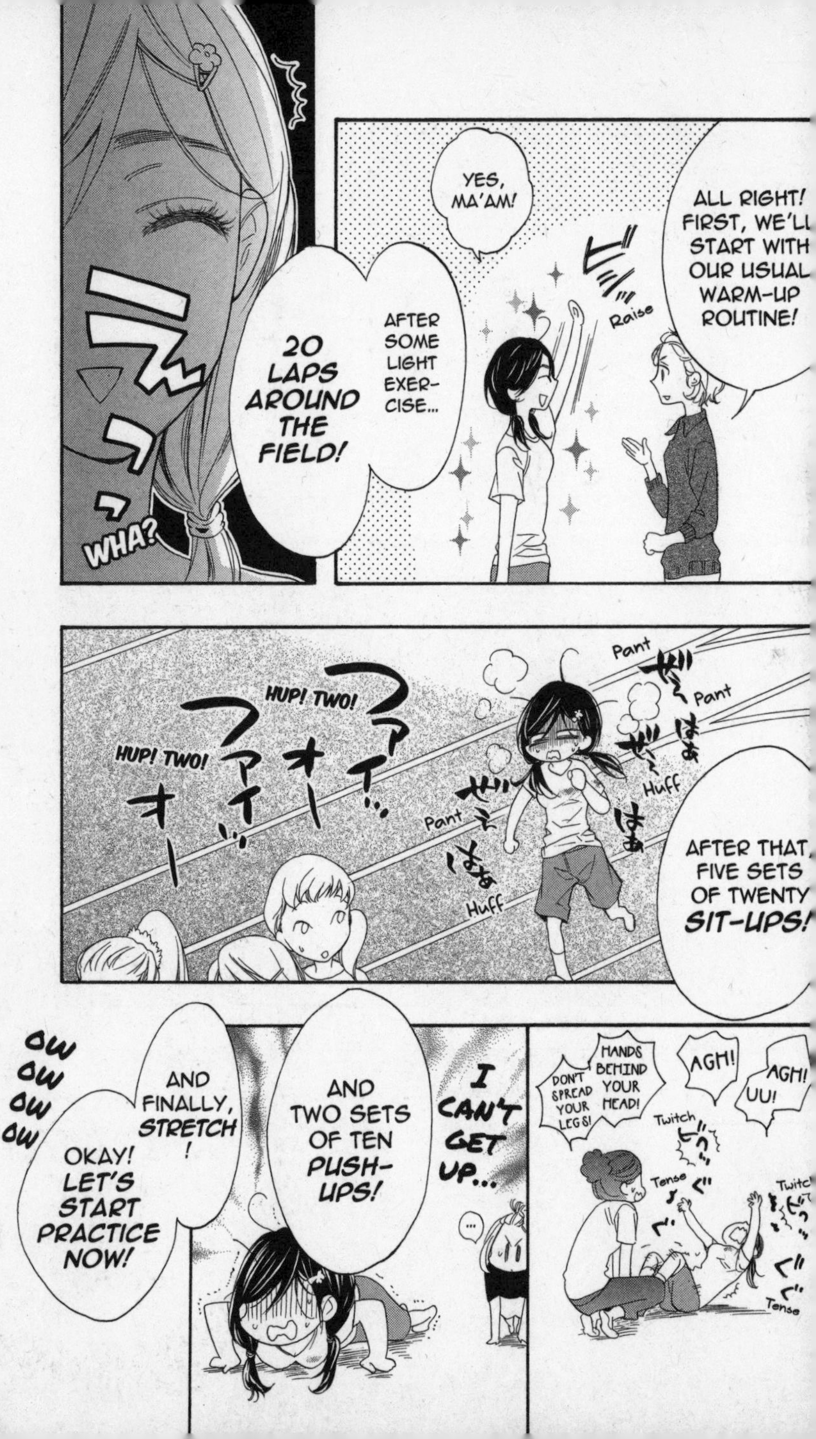
ALL RIGHT! FIRST, WE'LL START WITH OUR USUAL WARM-UP ROUTINE!
YES, MA'AM!
Raise
AFTER SOME LIGHT EXERCISE...
20 LAPS AROUND THE FIELD!
WHA?
AFTER THAT, FIVE SETS OF TWENTY SIT-UPS!
Pant
Pant
Huff
Pant
Huff
HUP! TWO!
HUP! TWO!
AGH! UU!
AGH!
HANDS BEHIND YOUR HEAD!
DON'T SPREAD YOUR LEGS!
Twitch
Tense
Twitch
Tense
I CAN'T GET UP...
...
AND TWO SETS OF TEN PUSH-UPS!
AND FINALLY, STRETCH!
OKAY! LET'S START PRACTICE NOW!
OW OW OW OW

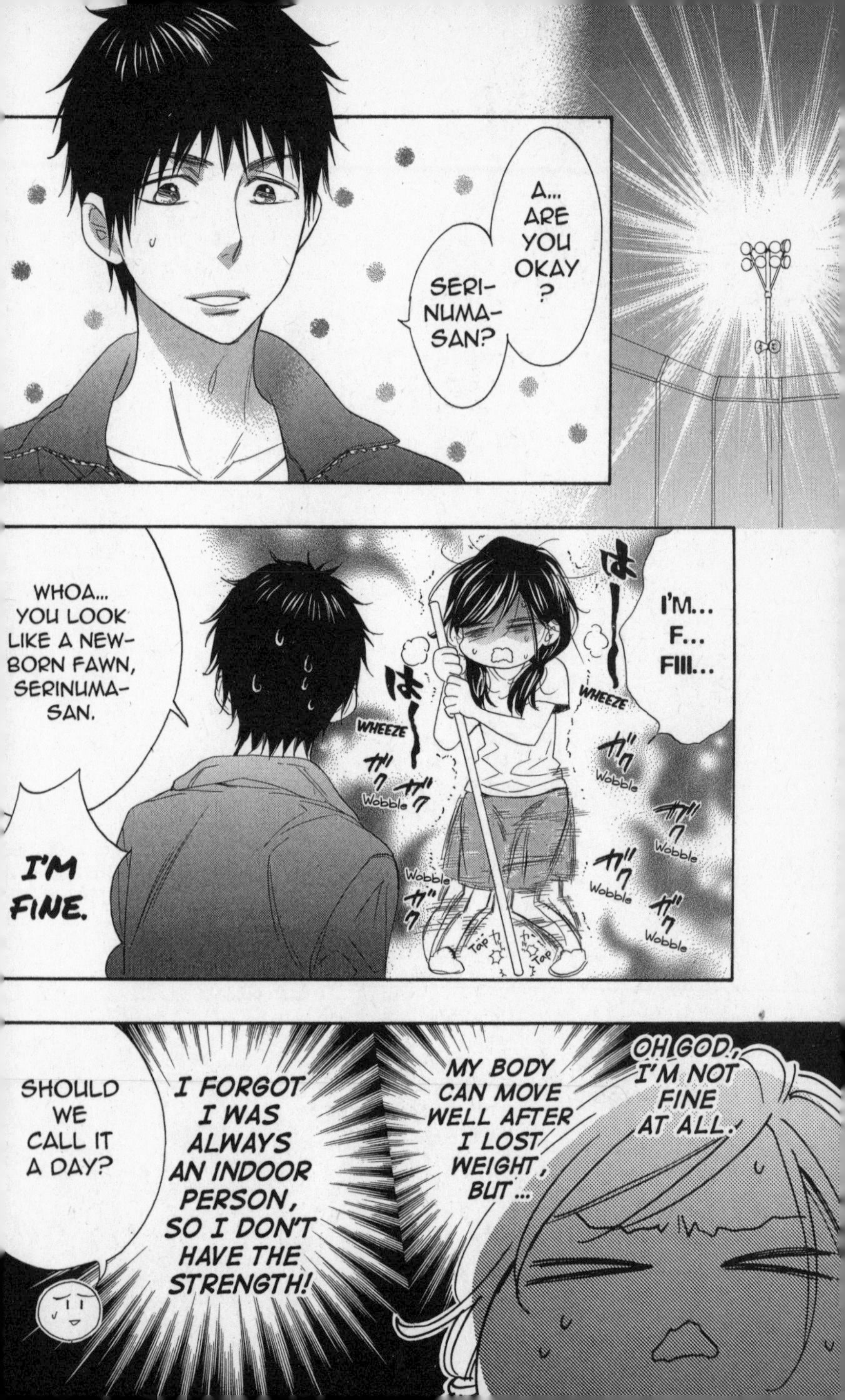

A... ARE YOU OKAY?
SERI-NUMA-SAN?
I'M... F... FIII...
WHEEZE
WHEEZE
Wobble
Wobble
Wobble
Wobble
Wobble
Wobble
Tap
Tap
WHOA... YOU LOOK LIKE A NEW-BORN FAWN, SERINUMA-SAN.
I'M FINE.
OH GOD, I'M NOT FINE AT ALL.
MY BODY CAN MOVE WELL AFTER I LOST WEIGHT, BUT...
I FORGOT I WAS ALWAYS AN INDOOR PERSON, SO I DON'T HAVE THE STRENGTH!
SHOULD WE CALL IT A DAY?

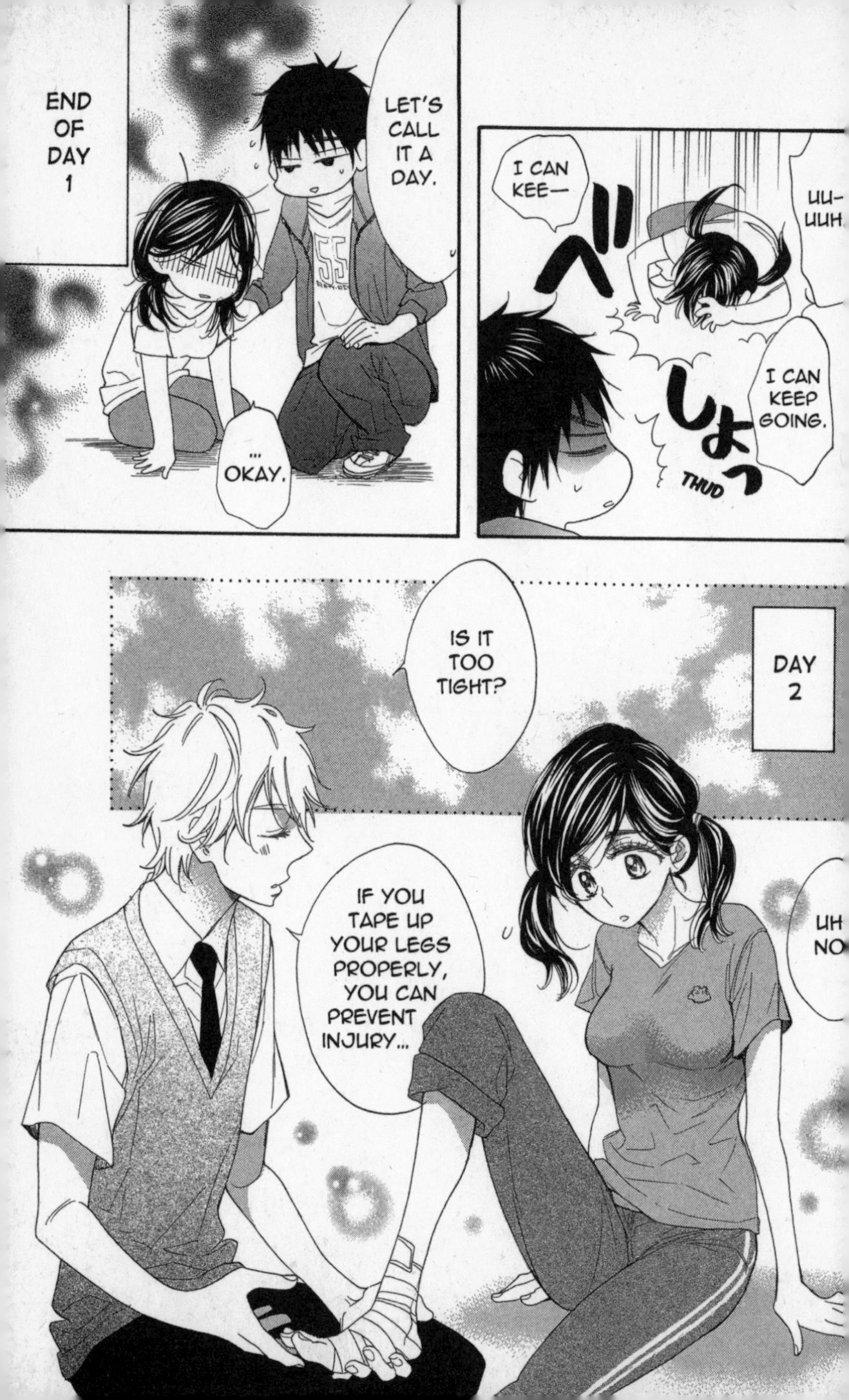
UU-UUH.
I CAN KEE—
べ
I CAN KEEP GOING.
しょっ
THUD
END OF DAY 1
LET'S CALL IT A DAY.
... OKAY.
DAY 2
UH NO
IS IT TOO TIGHT?
IF YOU TAPE UP YOUR LEGS PROPERLY, YOU CAN PREVENT INJURY...

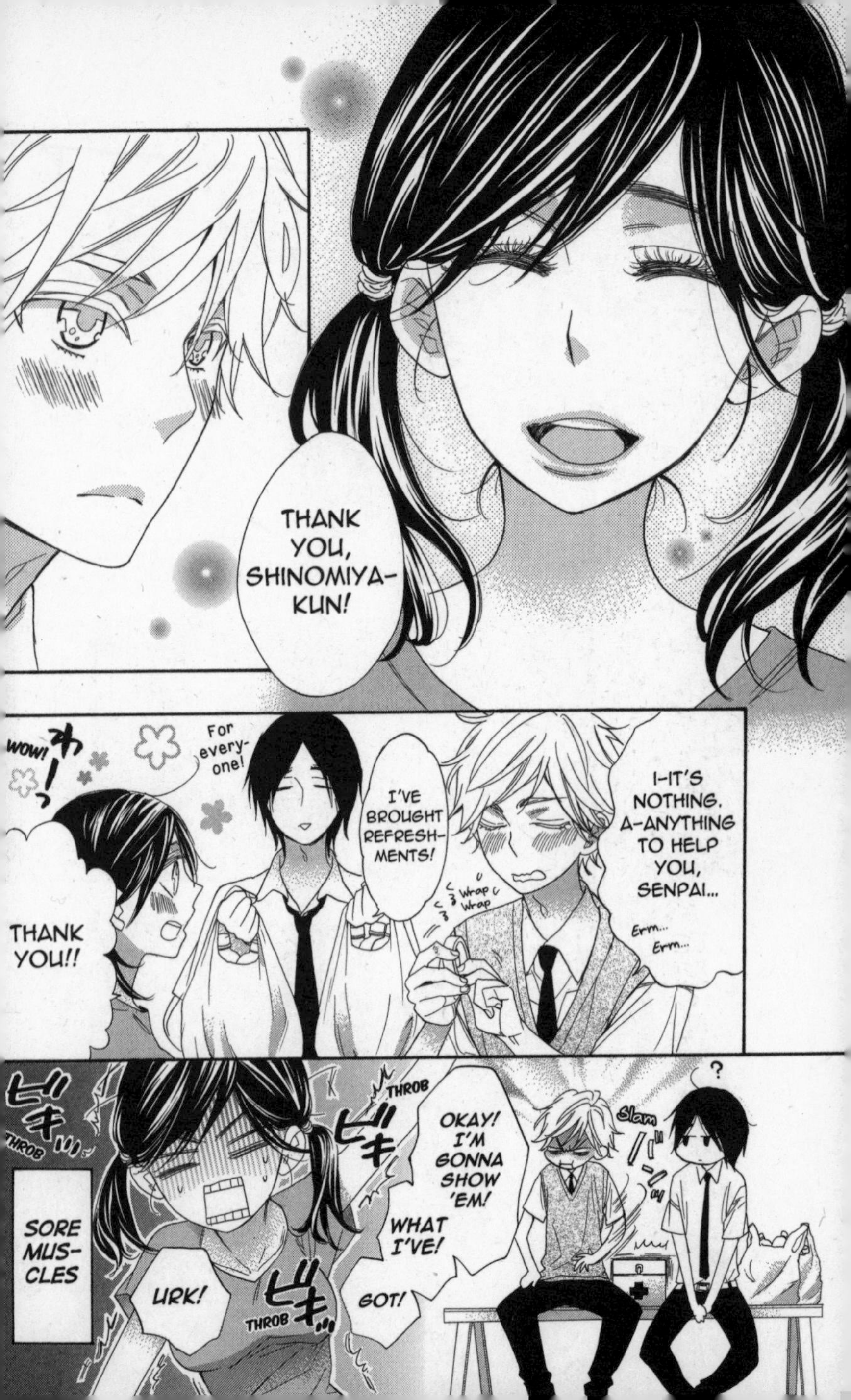
THANK YOU, SHINOMIYA-KUN!
I-IT'S NOTHING. A-ANYTHING TO HELP YOU, SENPAI...
Erm... Erm...
Wrap Wrap
I'VE BROUGHT REFRESHMENTS!
For every-one!
WOW!
THANK YOU!!
?
Slam
OKAY! I'M GONNA SHOW 'EM!
WHAT I'VE!
GOT!
THROB
URK!
THROB
THROB
SORE MUSCLES

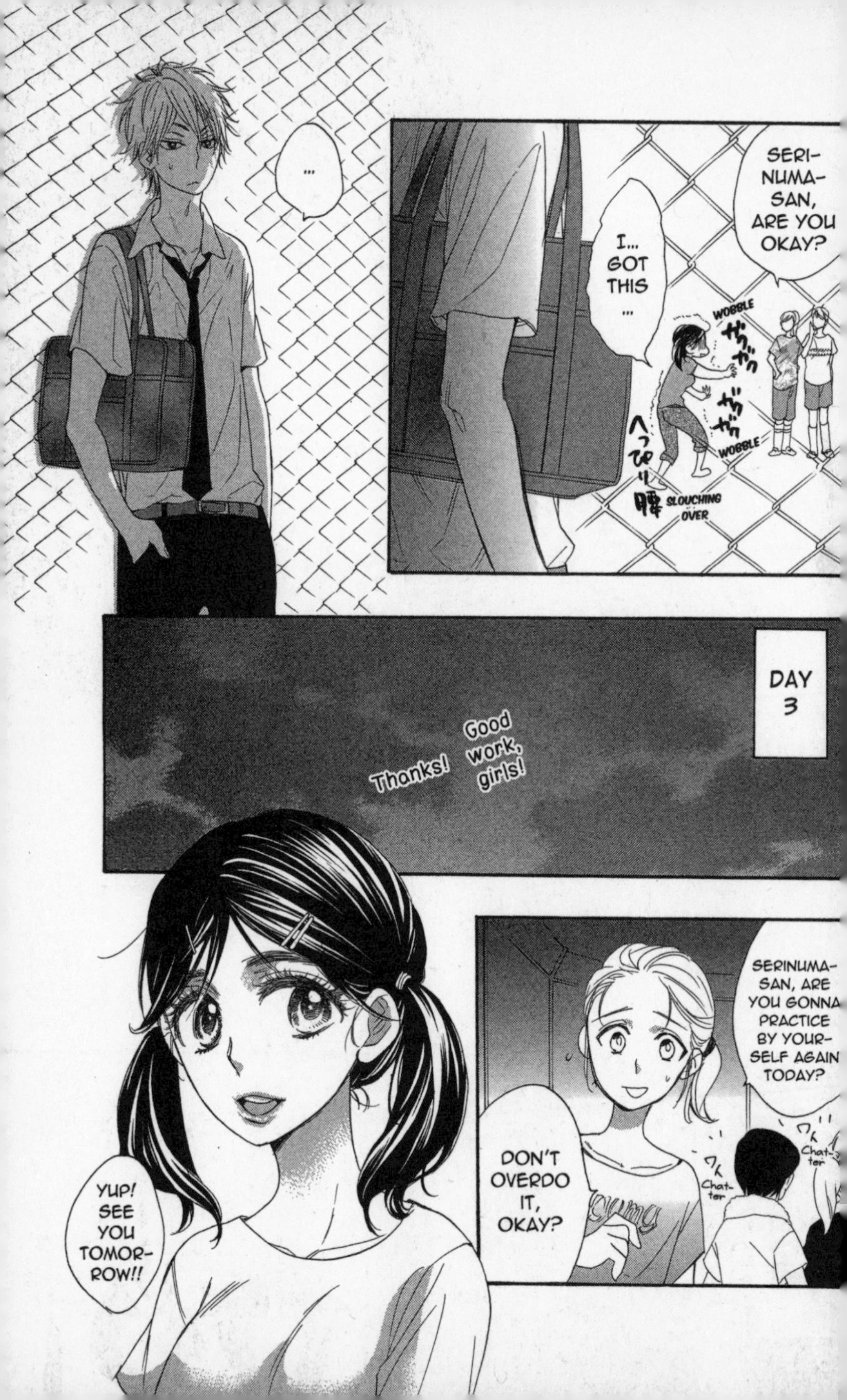
SERI-NUMA-SAN, ARE YOU OKAY?
I... GOT THIS ...
WOBBLE
WOBBLE
SLOUCHING OVER
...
DAY 3
Good work, girls!
Thanks!
SERINUMA-SAN, ARE YOU GONNA PRACTICE BY YOUR-SELF AGAIN TODAY?
DON'T OVERDO IT, OKAY?
Chat-ter
Chat-ter
YUP! SEE YOU TOMOR-ROW!!

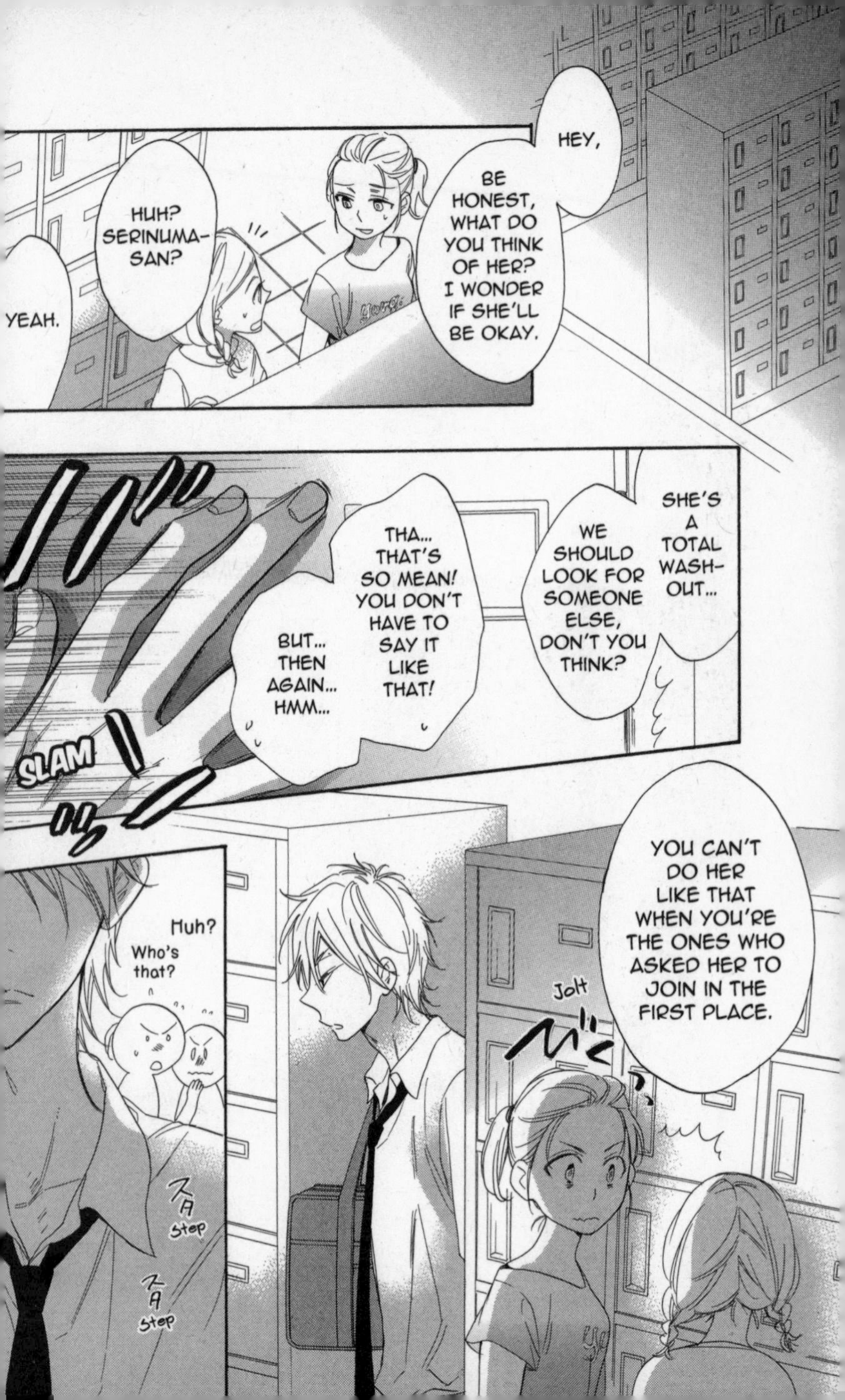
HEY,
BE HONEST, WHAT DO YOU THINK OF HER? I WONDER IF SHE'LL BE OKAY.
HUH? SERINUMA-SAN?
YEAH.
SHE'S A TOTAL WASH-OUT...
WE SHOULD LOOK FOR SOMEONE ELSE, DON'T YOU THINK?
THA... THAT'S SO MEAN! YOU DON'T HAVE TO SAY IT LIKE THAT!
BUT... THEN AGAIN... HMM...
SLAM
YOU CAN'T DO HER LIKE THAT WHEN YOU'RE THE ONES WHO ASKED HER TO JOIN IN THE FIRST PLACE.
Jolt
Huh? Who's that?
Step
Step

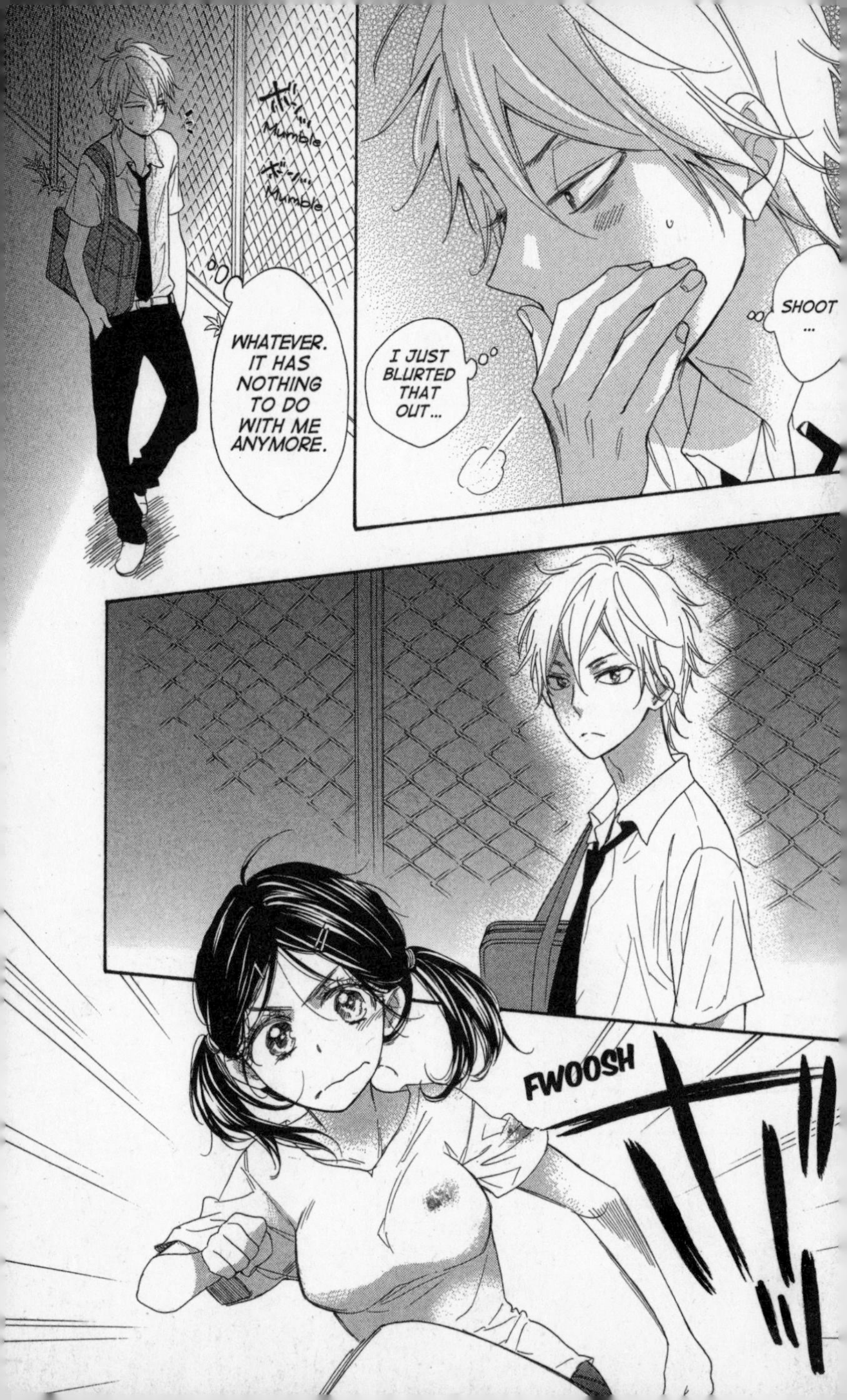
SHOOT ...
I JUST BLURTED THAT OUT...
Mumble
Mumble
WHATEVER. IT HAS NOTHING TO DO WITH ME ANYMORE.
FWOOSH

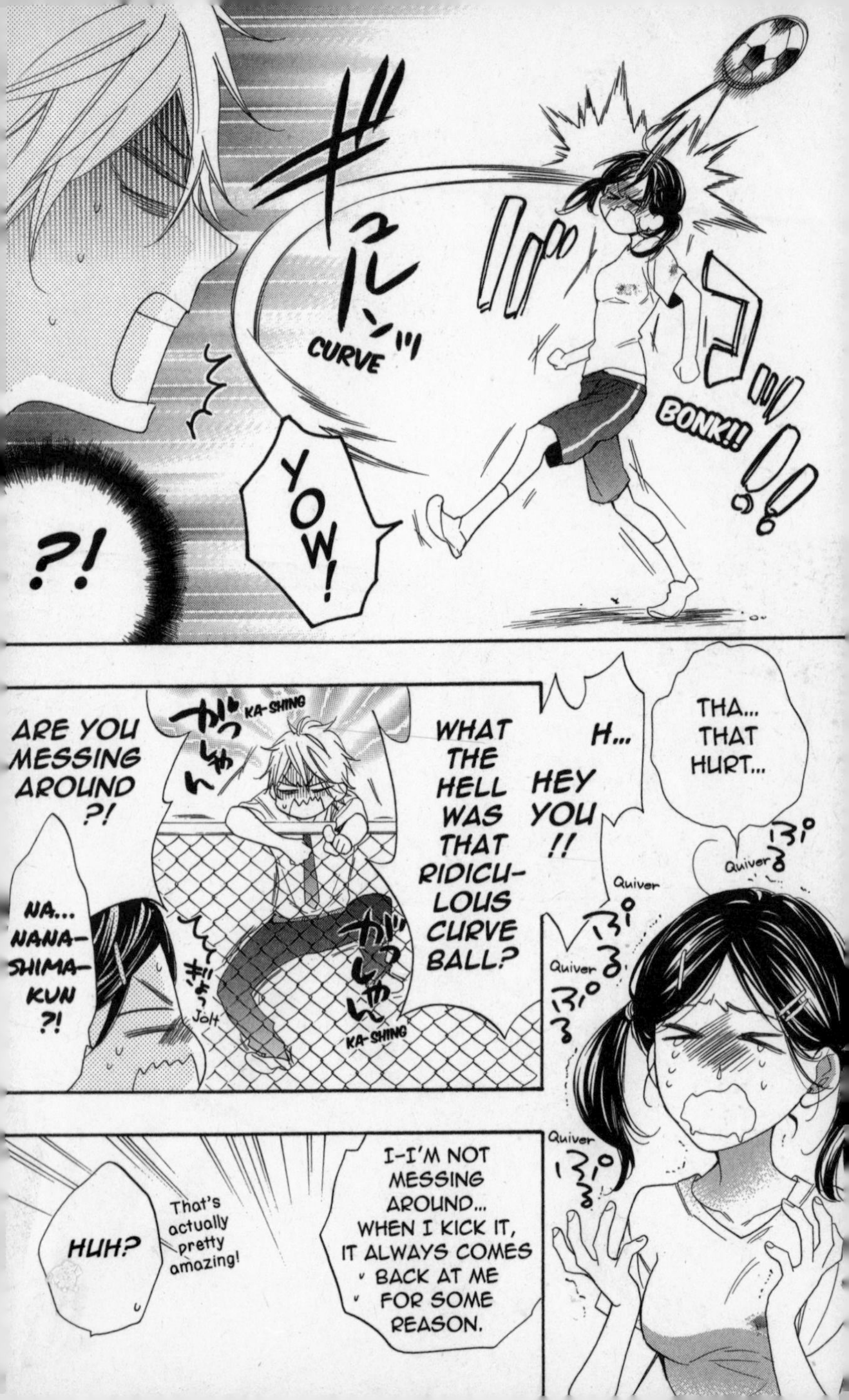
BONK!!
CURVE
YOW!
?!
THA... THAT HURT...
Quiver
Quiver
Quiver
H... HEY YOU!!
WHAT THE HELL WAS THAT RIDICULOUS CURVE BALL?
KA-SHING
ARE YOU MESSING AROUND?!
Jolt
KA-SHING
NA... NANA-SHIMA-KUN?!
Quiver
I-I'M NOT MESSING AROUND... WHEN I KICK IT, IT ALWAYS COMES BACK AT ME FOR SOME REASON.
HUH?
That's actually pretty amazing!

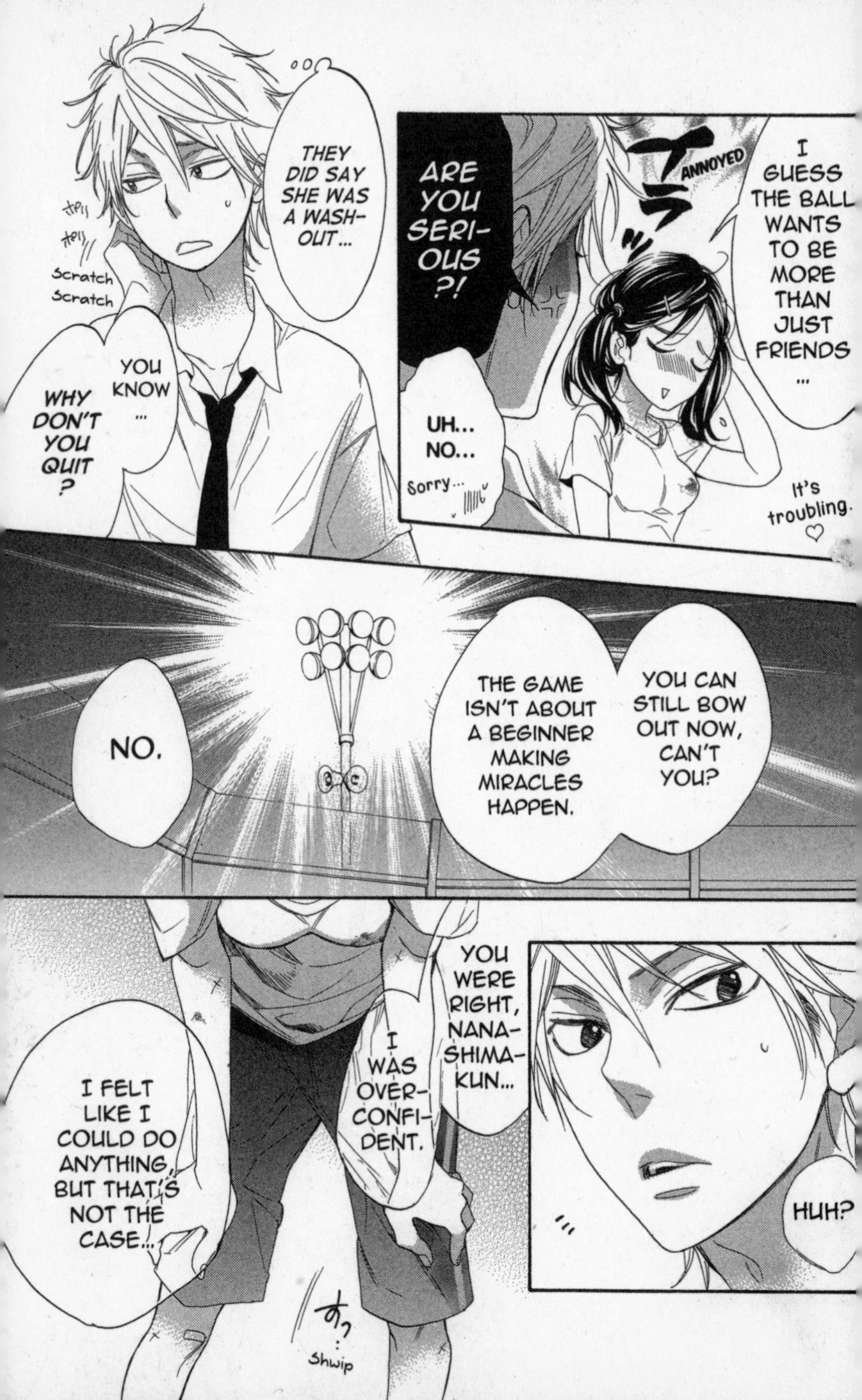
I GUESS THE BALL WANTS TO BE MORE THAN JUST FRIENDS...
ANNOYED
It's troubling. ♡
ARE YOU SERIOUS?!
UH... NO...
Sorry...
THEY DID SAY SHE WAS A WASH-OUT...
Scratch Scratch
YOU KNOW...
WHY DON'T YOU QUIT?
YOU CAN STILL BOW OUT NOW, CAN'T YOU?
THE GAME ISN'T ABOUT A BEGINNER MAKING MIRACLES HAPPEN.
NO.
HUH?
YOU WERE RIGHT, NANA-SHIMA-KUN...
I WAS OVER-CONFIDENT.
I FELT LIKE I COULD DO ANYTHING, BUT THAT'S NOT THE CASE...
Shwip

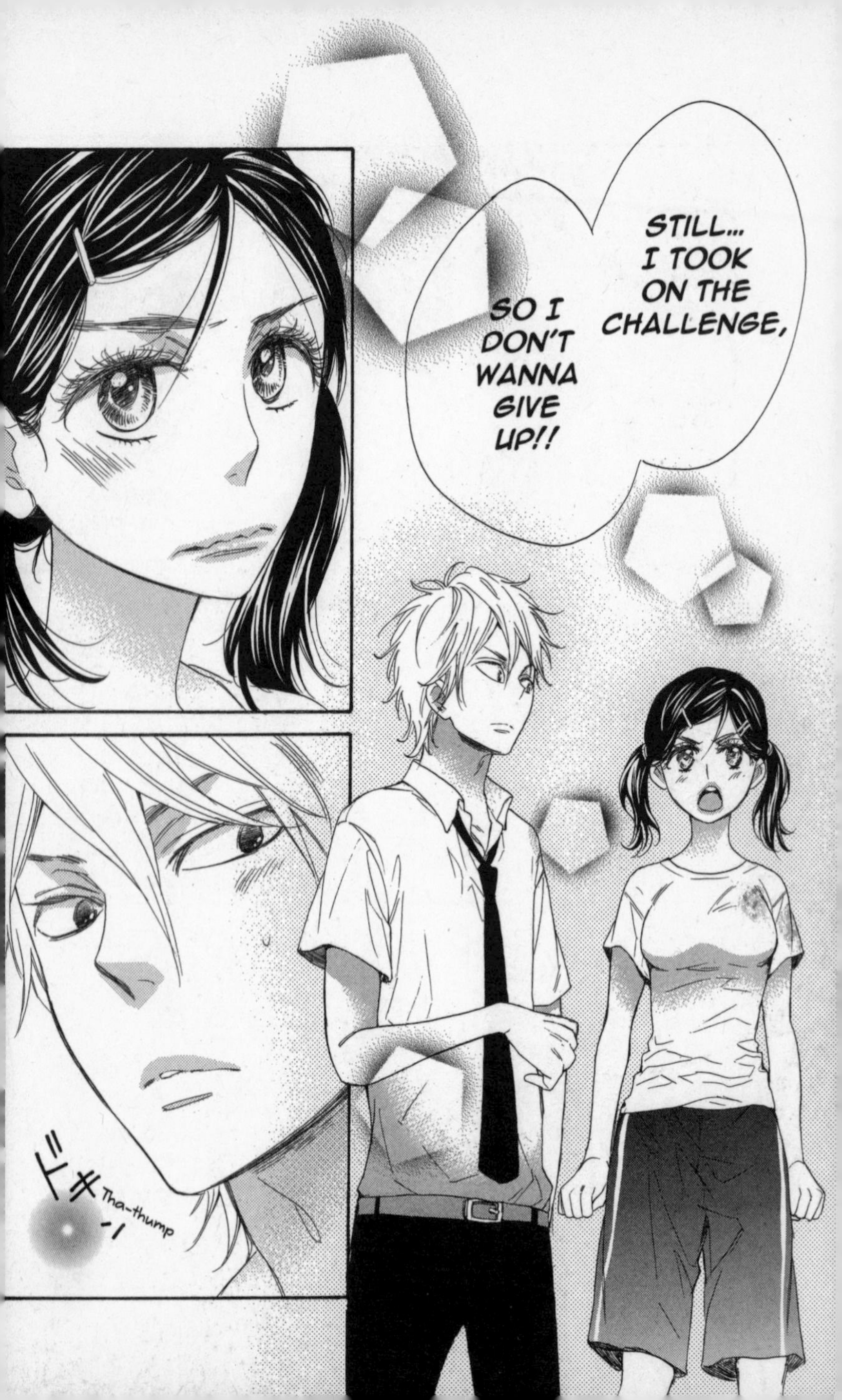
STILL... I TOOK ON THE CHALLENGE,
SO I DON'T WANNA GIVE UP!!
ドキッ Tha-thump

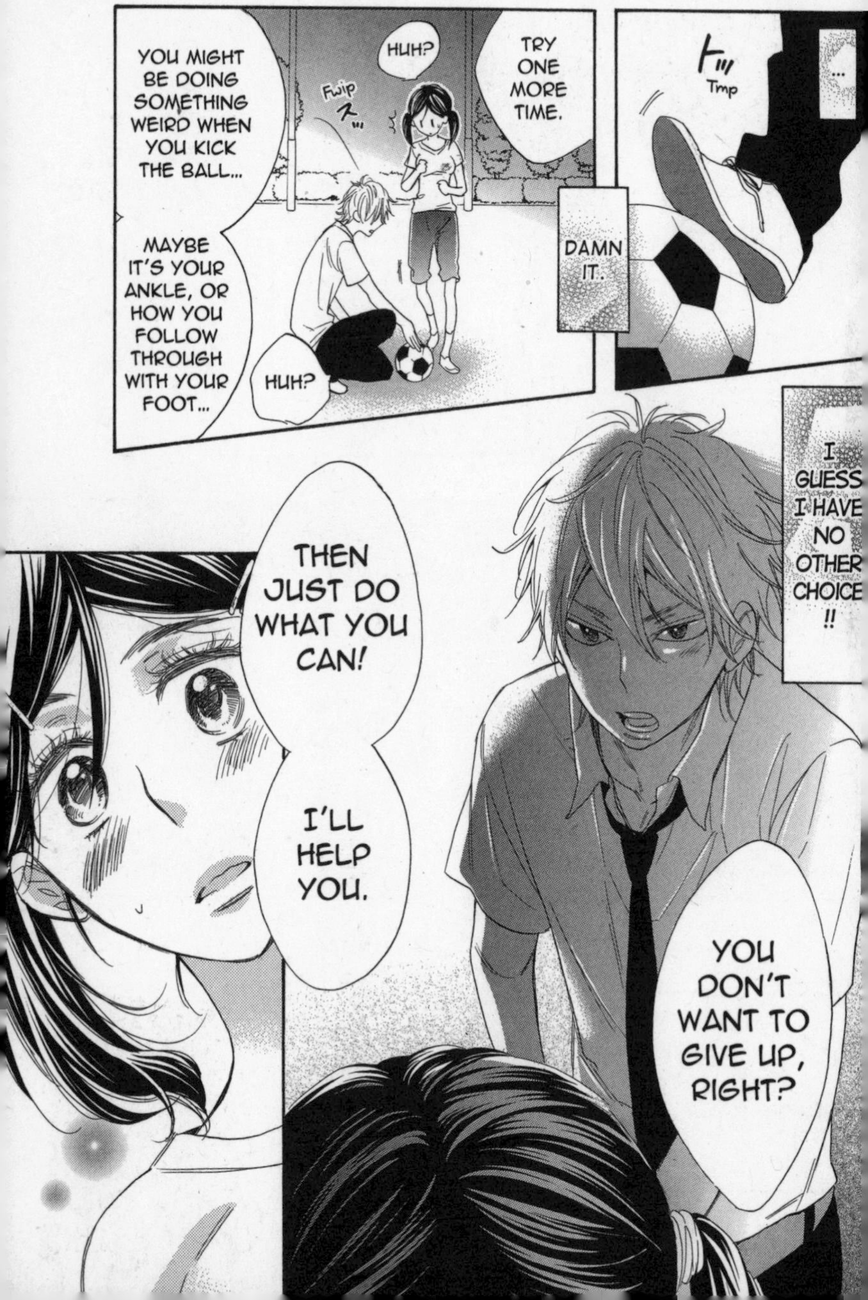
Tmp
...
DAMN IT.
TRY ONE MORE TIME.
HUH?
Fwip
YOU MIGHT BE DOING SOMETHING WEIRD WHEN YOU KICK THE BALL...
MAYBE IT'S YOUR ANKLE, OR HOW YOU FOLLOW THROUGH WITH YOUR FOOT...
HUH?
I GUESS I HAVE NO OTHER CHOICE!!
YOU DON'T WANT TO GIVE UP, RIGHT?
THEN JUST DO WHAT YOU CAN!
I'LL HELP YOU.

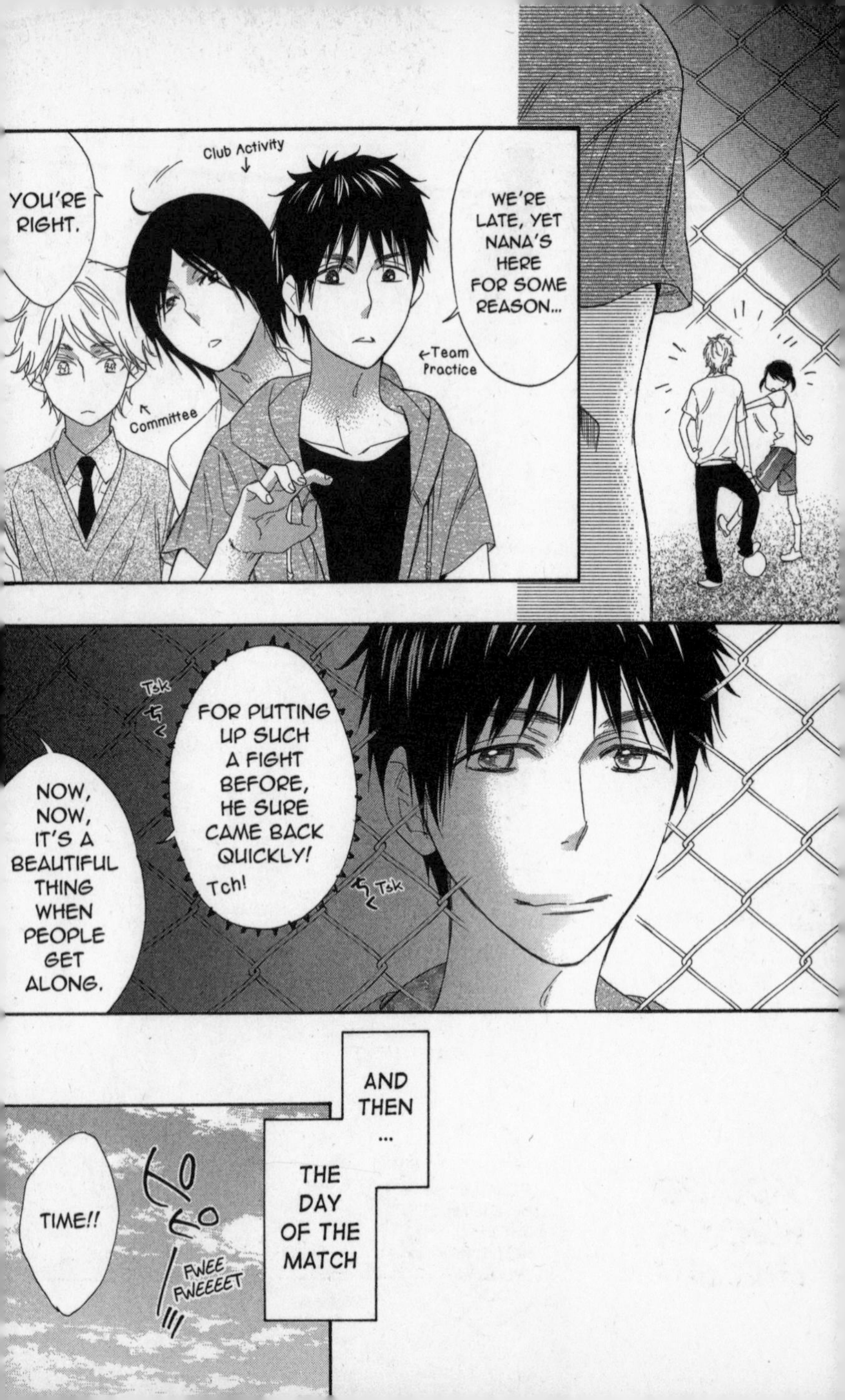
WE'RE LATE, YET NANA'S HERE FOR SOME REASON...
Club Activity
←Team Practice
Committee
YOU'RE RIGHT.
Tsk
FOR PUTTING UP SUCH A FIGHT BEFORE, HE SURE CAME BACK QUICKLY!
Tch!
Tsk
NOW, NOW, IT'S A BEAUTIFUL THING WHEN PEOPLE GET ALONG.
AND THEN ...
THE DAY OF THE MATCH
FWEE FWEEEET
TIME!!

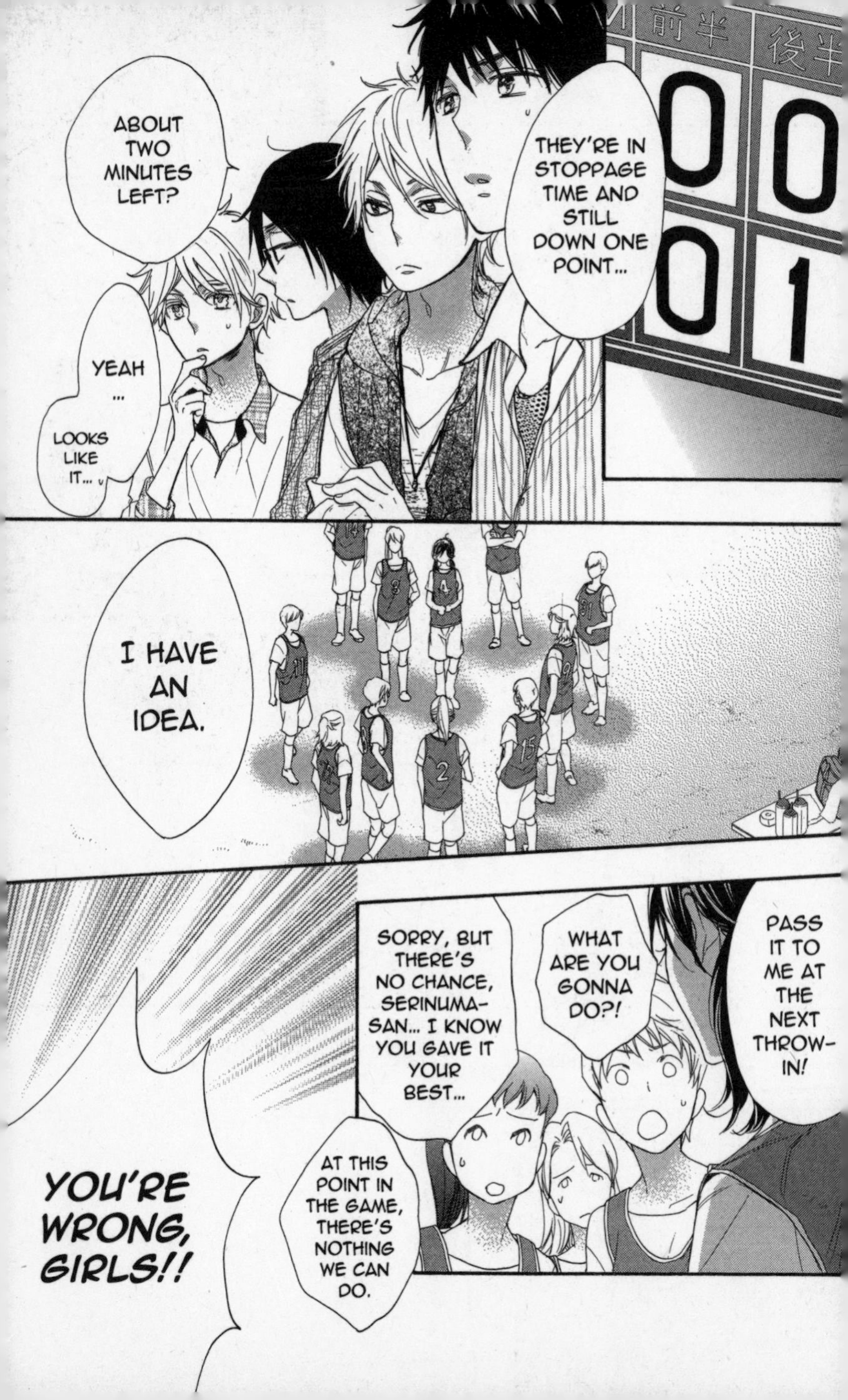

前半
後半
THEY'RE IN STOPPAGE TIME AND STILL DOWN ONE POINT...
ABOUT TWO MINUTES LEFT?
YEAH ... LOOKS LIKE IT...
I HAVE AN IDEA.
PASS IT TO ME AT THE NEXT THROW-IN!
WHAT ARE YOU GONNA DO?!
SORRY, BUT THERE'S NO CHANCE, SERINUMA-SAN... I KNOW YOU GAVE IT YOUR BEST...
AT THIS POINT IN THE GAME, THERE'S NOTHING WE CAN DO.
YOU'RE WRONG, GIRLS!!

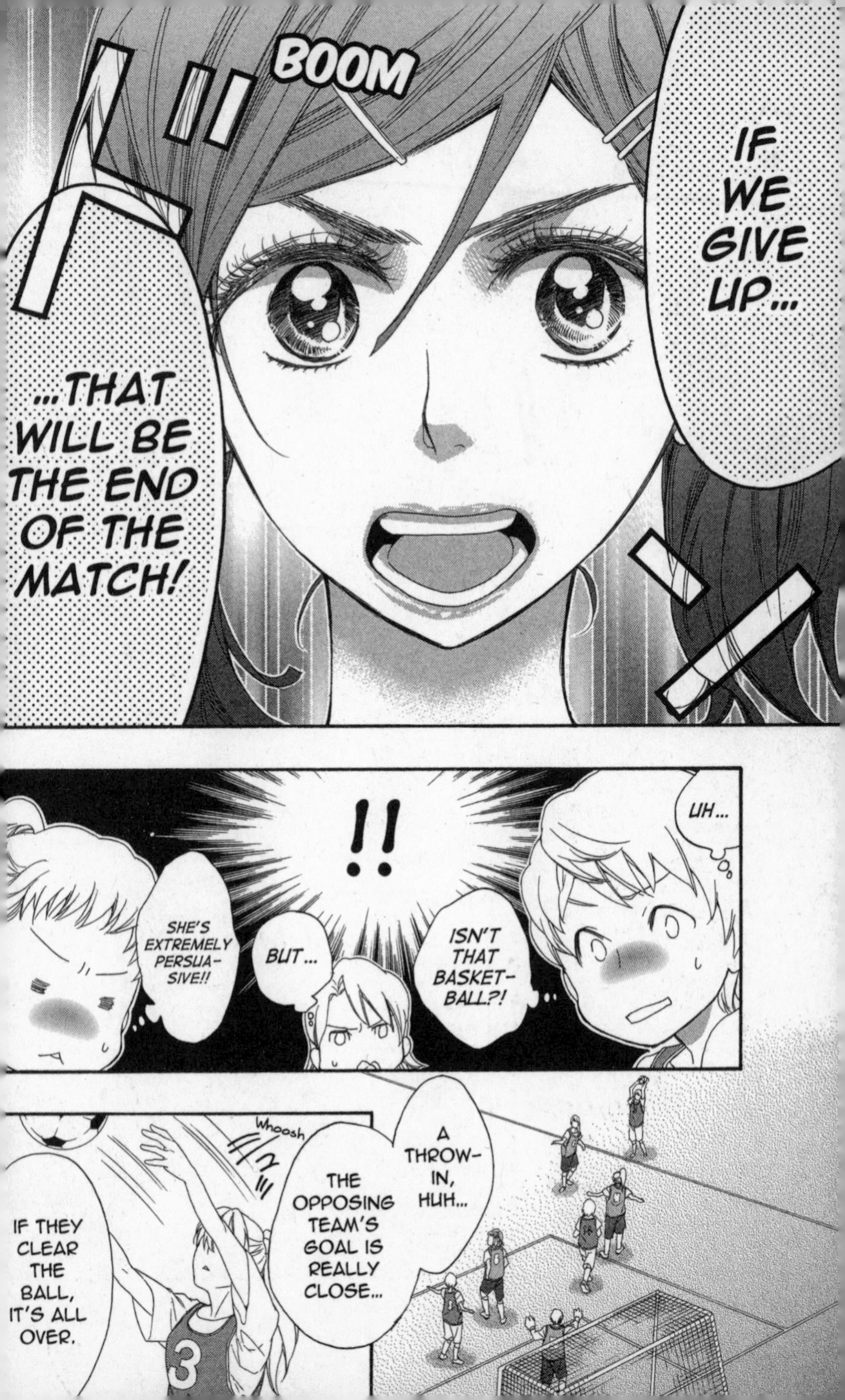
IF WE GIVE UP...
BOOM
...THAT WILL BE THE END OF THE MATCH!
UH...
!!
ISN'T THAT BASKET-BALL?!
BUT...
SHE'S EXTREMELY PERSUA-SIVE!!
A THROW-IN, HUH...
THE OPPOSING TEAM'S GOAL IS REALLY CLOSE...
Whoosh
IF THEY CLEAR THE BALL, IT'S ALL OVER.

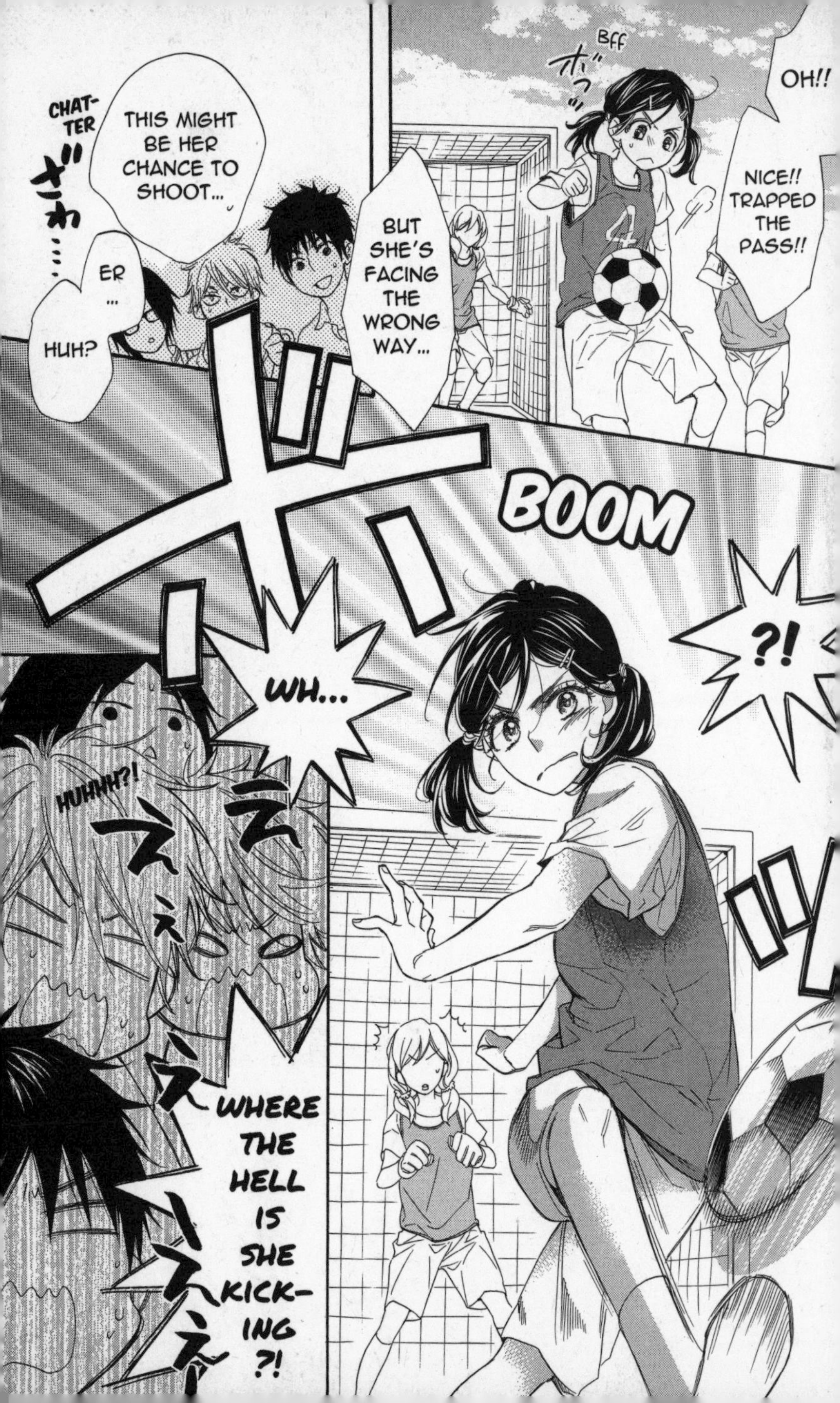
Bff
OH!!
NICE!! TRAPPED THE PASS!!
CHAT-TER
THIS MIGHT BE HER CHANCE TO SHOOT...
BUT SHE'S FACING THE WRONG WAY...
ER ...
HUH?
BOOM
?!
WH...
HUHHH?!
WHERE THE HELL IS SHE KICKING?!

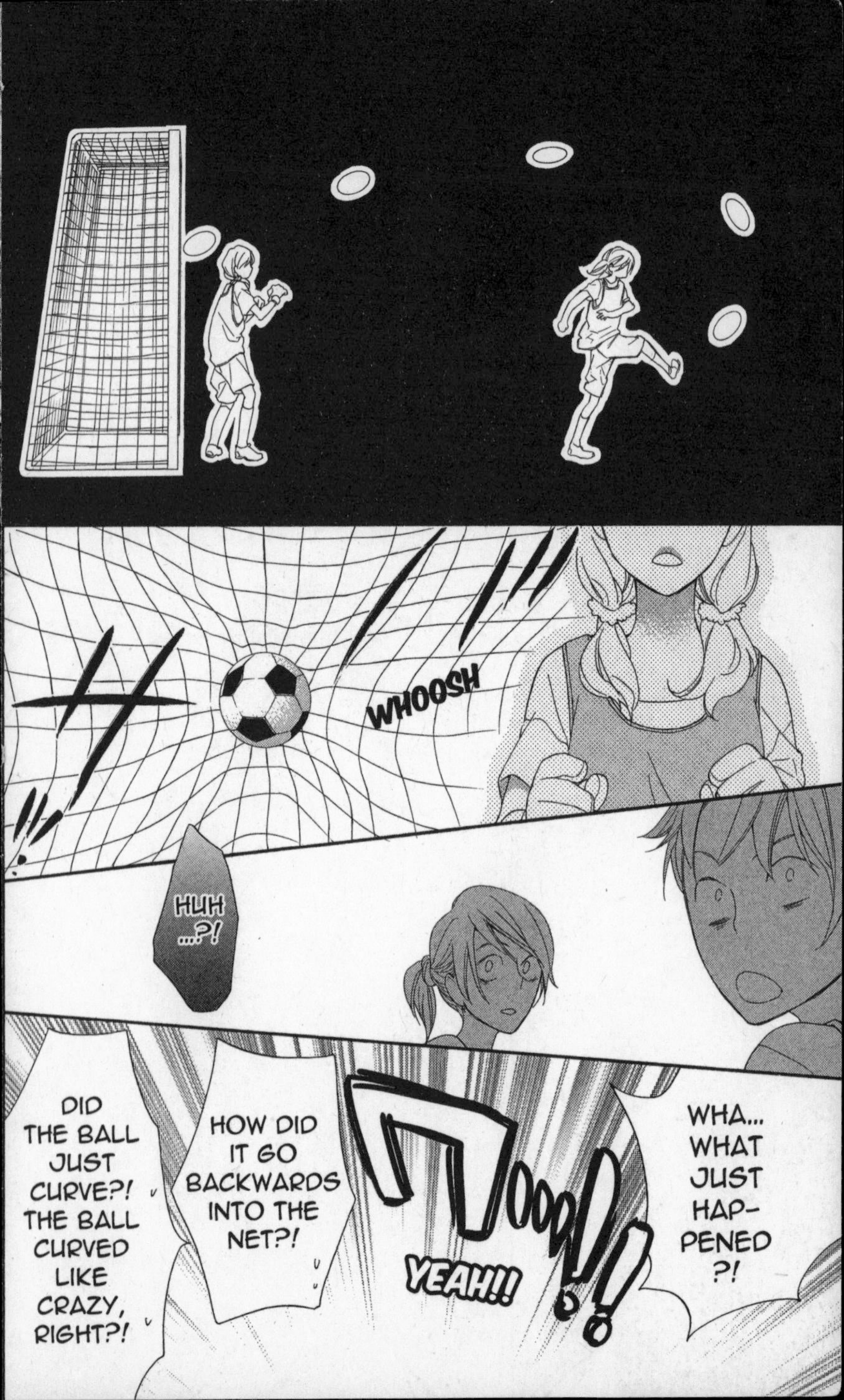
WHOOSH
HUH ...?!
WHA... WHAT JUST HAP-PENED ?!
YEAH!!
HOW DID IT GO BACKWARDS INTO THE NET?!
DID THE BALL JUST CURVE?! THE BALL CURVED LIKE CRAZY, RIGHT?!

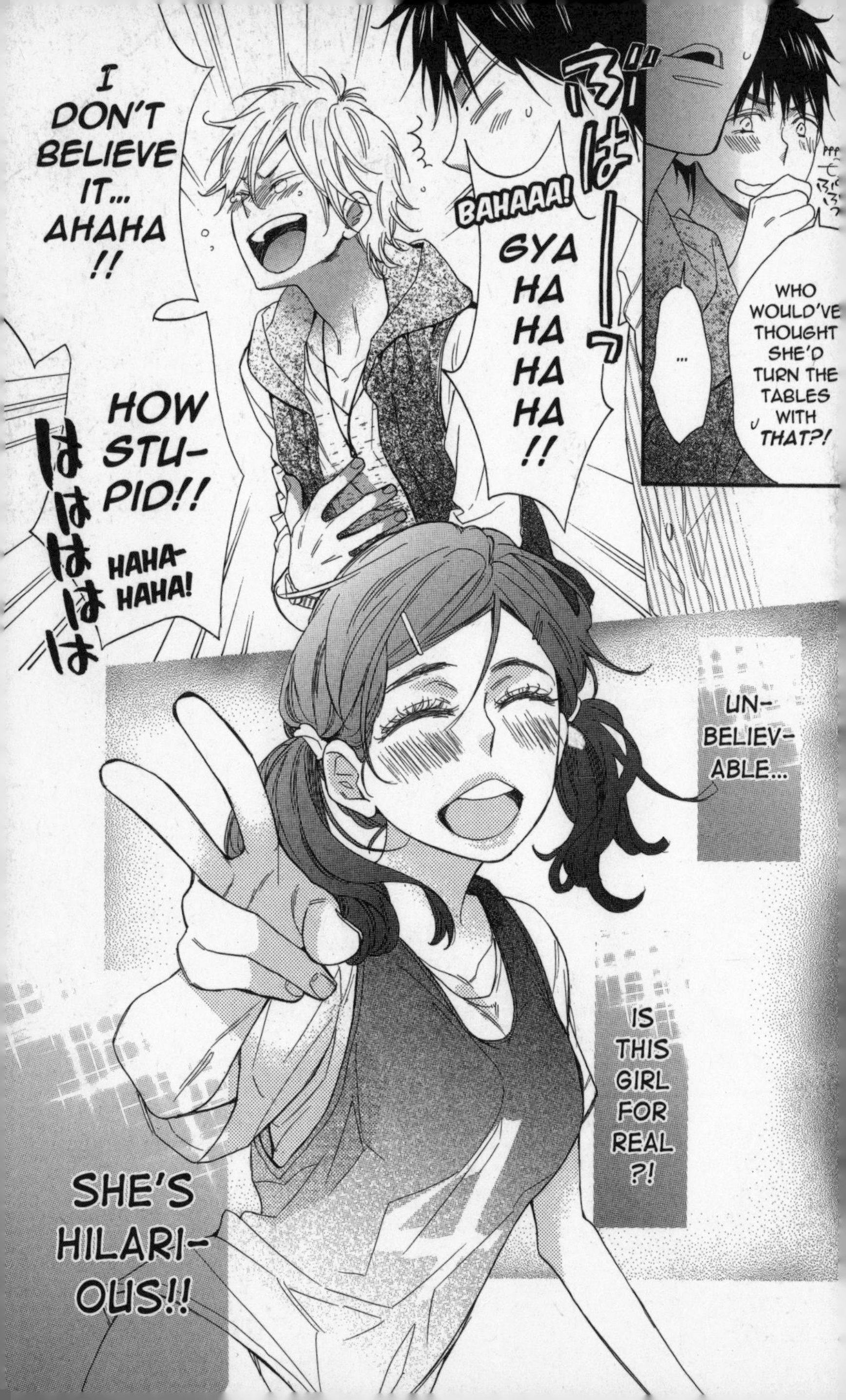

WHO WOULD'VE THOUGHT SHE'D TURN THE TABLES WITH THAT?!
...
ぶはー
BAHAAA!
GYA HA HA HA HA!!
I DON'T BELIEVE IT... AHAHA!!
HOW STUPID!!
ははははは
HAHA-HAHA!
UN-BELIEV-ABLE...
IS THIS GIRL FOR REAL?!
SHE'S HILARI-OUS!!

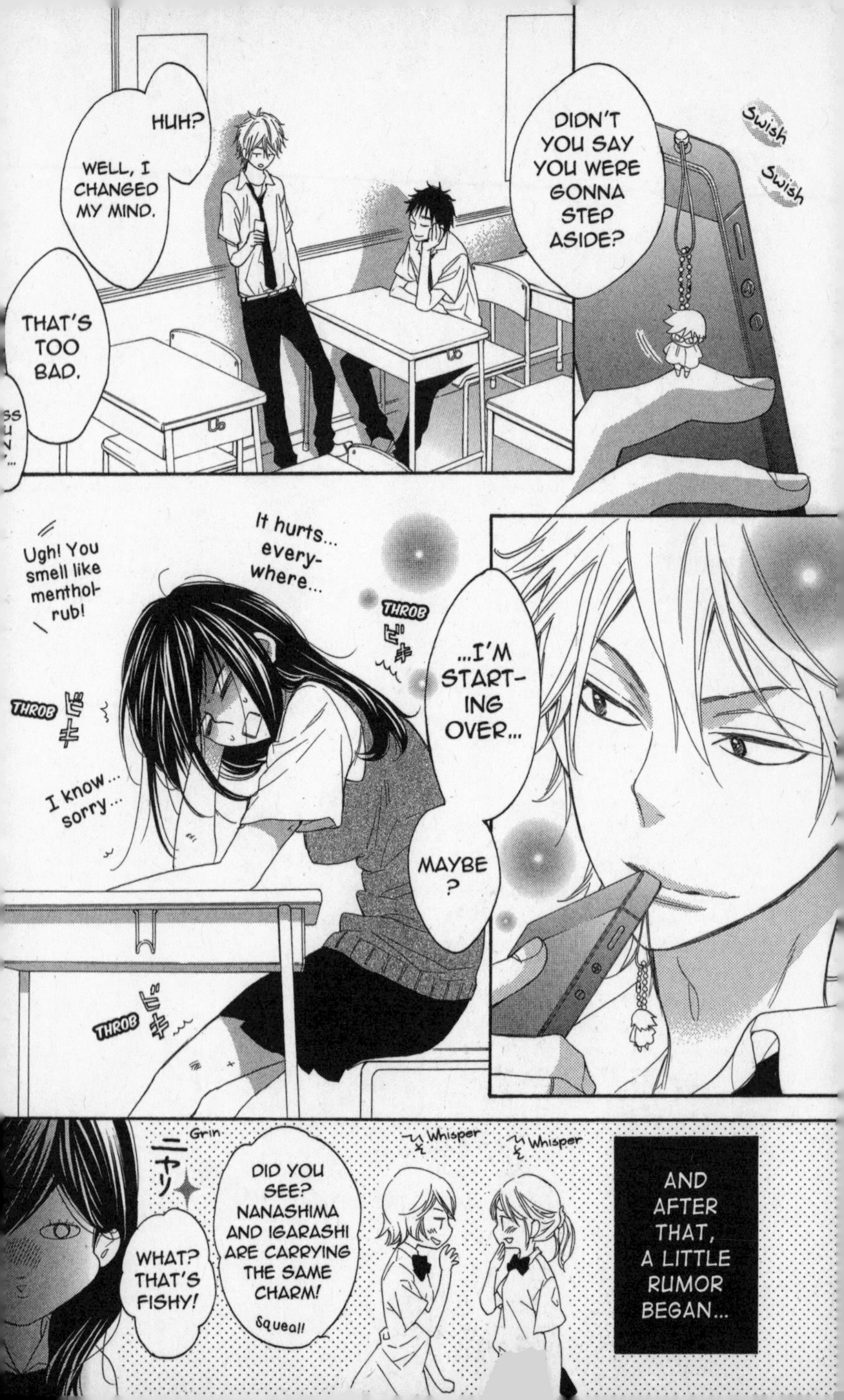

Swish
Swish
DIDN'T YOU SAY YOU WERE GONNA STEP ASIDE?
HUH?
WELL, I CHANGED MY MIND.
THAT'S TOO BAD.
...I'M STARTING-ING OVER...
MAYBE?
It hurts... every-where...
THROB
Ugh! You smell like menthol-rub!
THROB
I know... sorry...
THROB
AND AFTER THAT, A LITTLE RUMOR BEGAN...
Whisper
Whisper
DID YOU SEE? NANASHIMA AND IGARASHI ARE CARRYING THE SAME CHARM!
Squeal!
WHAT? THAT'S FISHY!
Grin

KiSS HiM, NOT ME!

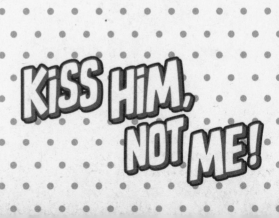

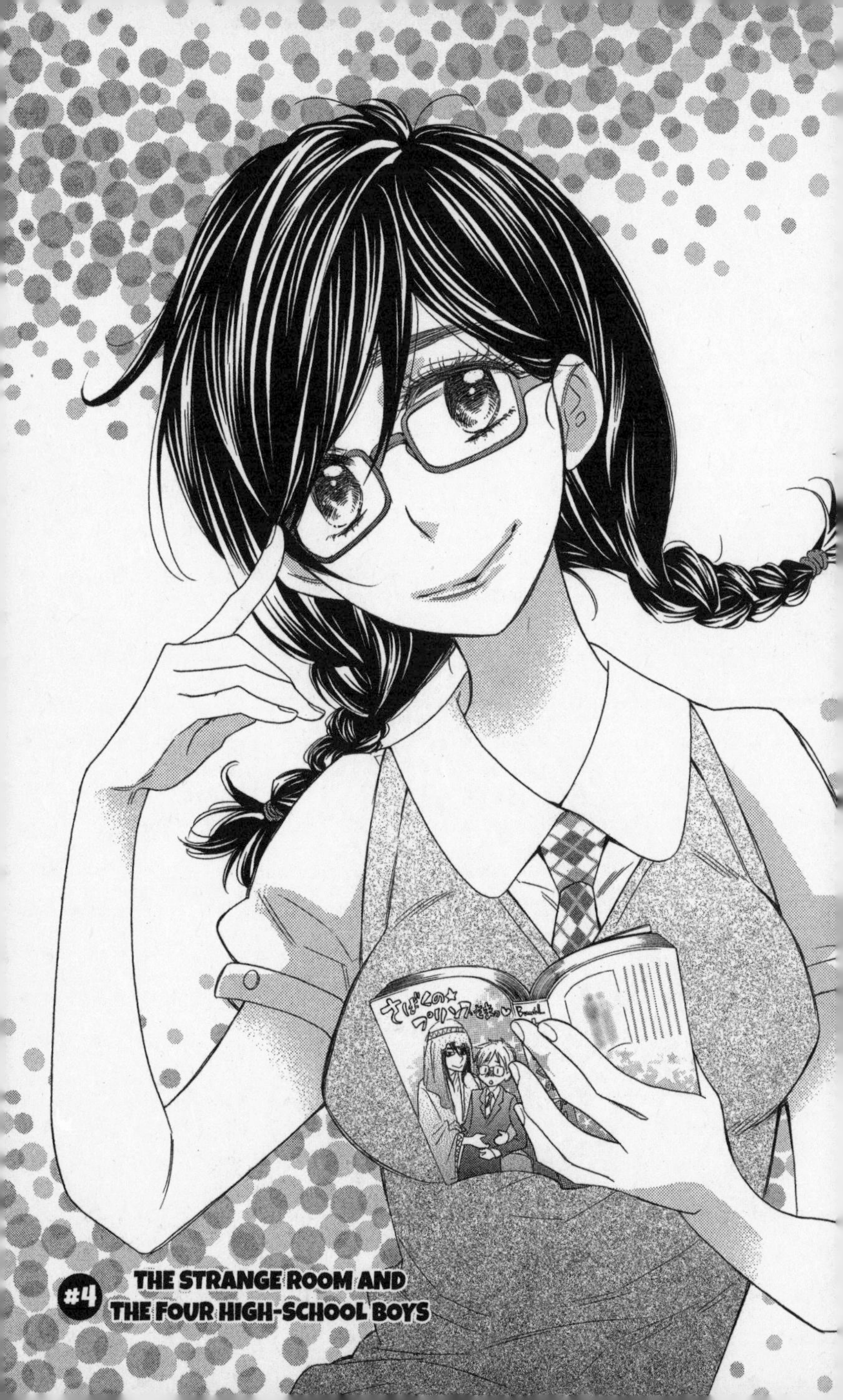
#4 THE STRANGE ROOM AND THE FOUR HIGH-SCHOOL BOYS
さばくの☆プリンスさまっ♡

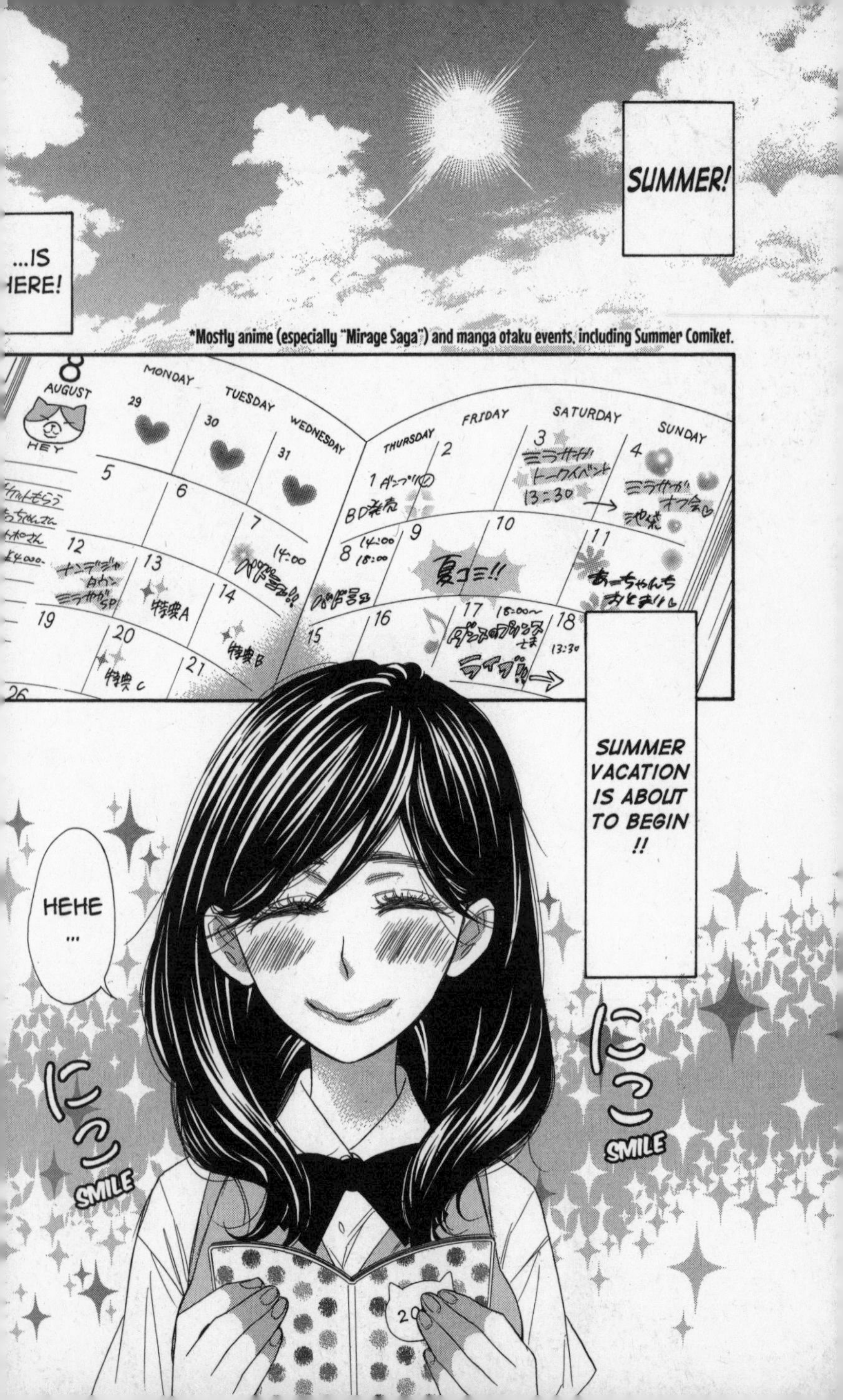
SUMMER!
...IS HERE!
*Mostly anime (especially "Mirage Saga") and manga otaku events, including Summer Comiket.
8 AUGUST
HEY
MONDAY
TUESDAY
WEDNESDAY
THURSDAY
FRIDAY
SATURDAY
SUNDAY
SUMMER VACATION IS ABOUT TO BEGIN !!
SMILE
HEHE ...
SMILE

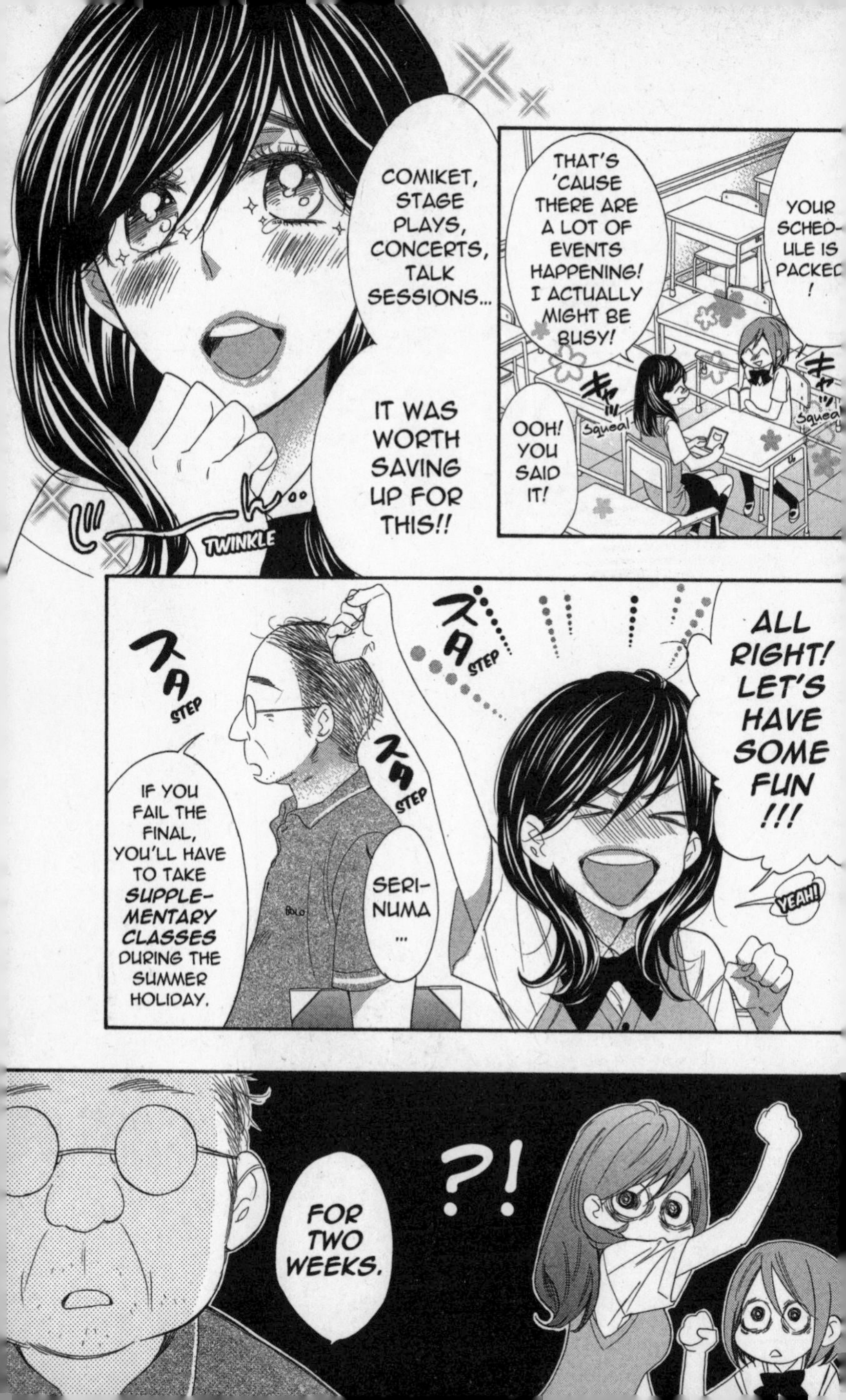
YOUR SCHED-ULE IS PACKED!
THAT'S 'CAUSE THERE ARE A LOT OF EVENTS HAPPENING! I ACTUALLY MIGHT BE BUSY!
Squeal
Squeal
OOH! YOU SAID IT!
COMIKET, STAGE PLAYS, CONCERTS, TALK SESSIONS...
IT WAS WORTH SAVING UP FOR THIS!!
TWINKLE
ALL RIGHT! LET'S HAVE SOME FUN!!!
YEAH!
STEP
STEP
STEP
SERI-NUMA...
IF YOU FAIL THE FINAL, YOU'LL HAVE TO TAKE SUPPLE-MENTARY CLASSES DURING THE SUMMER HOLIDAY.
?!
FOR TWO WEEKS.

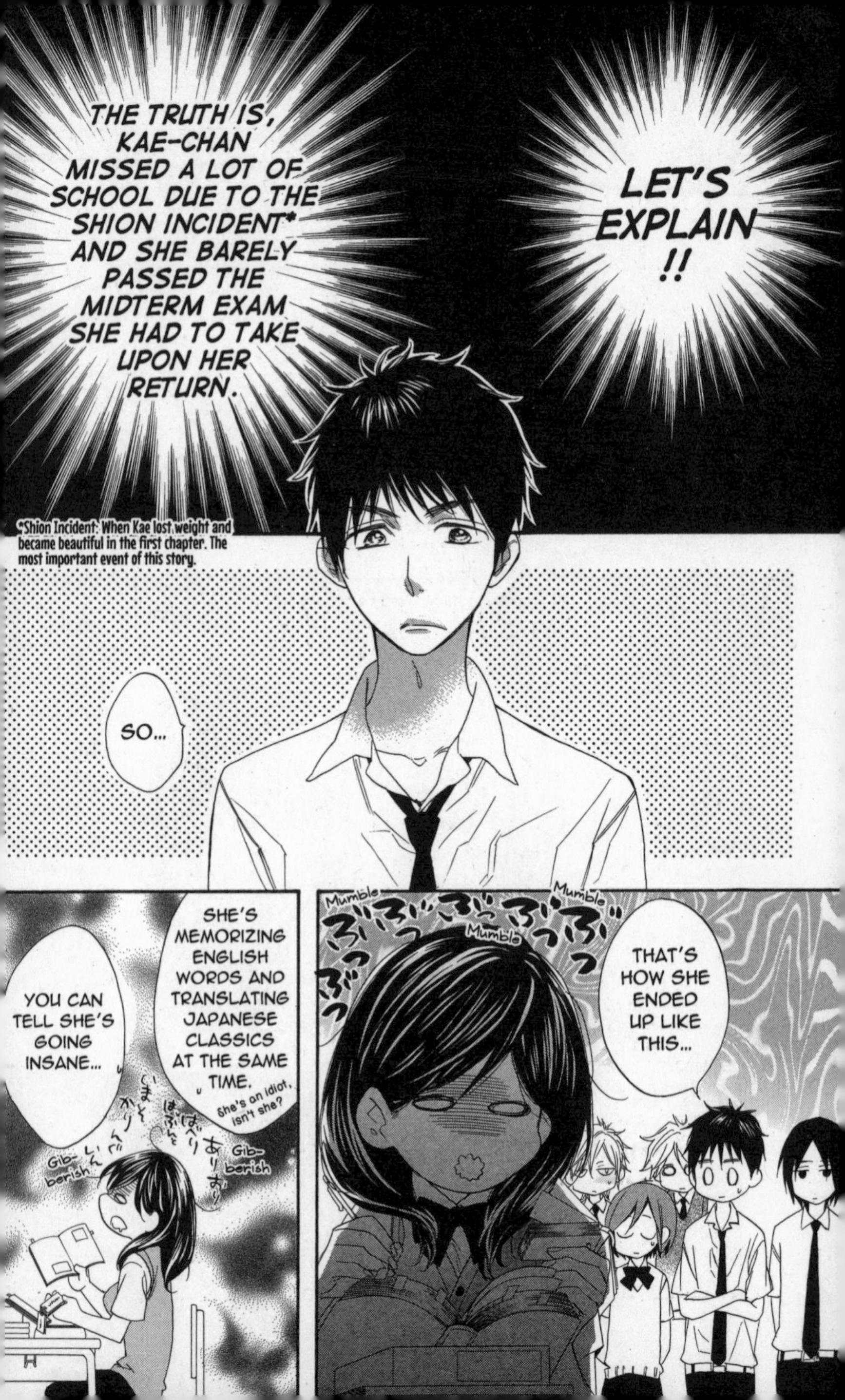
LET'S EXPLAIN !!
THE TRUTH IS, KAE-CHAN MISSED A LOT OF SCHOOL DUE TO THE SHION INCIDENT* AND SHE BARELY PASSED THE MIDTERM EXAM SHE HAD TO TAKE UPON HER RETURN.
*Shion Incident: When Kae lost weight and became beautiful in the first chapter. The most important event of this story.
SO...
Mumble
Mumble
Mumble
THAT'S HOW SHE ENDED UP LIKE THIS...
She's an idiot, isn't she?
SHE'S MEMORIZING ENGLISH WORDS AND TRANSLATING JAPANESE CLASSICS AT THE SAME TIME.
YOU CAN TELL SHE'S GOING INSANE...
Gib-berish
Gib-berish

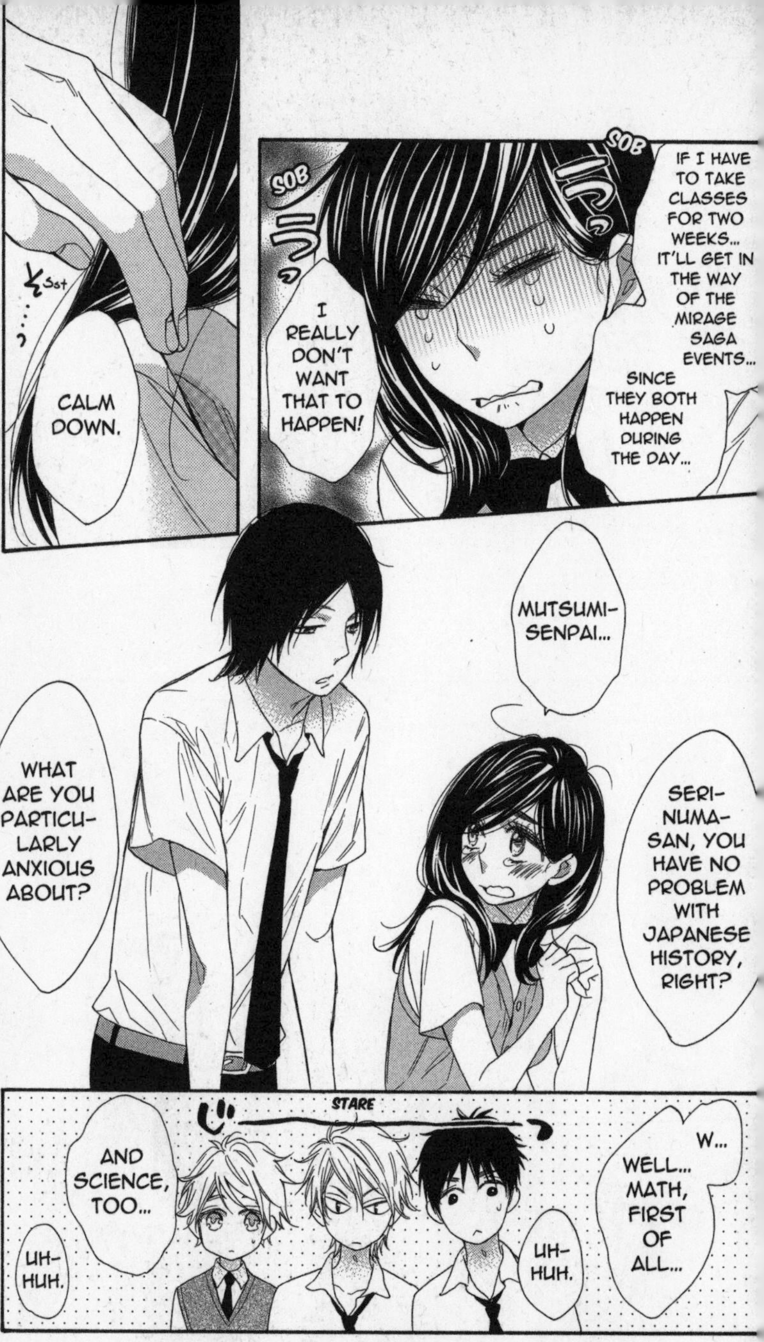
SOB
SOB
IF I HAVE TO TAKE CLASSES FOR TWO WEEKS... IT'LL GET IN THE WAY OF THE MIRAGE SAGA EVENTS...
SINCE THEY BOTH HAPPEN DURING THE DAY...
I REALLY DON'T WANT THAT TO HAPPEN!
Sst
...
CALM DOWN.
MUTSUMI-SENPAI...
SERI-NUMA-SAN, YOU HAVE NO PROBLEM WITH JAPANESE HISTORY, RIGHT?
WHAT ARE YOU PARTICU-LARLY ANXIOUS ABOUT?
STARE
W... WELL... MATH, FIRST OF ALL...
UH-HUH.
AND SCIENCE, TOO...
UH-HUH.

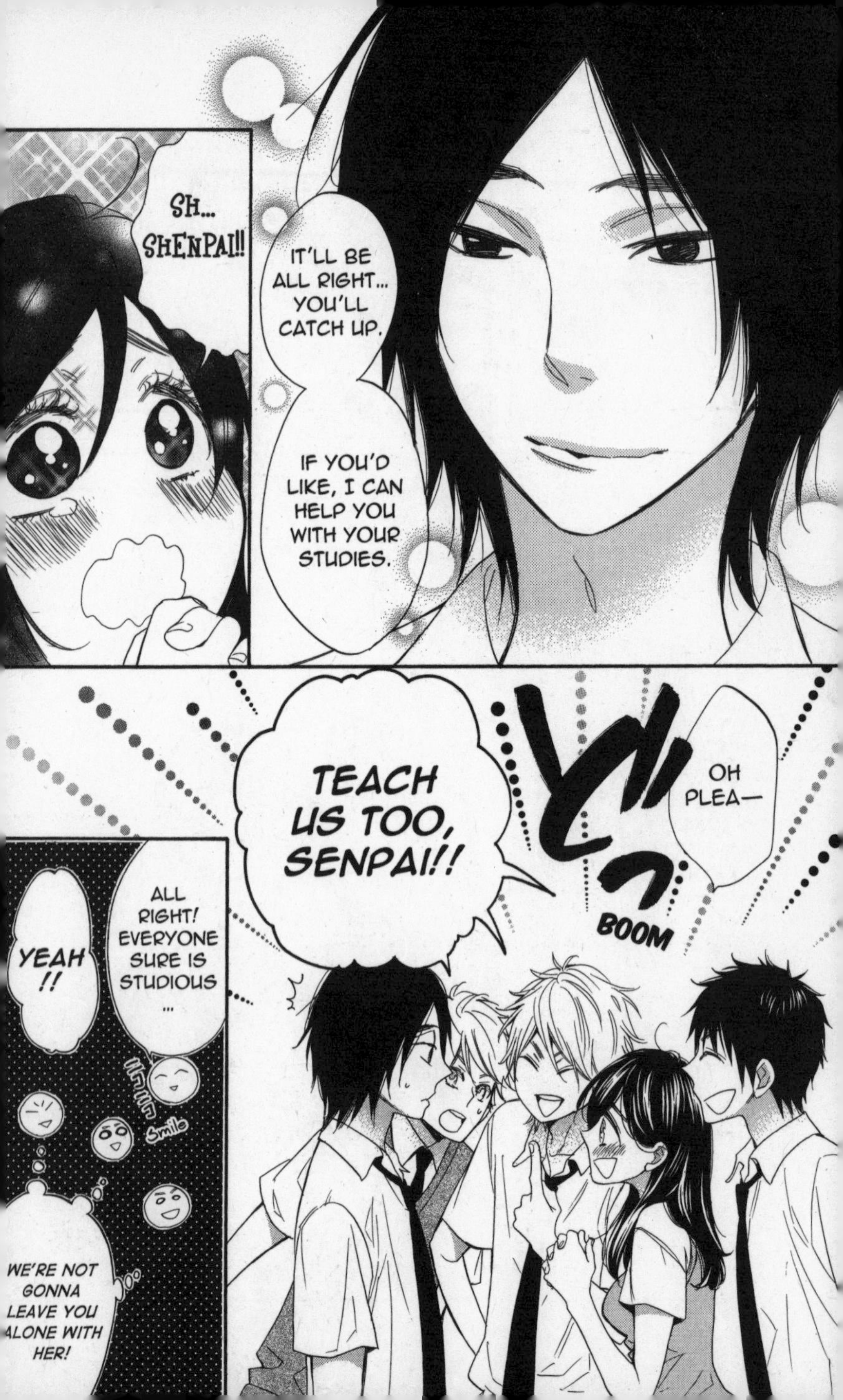
IT'LL BE ALL RIGHT... YOU'LL CATCH UP.
IF YOU'D LIKE, I CAN HELP YOU WITH YOUR STUDIES.
SH... SHENPAI!!
OH PLEA—
BOOM
TEACH US TOO, SENPAI!!
ALL RIGHT! EVERYONE SURE IS STUDIOUS ...
YEAH !!
Smile
WE'RE NOT GONNA LEAVE YOU ALONE WITH HER!

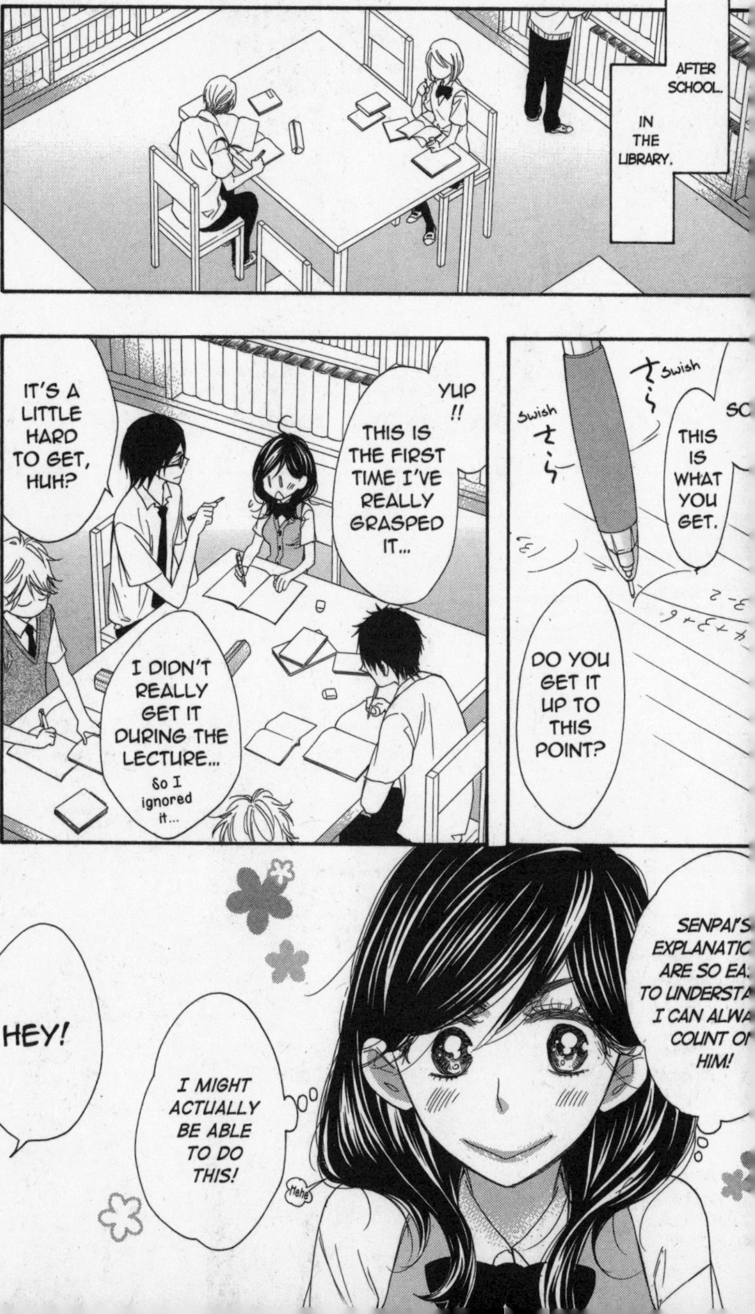
AFTER SCHOOL.
IN THE LIBRARY.
Swish
Swish
SO
THIS IS WHAT YOU GET.
DO YOU GET IT UP TO THIS POINT?
YUP !!
THIS IS THE FIRST TIME I'VE REALLY GRASPED IT...
IT'S A LITTLE HARD TO GET, HUH?
I DIDN'T REALLY GET IT DURING THE LECTURE...
So I ignored it...
SENPAI'S EXPLANATIC ARE SO EA: TO UNDERSTA I CAN ALWA COUNT OI HIM!
I MIGHT ACTUALLY BE ABLE TO DO THIS!
Hehe
HEY!

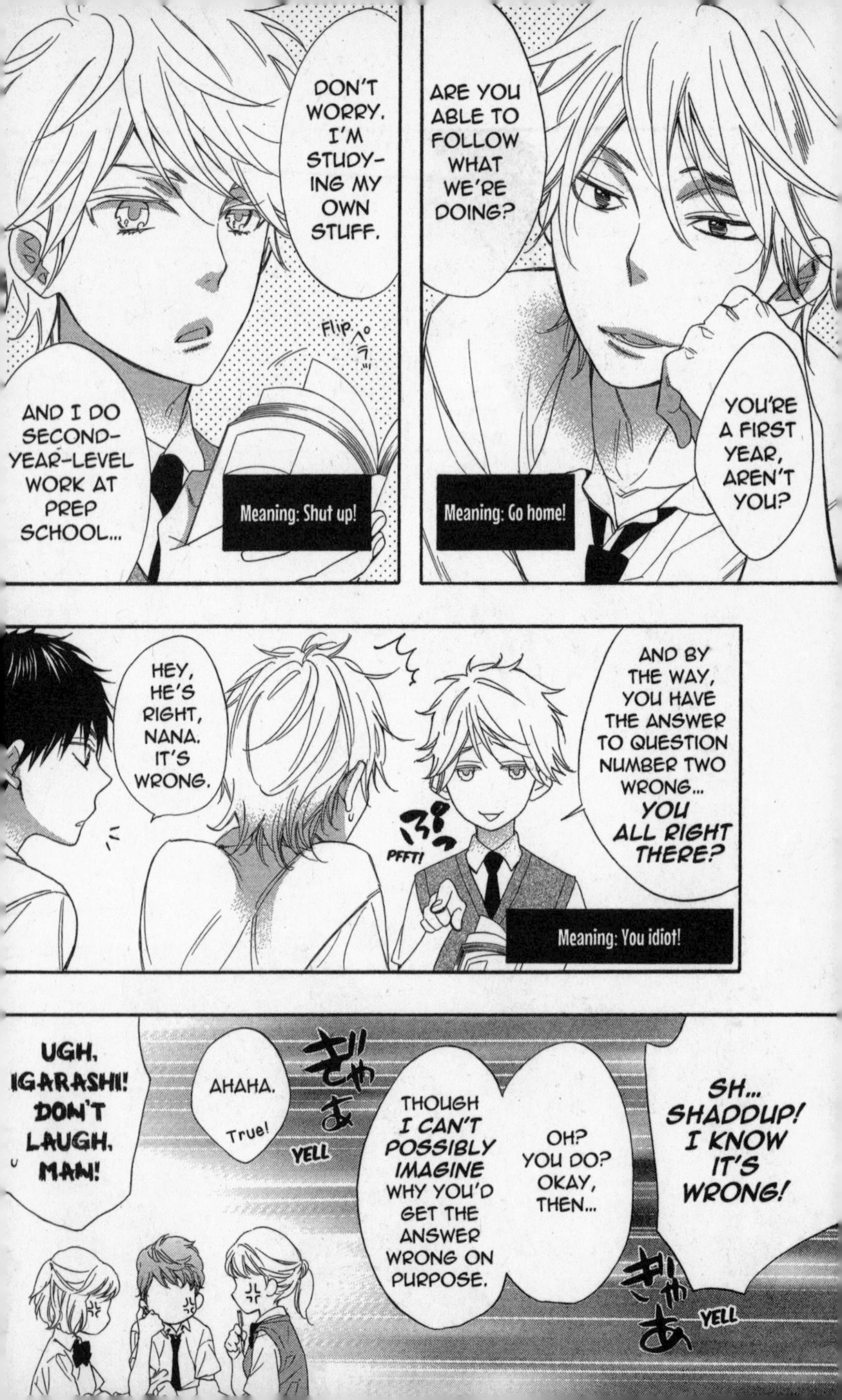
ARE YOU ABLE TO FOLLOW WHAT WE'RE DOING?
YOU'RE A FIRST YEAR, AREN'T YOU?
Meaning: Go home!
DON'T WORRY. I'M STUDYING MY OWN STUFF.
Flip
AND I DO SECOND-YEAR-LEVEL WORK AT PREP SCHOOL...
Meaning: Shut up!
AND BY THE WAY, YOU HAVE THE ANSWER TO QUESTION NUMBER TWO WRONG... *YOU ALL RIGHT THERE?*
PFFT!
Meaning: You idiot!
HEY, HE'S RIGHT, NANA. IT'S WRONG.
SH... SHADDUP! I KNOW IT'S WRONG!
YELL
OH? YOU DO? OKAY, THEN...
THOUGH *I CAN'T POSSIBLY IMAGINE* WHY YOU'D GET THE ANSWER WRONG ON PURPOSE.
YELL
AHAHA.
True!
UGH, IGARASHI! DON'T LAUGH, MAN!

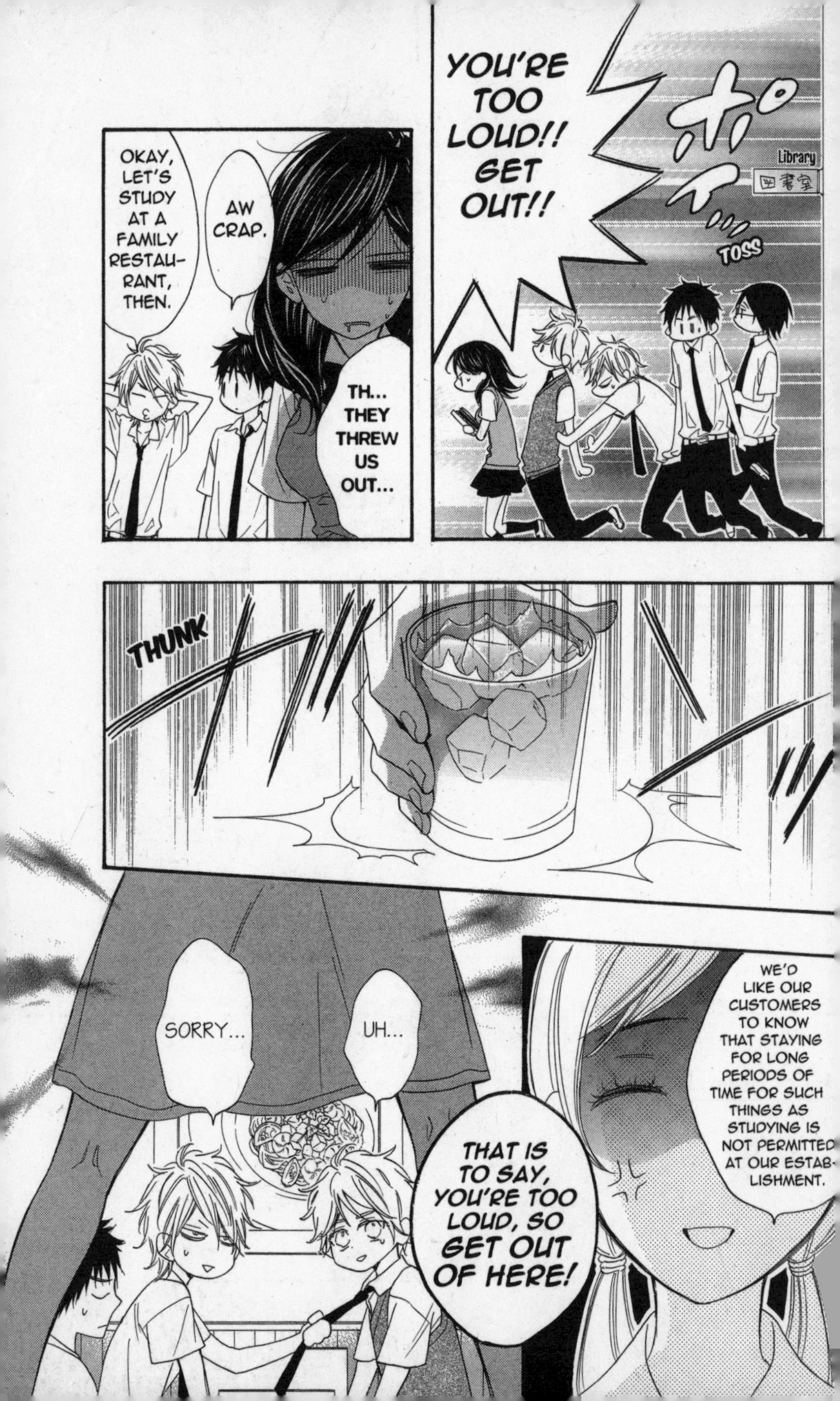
YOU'RE TOO LOUD!! GET OUT!!
ポイ…
TOSS
Library
図書室
TH... THEY THREW US OUT...
AW CRAP.
OKAY, LET'S STUDY AT A FAMILY RESTAURANT, THEN.
THUNK
WE'D LIKE OUR CUSTOMERS TO KNOW THAT STAYING FOR LONG PERIODS OF TIME FOR SUCH THINGS AS STUDYING IS NOT PERMITTED AT OUR ESTABLISHMENT.
THAT IS TO SAY, YOU'RE TOO LOUD, SO GET OUT OF HERE!
UH...
SORRY...

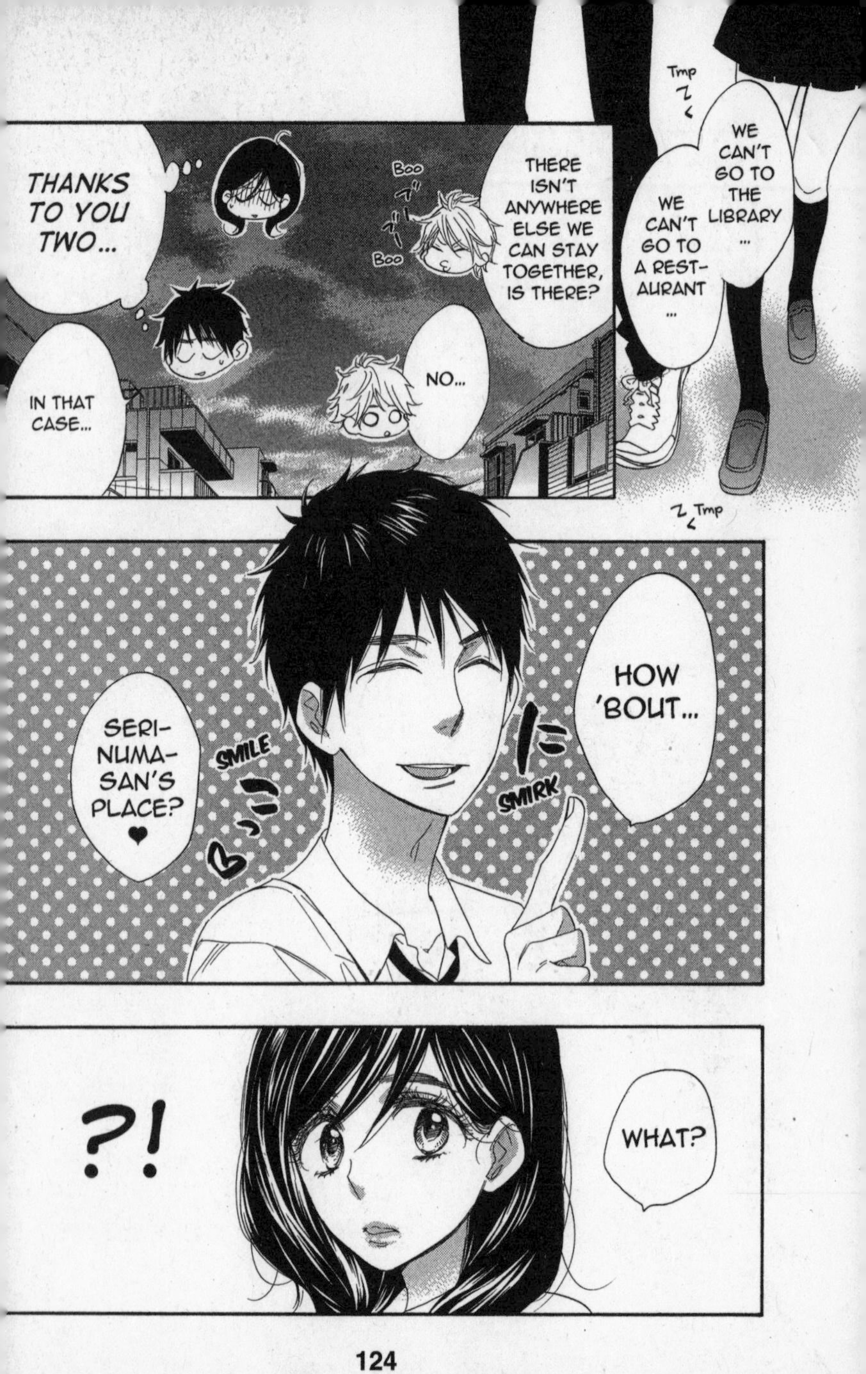
Tmp
WE CAN'T GO TO THE LIBRARY...
WE CAN'T GO TO A REST-AURANT...
Tmp
THERE ISN'T ANYWHERE ELSE WE CAN STAY TOGETHER, IS THERE?
Boo
Boo
NO...
THANKS TO YOU TWO...
IN THAT CASE...
HOW 'BOUT...
SMIRK
SMILE
SERI-NUMA-SAN'S PLACE? ♥
WHAT?
?!

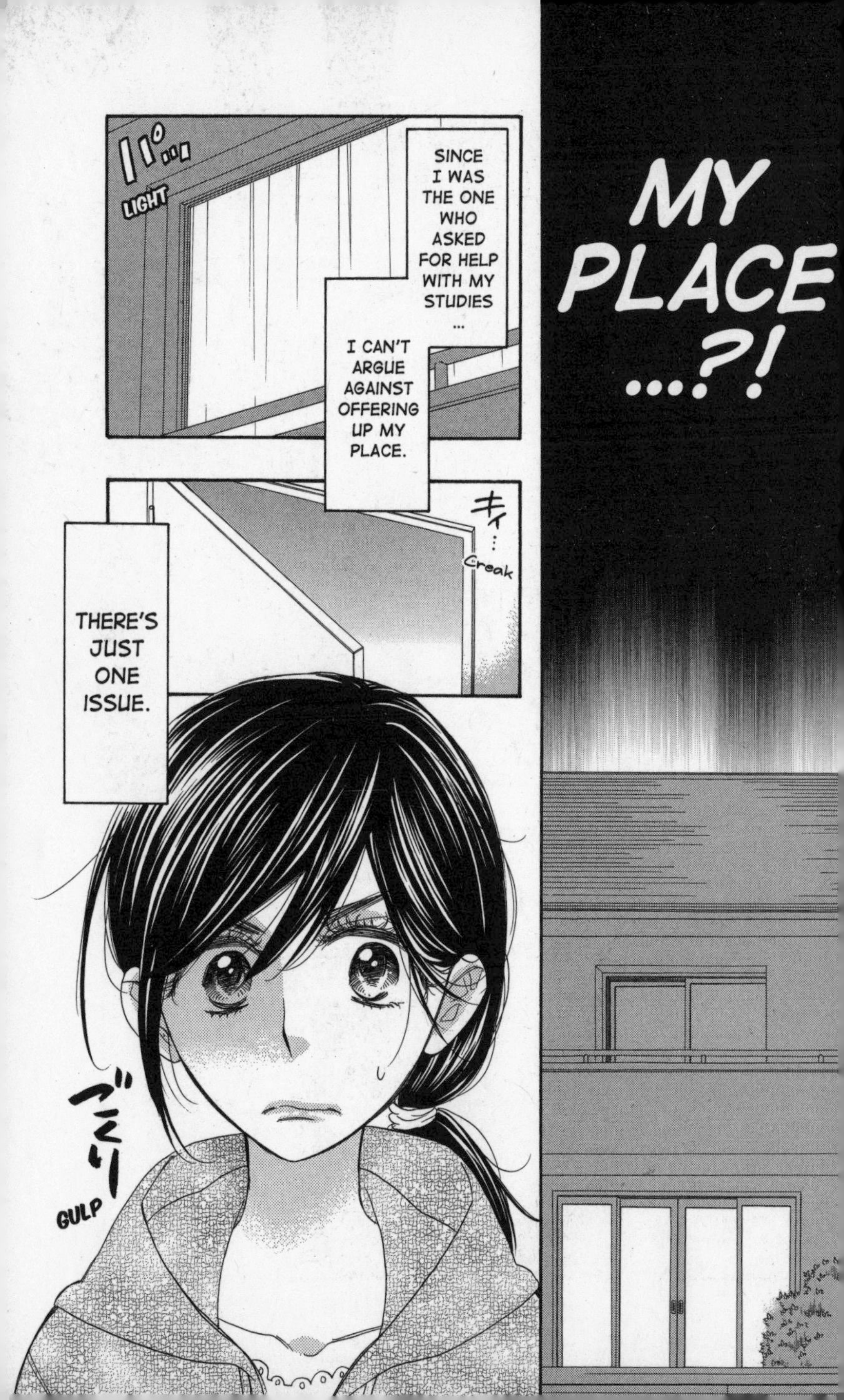
MY PLACE ...?!
LIGHT
SINCE I WAS THE ONE WHO ASKED FOR HELP WITH MY STUDIES ...
I CAN'T ARGUE AGAINST OFFERING UP MY PLACE.
Creak
THERE'S JUST ONE ISSUE.
GULP

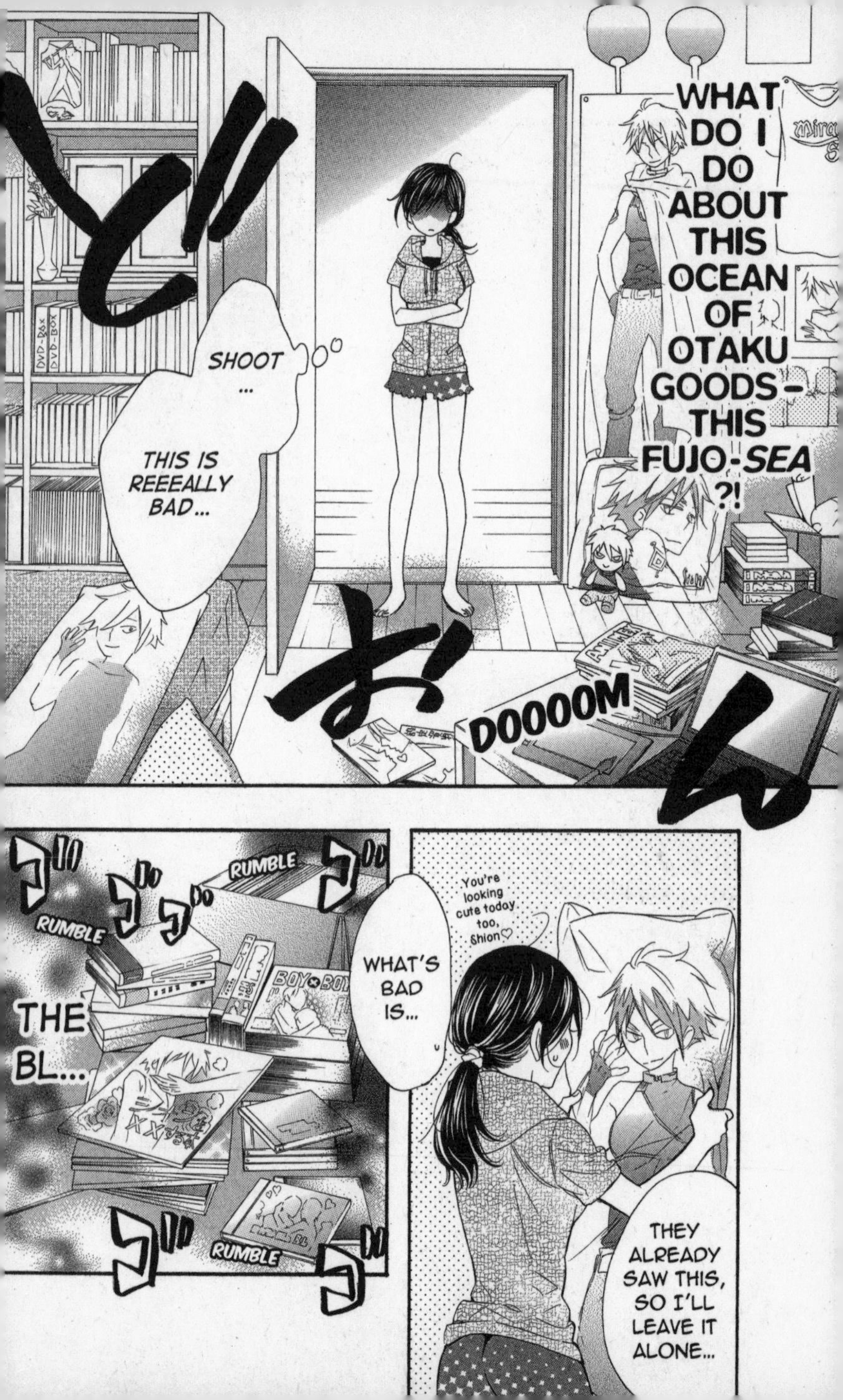
WHAT DO I DO ABOUT THIS OCEAN OF OTAKU GOODS–THIS FUJO-*SEA*?!
SHOOT ...
THIS IS REEEALLY BAD...
DOOOOM
You're looking cute today too, Shion♡
WHAT'S BAD IS...
THEY ALREADY SAW THIS, SO I'LL LEAVE IT ALONE...
RUMBLE
RUMBLE
THE BL...
RUMBLE

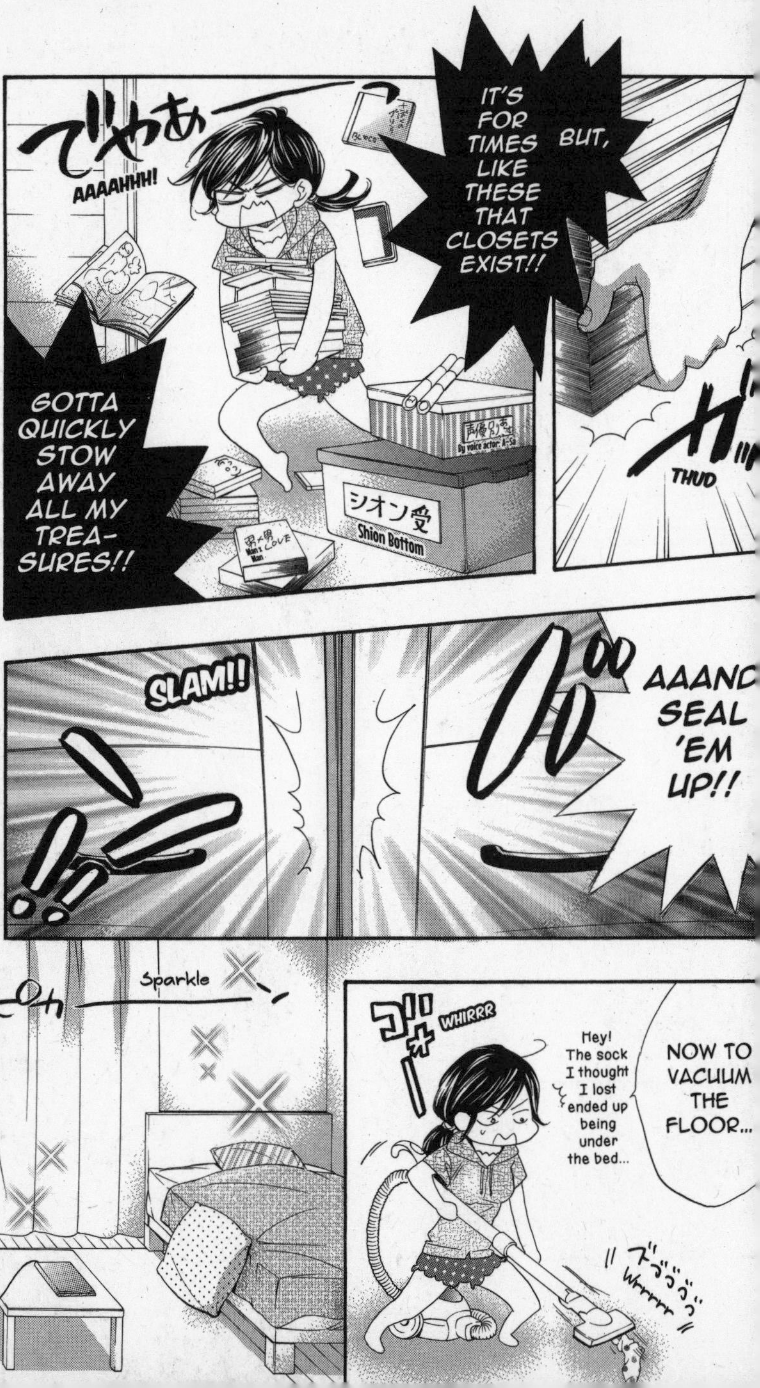

THUD
でやあー
AAAAHHH!
BUT, IT'S FOR TIMES LIKE THESE THAT CLOSETS EXIST!!
GOTTA QUICKLY STOW AWAY ALL MY TREASURES!!
By voice actor: A-Sa
シオン受
Shion Bottom
Man x Man LOVE
AAAND SEAL 'EM UP!!
SLAM!!
WHIRRR
NOW TO VACUUM THE FLOOR...
Hey! The sock I thought I lost ended up being under the bed...
Wrrrrr
Sparkle

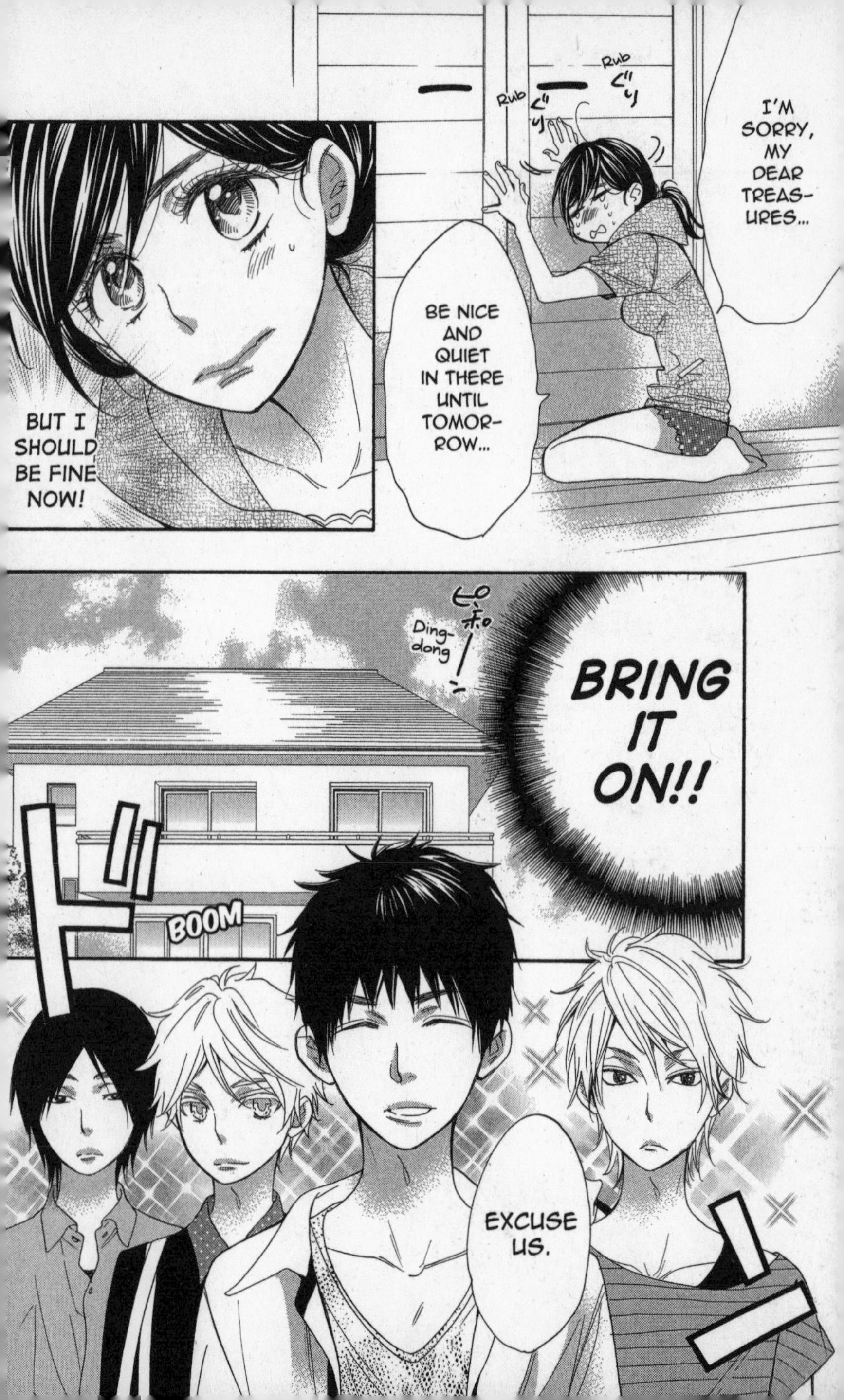
Rub
Rub
I'M SORRY, MY DEAR TREASURES...
BE NICE AND QUIET IN THERE UNTIL TOMORROW...
BUT I SHOULD BE FINE NOW!
Ding-dong
BRING IT ON!!
BOOM
EXCUSE US.

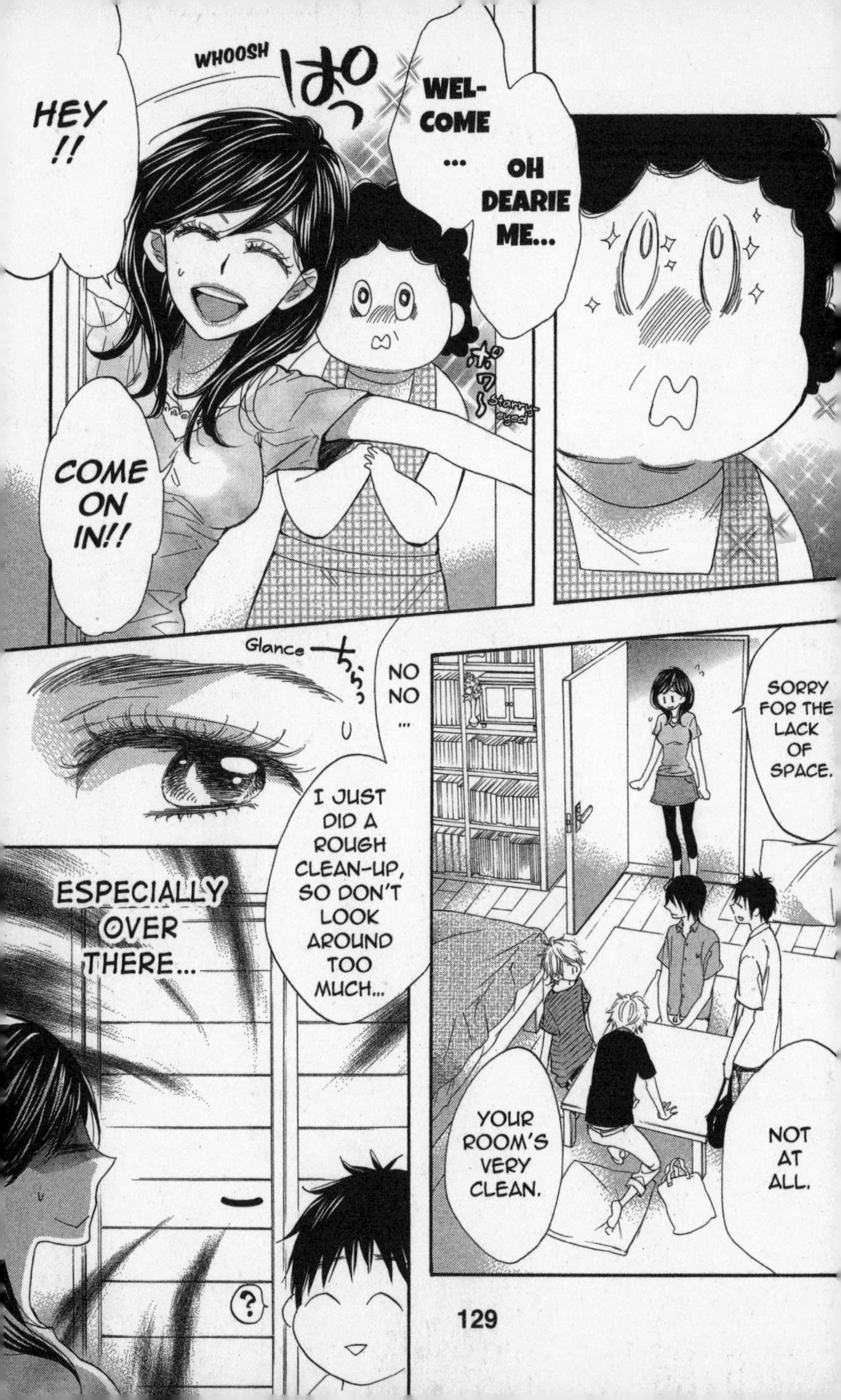

WEL-COME ... OH DEARIE ME...
WHOOSH
HEY !!
Starry-eyed
COME ON IN!!
SORRY FOR THE LACK OF SPACE.
NOT AT ALL.
YOUR ROOM'S VERY CLEAN.
Glance
NO NO ...
I JUST DID A ROUGH CLEAN-UP, SO DON'T LOOK AROUND TOO MUCH...
ESPECIALLY OVER THERE...
?

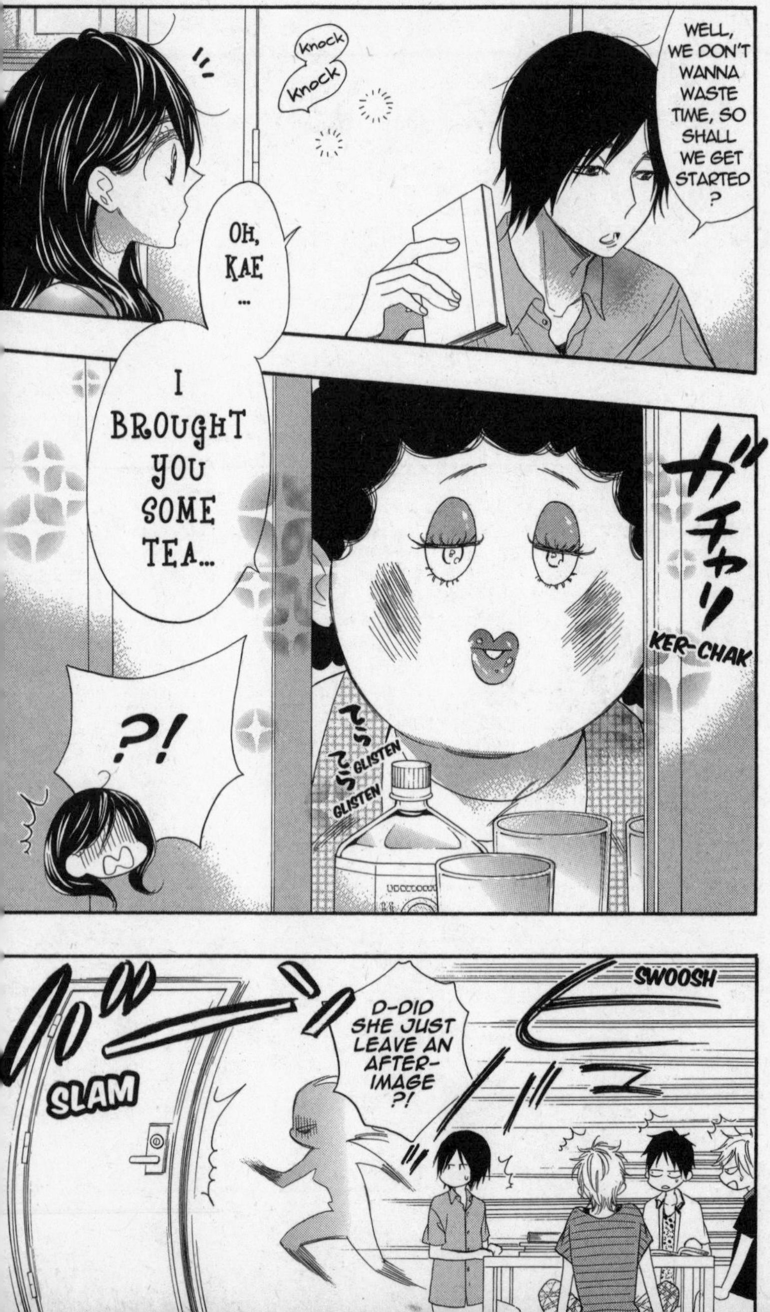
WELL, WE DON'T WANNA WASTE TIME, SO SHALL WE GET STARTED?
knock knock
OH, KAE...
ガチャリ
KER-CHAK
I BROUGHT YOU SOME TEA...
てらてら
GLISTEN GLISTEN
?!
SWOOSH
D-DID SHE JUST LEAVE AN AFTER-IMAGE?!
SLAM

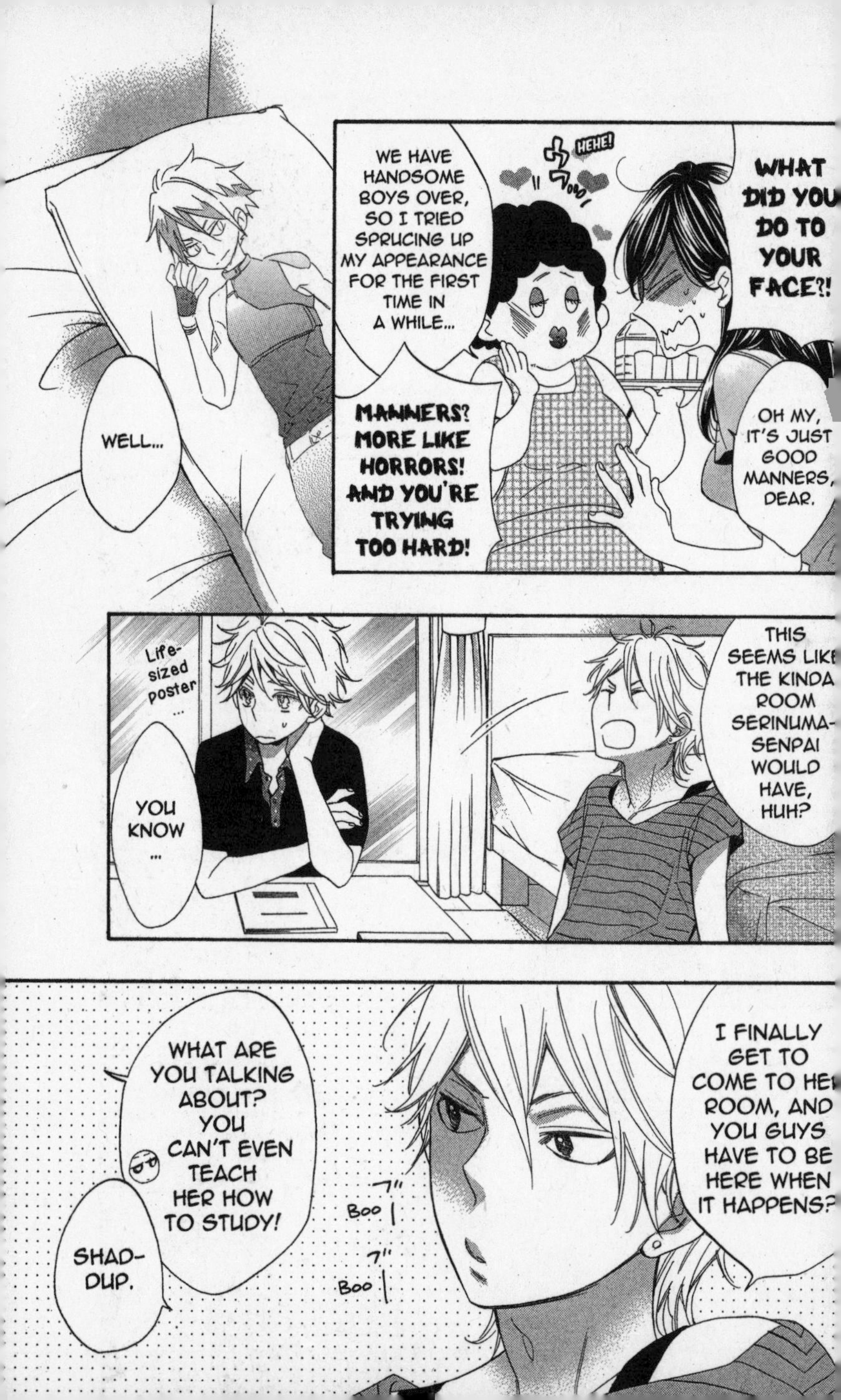

WHAT DID YOU DO TO YOUR FACE?!
HEHE!
WE HAVE HANDSOME BOYS OVER, SO I TRIED SPRUCING UP MY APPEARANCE FOR THE FIRST TIME IN A WHILE...
OH MY, IT'S JUST GOOD MANNERS, DEAR.
MANNERS? MORE LIKE HORRORS! AND YOU'RE TRYING TOO HARD!
WELL...
THIS SEEMS LIK THE KINDA ROOM SERINUMA-SENPAI WOULD HAVE, HUH?
Life-sized poster ...
YOU KNOW ...
I FINALLY GET TO COME TO HE ROOM, AND YOU GUYS HAVE TO BE HERE WHEN IT HAPPENS?
WHAT ARE YOU TALKING ABOUT? YOU CAN'T EVEN TEACH HER HOW TO STUDY!
Boo
Boo
SHAD-DUP.

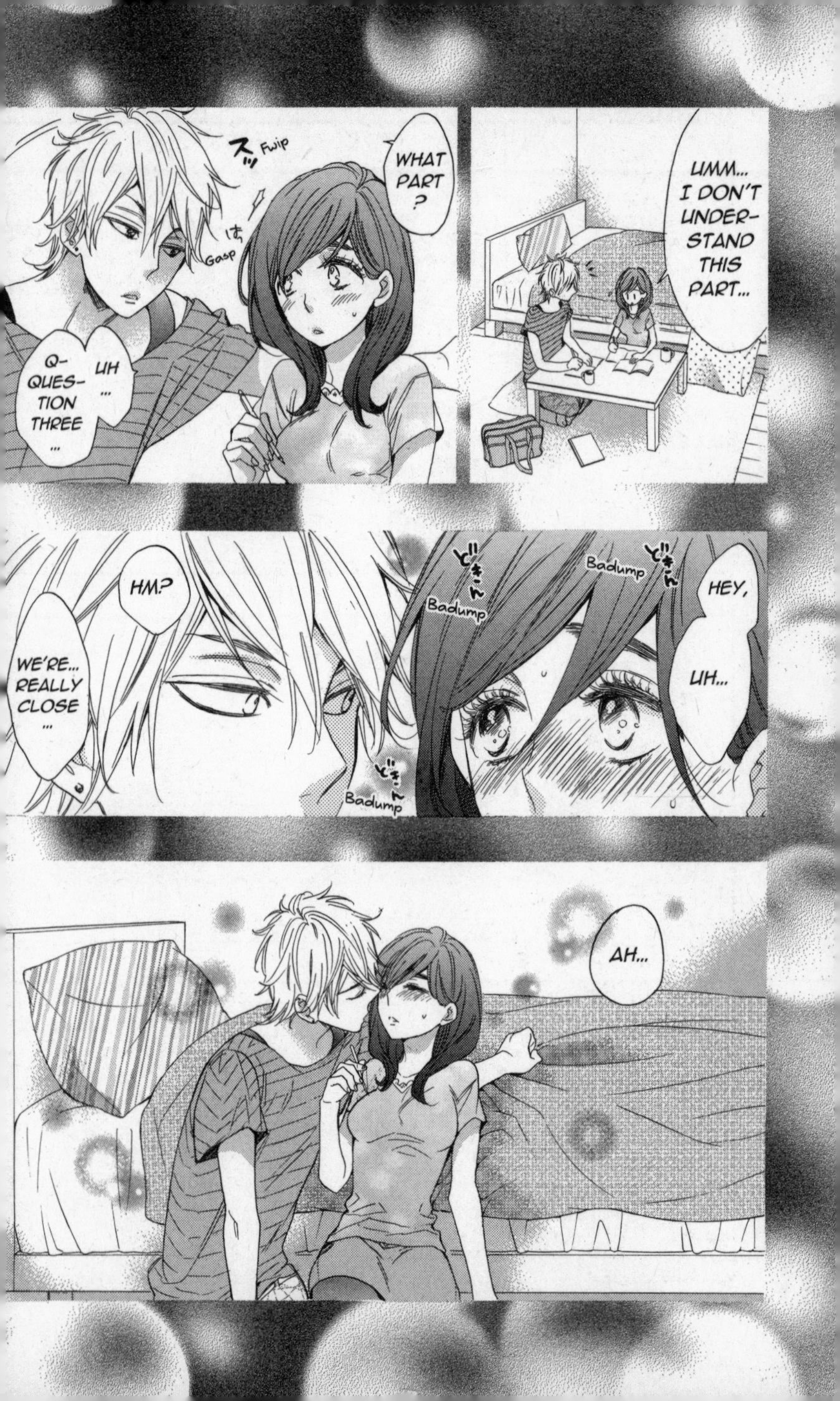
UMM... I DON'T UNDER-STAND THIS PART...
WHAT PART?
スッ Fwip
はっ Gasp
UH ...
Q-QUES-TION THREE ...
HEY,
UH...
どきん Badump
どきん Badump
どきん Badump
HM?
WE'RE... REALLY CLOSE ...
AH...

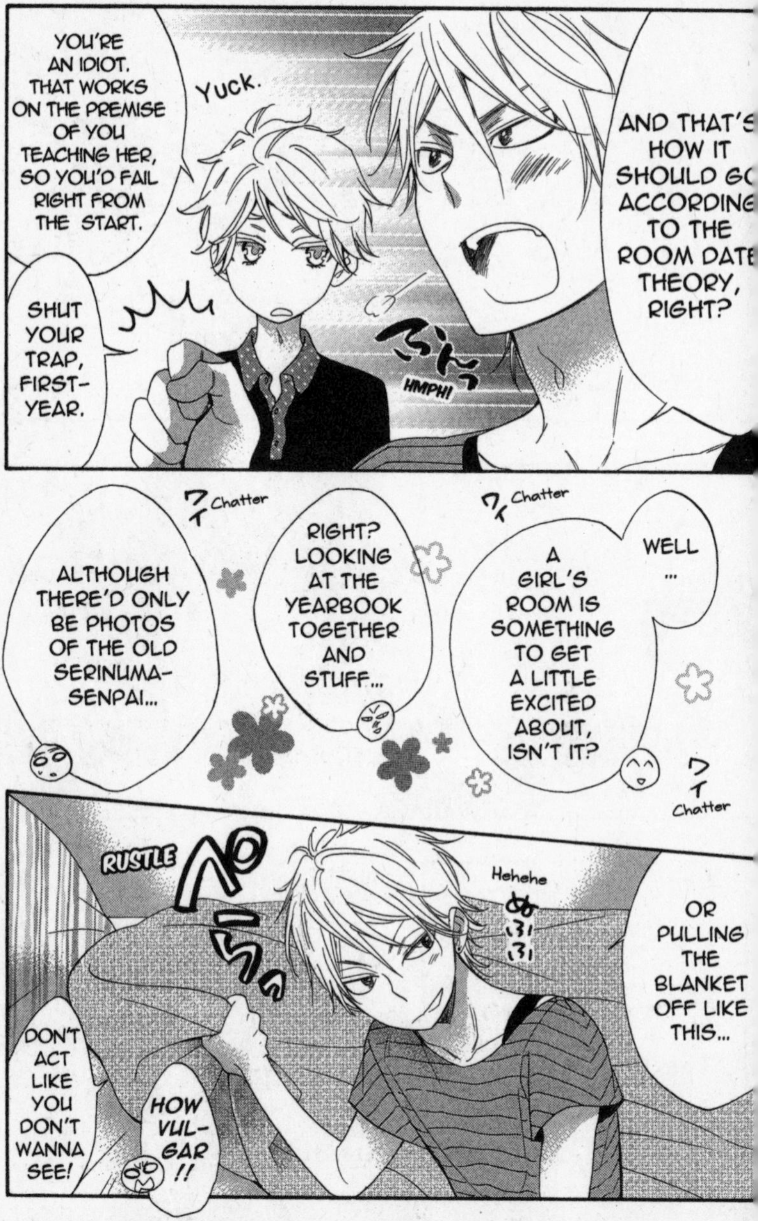
AND THAT'S HOW IT SHOULD GO ACCORDING TO THE ROOM DATE THEORY, RIGHT?
HMPH!
Yuck.
YOU'RE AN IDIOT. THAT WORKS ON THE PREMISE OF YOU TEACHING HER, SO YOU'D FAIL RIGHT FROM THE START.
SHUT YOUR TRAP, FIRST-YEAR.
WELL...
Chatter
A GIRL'S ROOM IS SOMETHING TO GET A LITTLE EXCITED ABOUT, ISN'T IT?
Chatter
RIGHT? LOOKING AT THE YEARBOOK TOGETHER AND STUFF...
Chatter
ALTHOUGH THERE'D ONLY BE PHOTOS OF THE OLD SERINUMA-SENPAI...
OR PULLING THE BLANKET OFF LIKE THIS...
Hehehe
RUSTLE
HOW VULGAR!!
DON'T ACT LIKE YOU DON'T WANNA SEE!

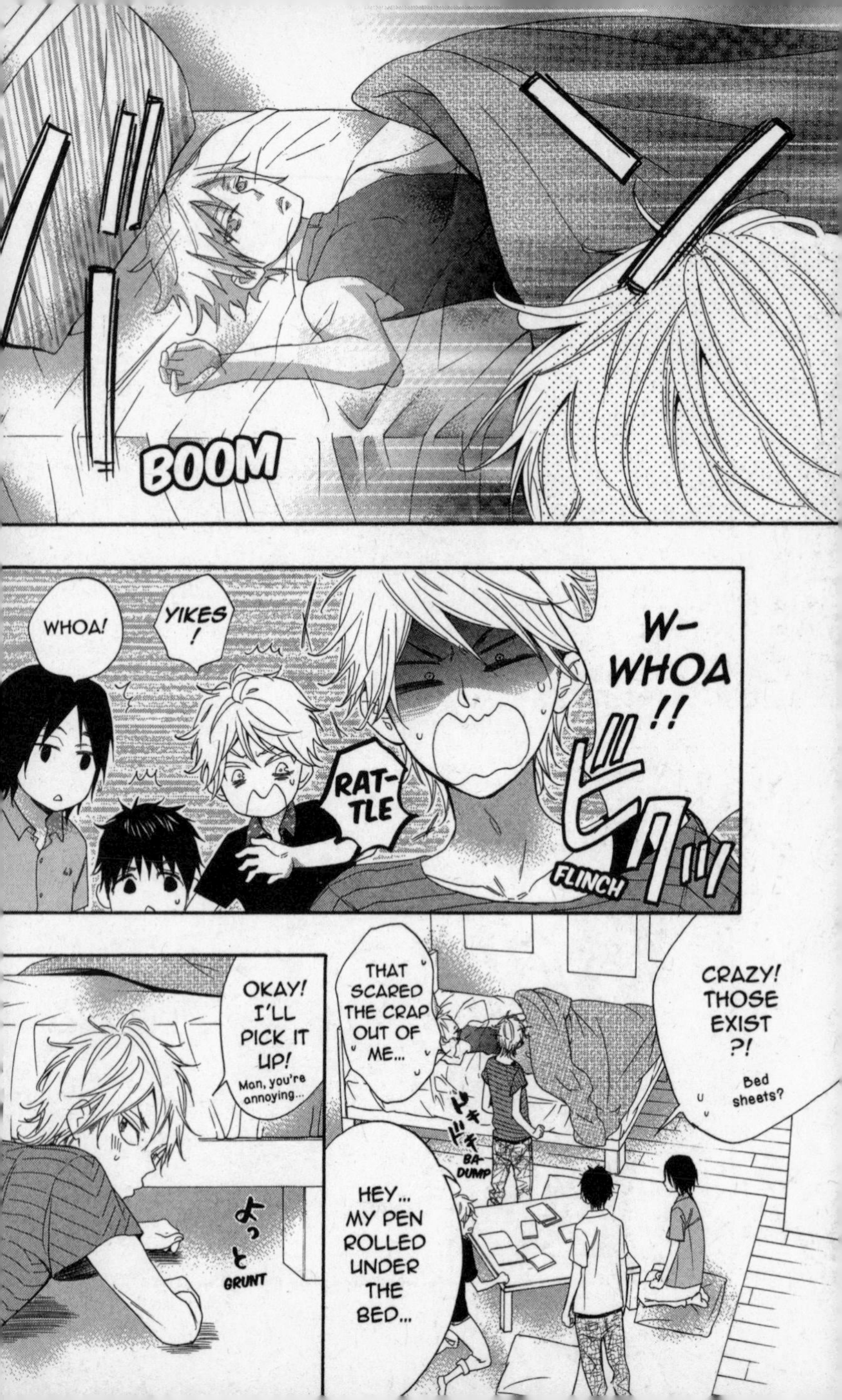
BOOM
W-WHOA!!
ビクッ
FLINCH
RAT-TLE
YIKES!
WHOA!
CRAZY! THOSE EXIST?!
Bed sheets?
THAT SCARED THE CRAP OUT OF ME...
ドキドキ
BA-DUMP
HEY... MY PEN ROLLED UNDER THE BED...
OKAY! I'LL PICK IT UP!
Man, you're annoying...
よっと
GRUNT

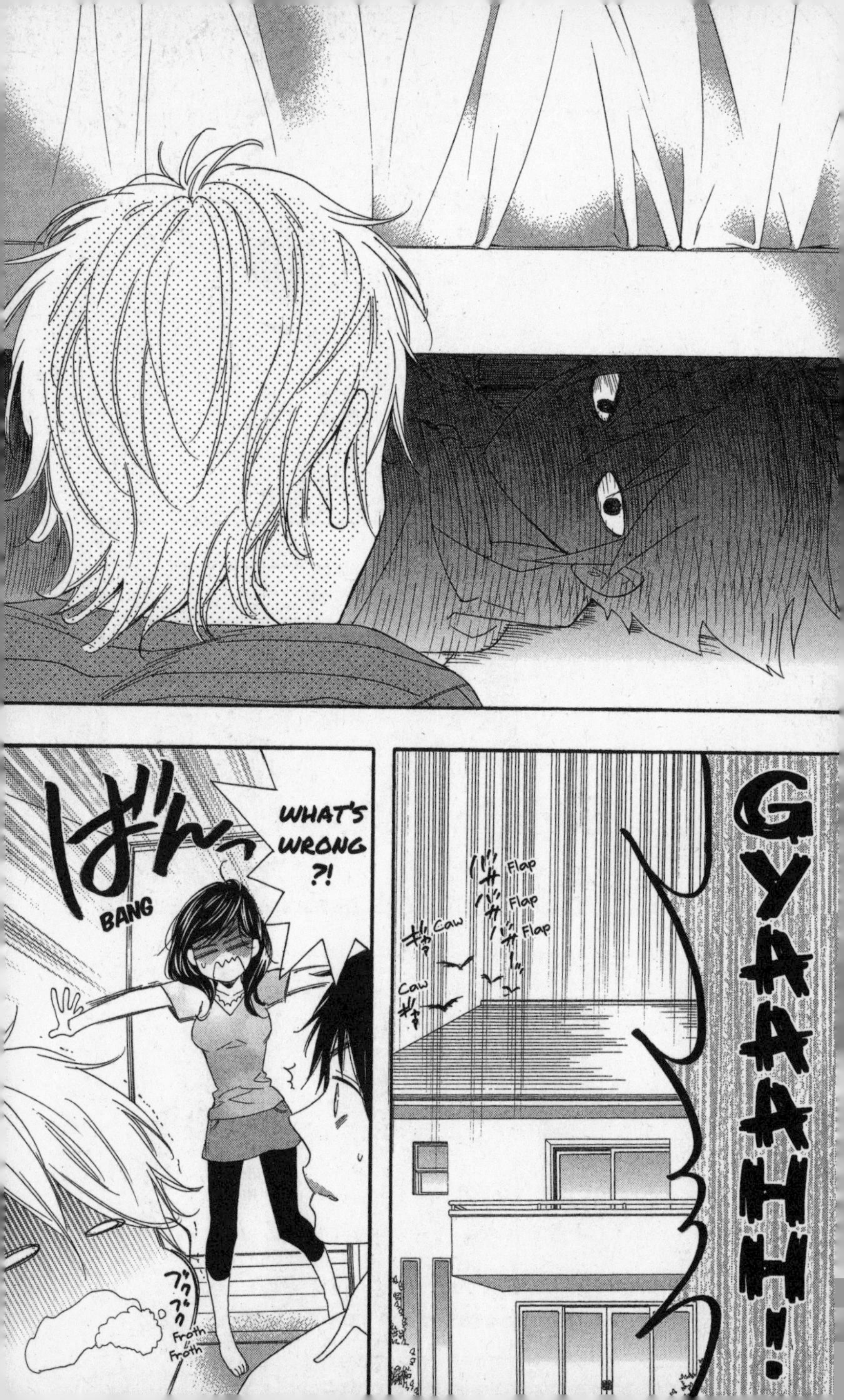
GYAAHH!!
Flap
Flap
Flap
Caw
Caw
ばんっ
BANG
WHAT'S WRONG ?!
Froth
Froth

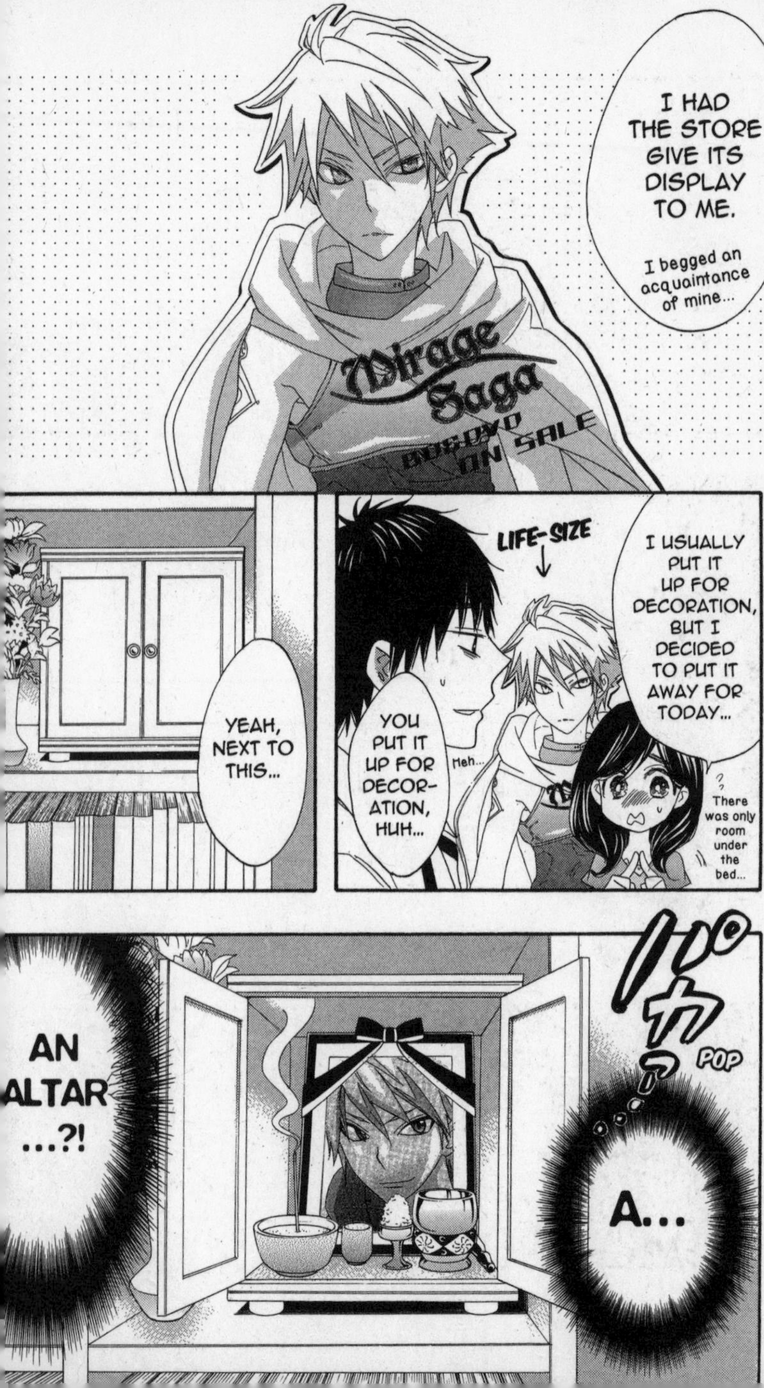
I HAD THE STORE GIVE ITS DISPLAY TO ME.
I begged an acquaintance of mine...
Mirage Saga
ON SALE
LIFE-SIZE
I USUALLY PUT IT UP FOR DECORATION, BUT I DECIDED TO PUT IT AWAY FOR TODAY...
There was only room under the bed...
YOU PUT IT UP FOR DECORATION, HUH...
Heh...
YEAH, NEXT TO THIS...
パカッ
POP
A...
AN ALTAR ...?!

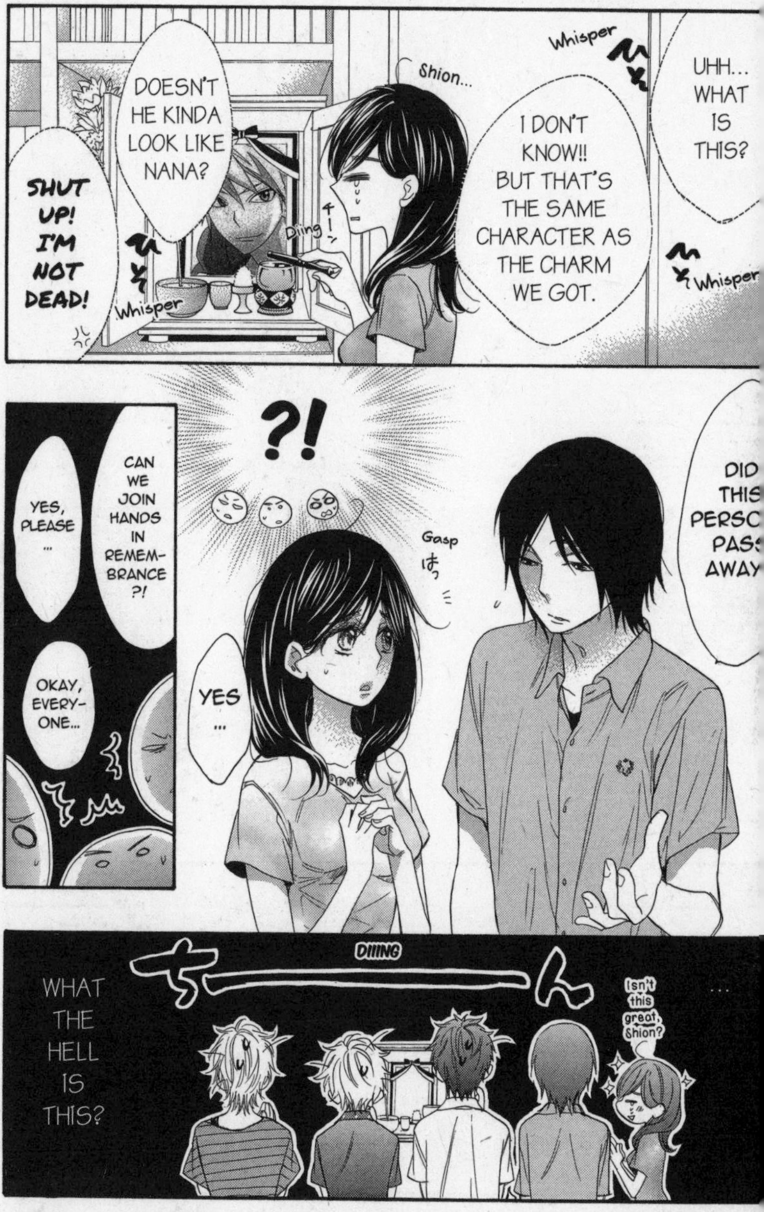
Whisper
UHH... WHAT IS THIS?
Whisper
I DON'T KNOW!! BUT THAT'S THE SAME CHARACTER AS THE CHARM WE GOT.
Shion...
DOESN'T HE KINDA LOOK LIKE NANA?
Diiing
SHUT UP! I'M NOT DEAD!
Whisper
DID THIS PERSO PAS AWAY
?!
Gasp
YES ...
CAN WE JOIN HANDS IN REMEMBRANCE?!
YES, PLEASE ...
OKAY, EVERYONE...
...
Isn't this great, Shion?
DIIING
WHAT THE HELL IS THIS?

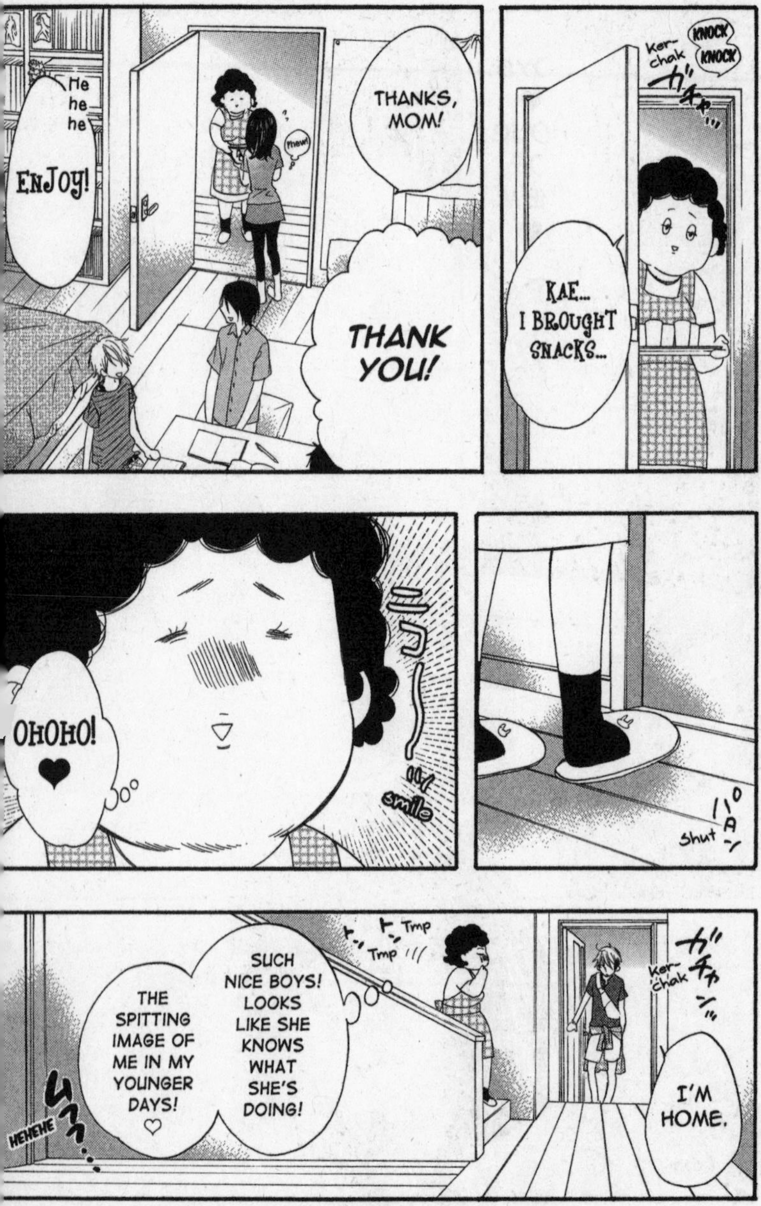
KNOCK KNOCK
Ker-chak
KAE... I BROUGHT SNACKS...
THANKS, MOM!
Phew!
THANK YOU!
He he he
ENJOY!
Shut
OHOHO! ♥
smile
Ker-chak
I'M HOME.
Tmp Tmp
SUCH NICE BOYS! LOOKS LIKE SHE KNOWS WHAT SHE'S DOING!
THE SPITTING IMAGE OF ME IN MY YOUNGER DAYS! ♡
HEHEHE

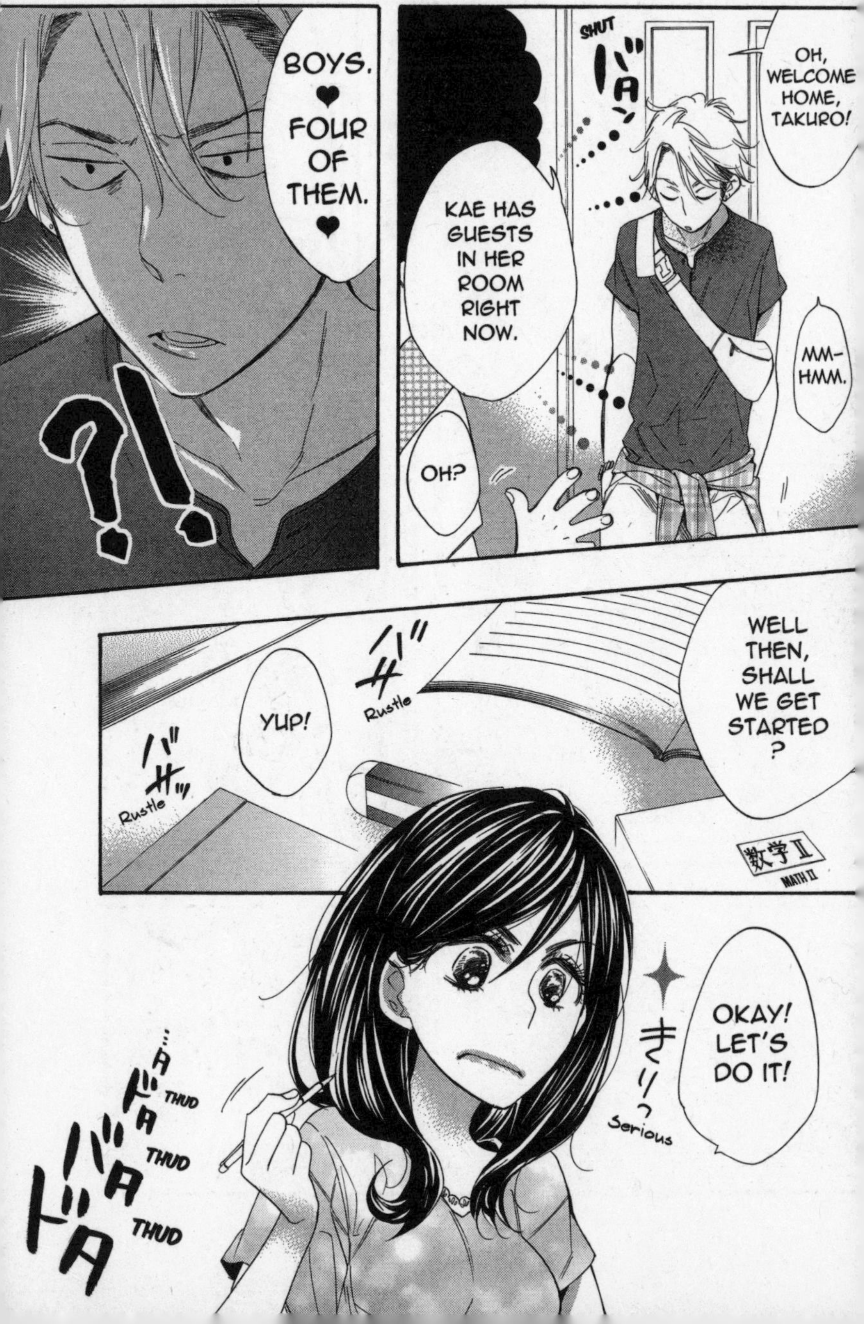
SHUT
OH, WELCOME HOME, TAKURO!
MM-HMM.
KAE HAS GUESTS IN HER ROOM RIGHT NOW.
OH?
BOYS. ❤ FOUR OF THEM. ❤
?!
WELL THEN, SHALL WE GET STARTED?
Rustle
YUP!
Rustle
数学II
MATH II
OKAY! LET'S DO IT!
Serious
THUD
THUD
THUD

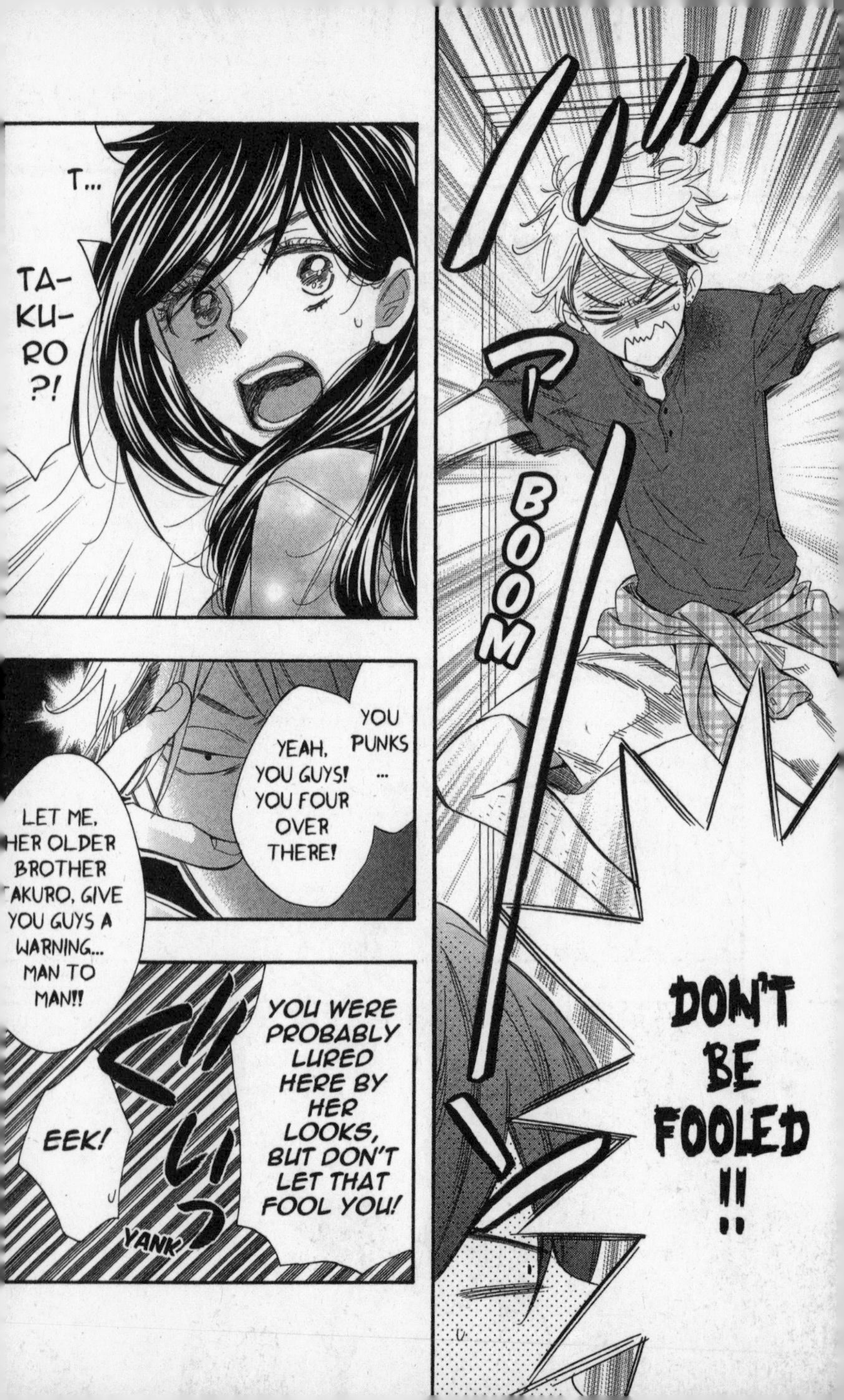
BOOM
DON'T BE FOOLED!!
T...
TA-KU-RO?!
YOU PUNKS...
YEAH, YOU GUYS! YOU FOUR OVER THERE!
LET ME, HER OLDER BROTHER TAKURO, GIVE YOU GUYS A WARNING... MAN TO MAN!!
YOU WERE PROBABLY LURED HERE BY HER LOOKS, BUT DON'T LET THAT FOOL YOU!
EEK!
YANK

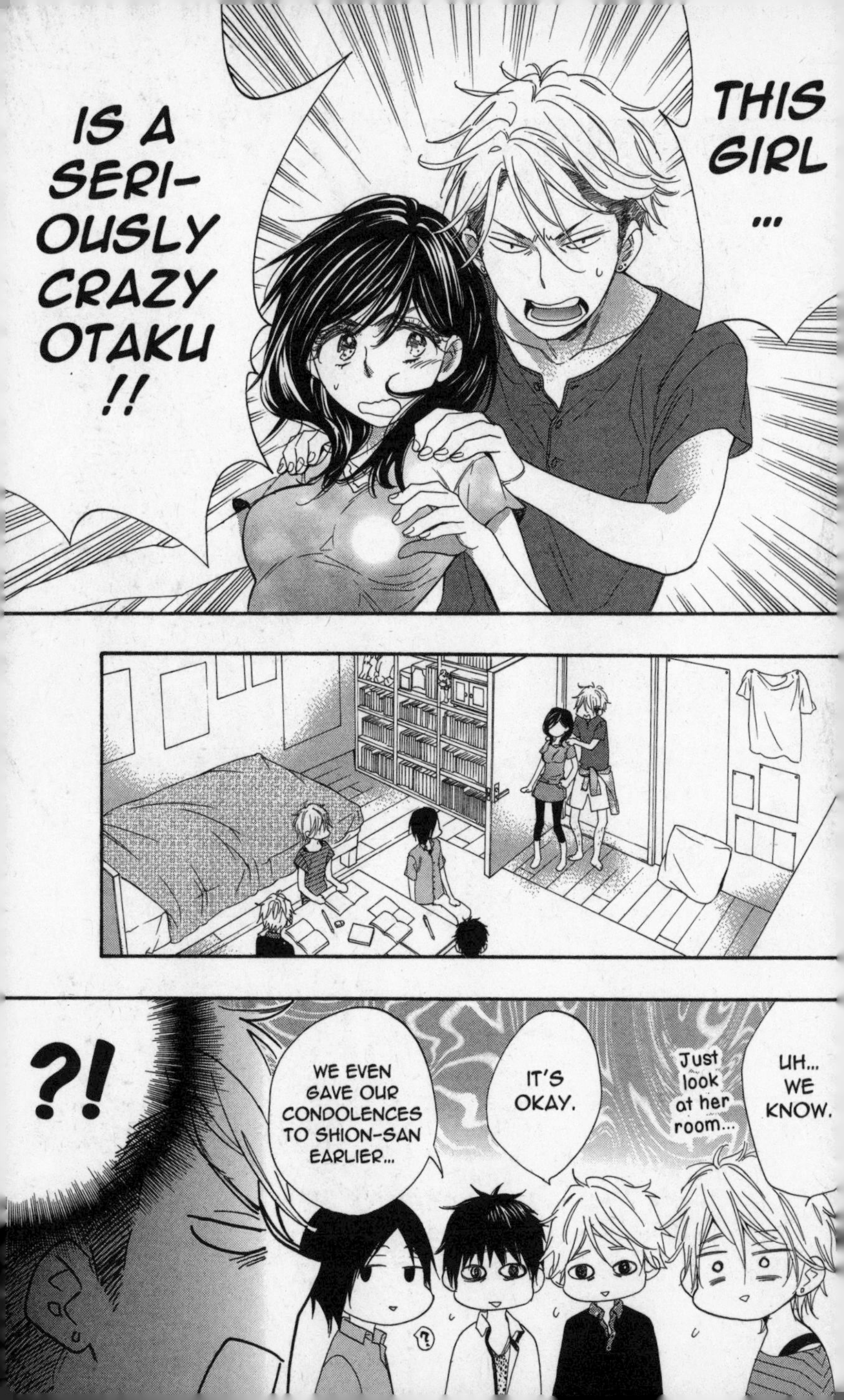
THIS GIRL ...
IS A SERIOUSLY CRAZY OTAKU !!
UH... WE KNOW.
Just look at her room...
IT'S OKAY.
WE EVEN GAVE OUR CONDOLENCES TO SHION-SAN EARLIER...
?!

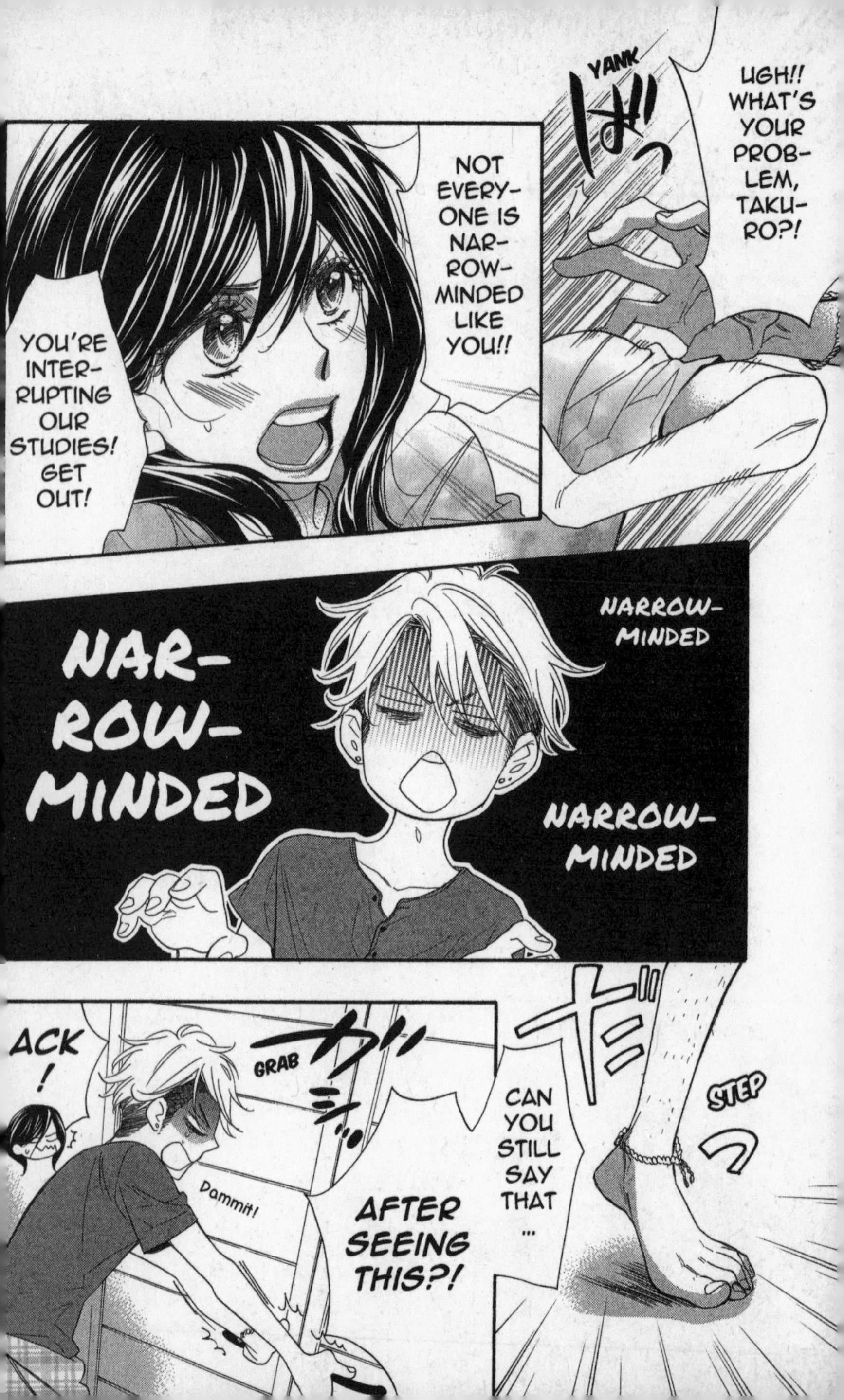
YANK
UGH!! WHAT'S YOUR PROBLEM, TAKURO?!
NOT EVERYONE IS NARROW-MINDED LIKE YOU!!
YOU'RE INTERRUPTING OUR STUDIES! GET OUT!
NARROW-MINDED
NARROW-MINDED
NARROW-MINDED
STEP
CAN YOU STILL SAY THAT ...
AFTER SEEING THIS?!
GRAB
Dammit!
ACK!

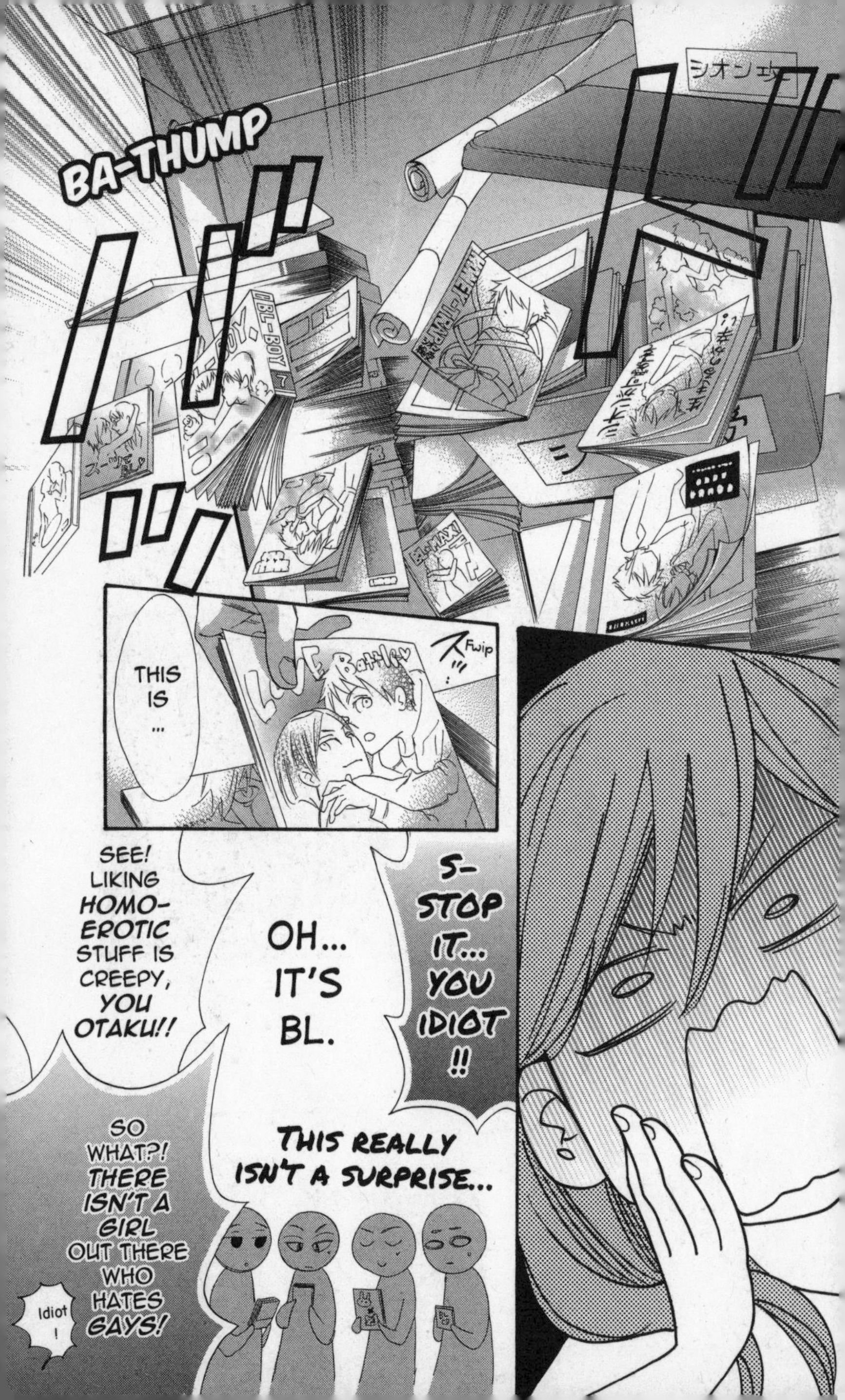
BA-THUMP
Fwip
THIS IS ...
S- STOP IT... YOU IDIOT !!
OH... IT'S BL.
SEE! LIKING HOMO-EROTIC STUFF IS CREEPY, YOU OTAKU!!
THIS REALLY ISN'T A SURPRISE...
SO WHAT?! THERE ISN'T A GIRL OUT THERE WHO HATES GAYS!
Idiot !

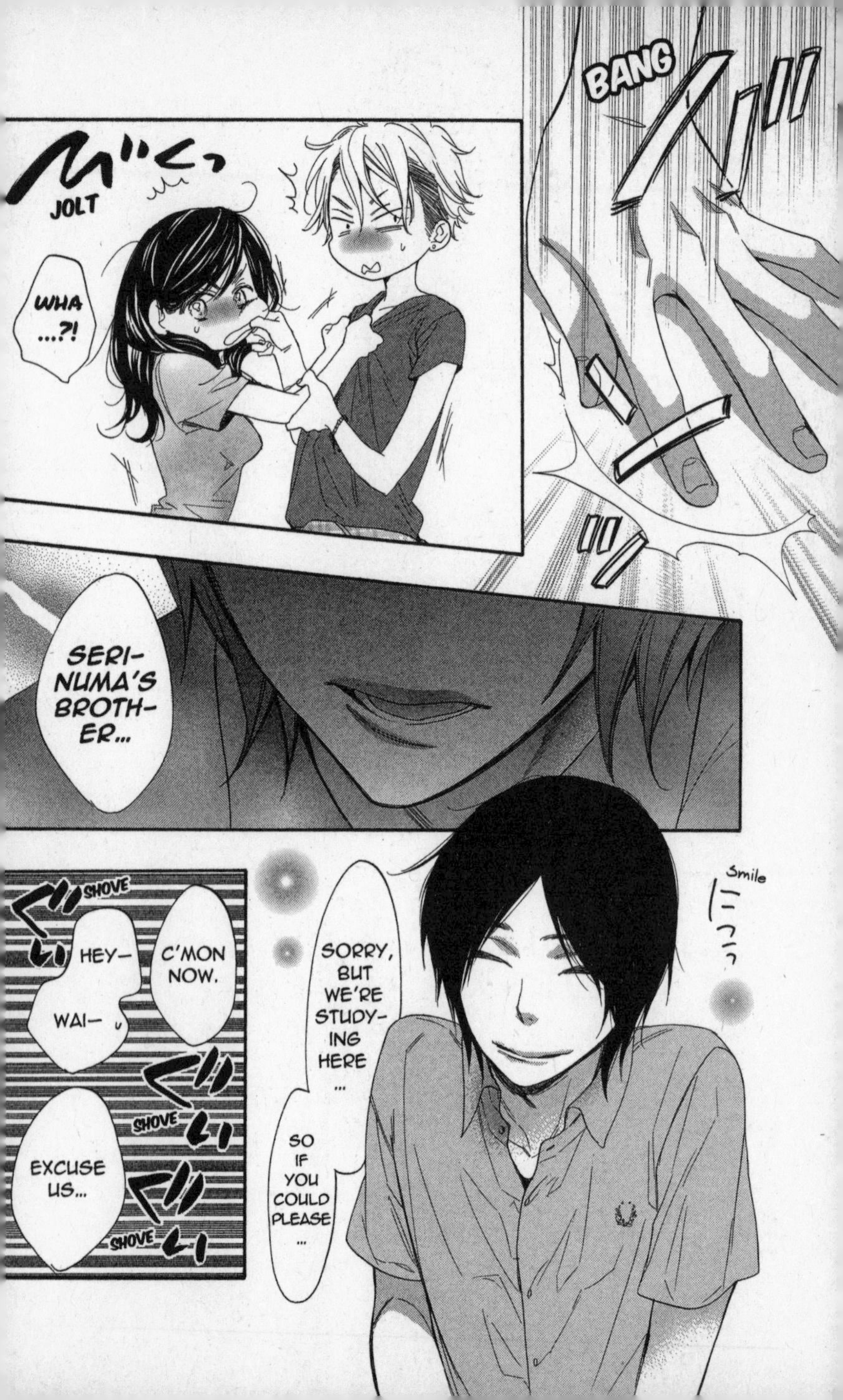
BANG
JOLT
WHA ...?!
SERI-NUMA'S BROTH-ER...
Smile
SORRY, BUT WE'RE STUDY-ING HERE ...
SO IF YOU COULD PLEASE ...
SHOVE
C'MON NOW.
HEY—
WAI—
SHOVE
EXCUSE US...
SHOVE

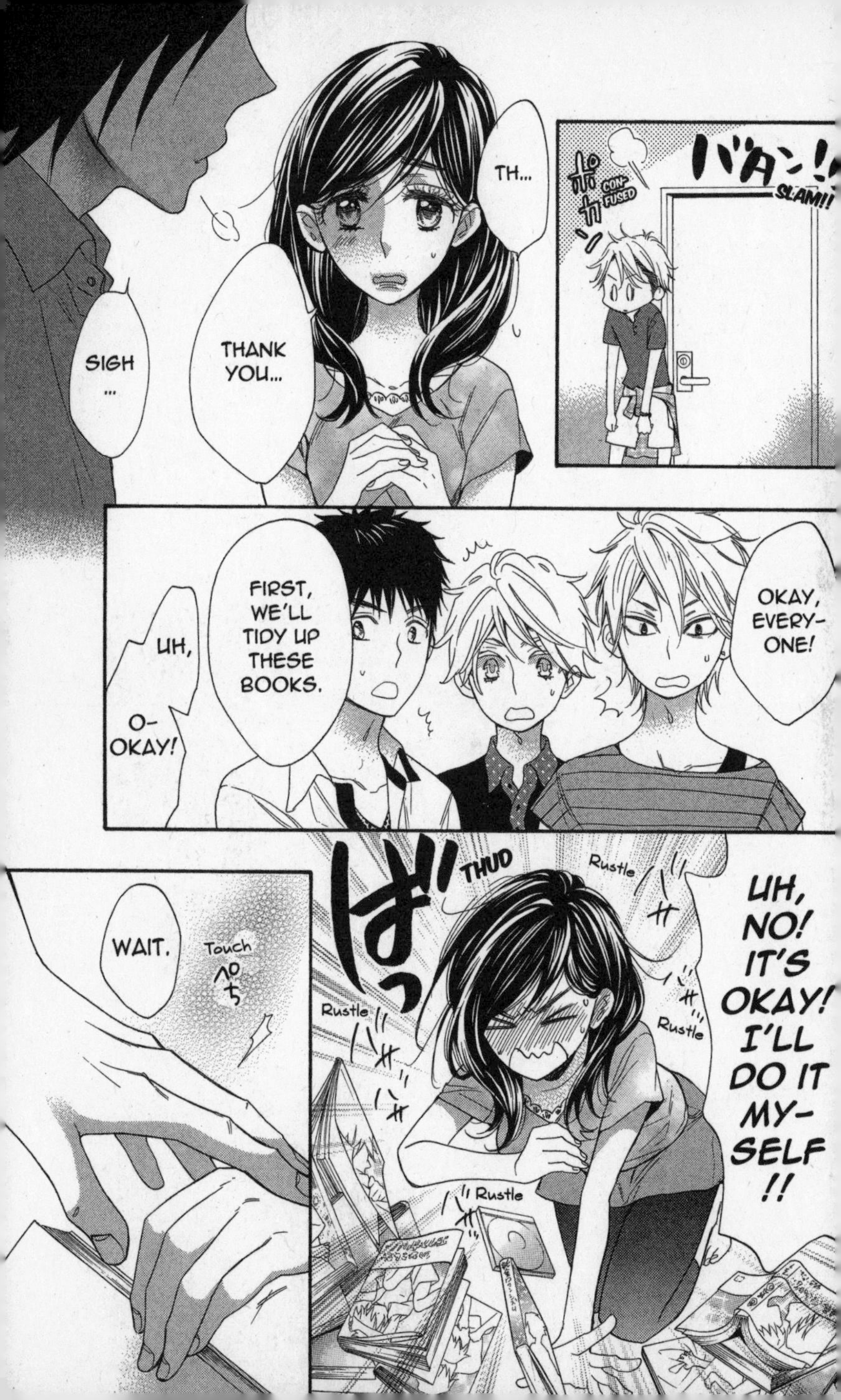
バタン!!
SLAM!!
CON-FUSED
TH...
THANK YOU...
SIGH ...
OKAY, EVERY-ONE!
FIRST, WE'LL TIDY UP THESE BOOKS.
UH,
O-OKAY!
THUD
Rustle
UH, NO! IT'S OKAY! I'LL DO IT MY-SELF!!
Rustle
Rustle
Rustle
WAIT.
Touch

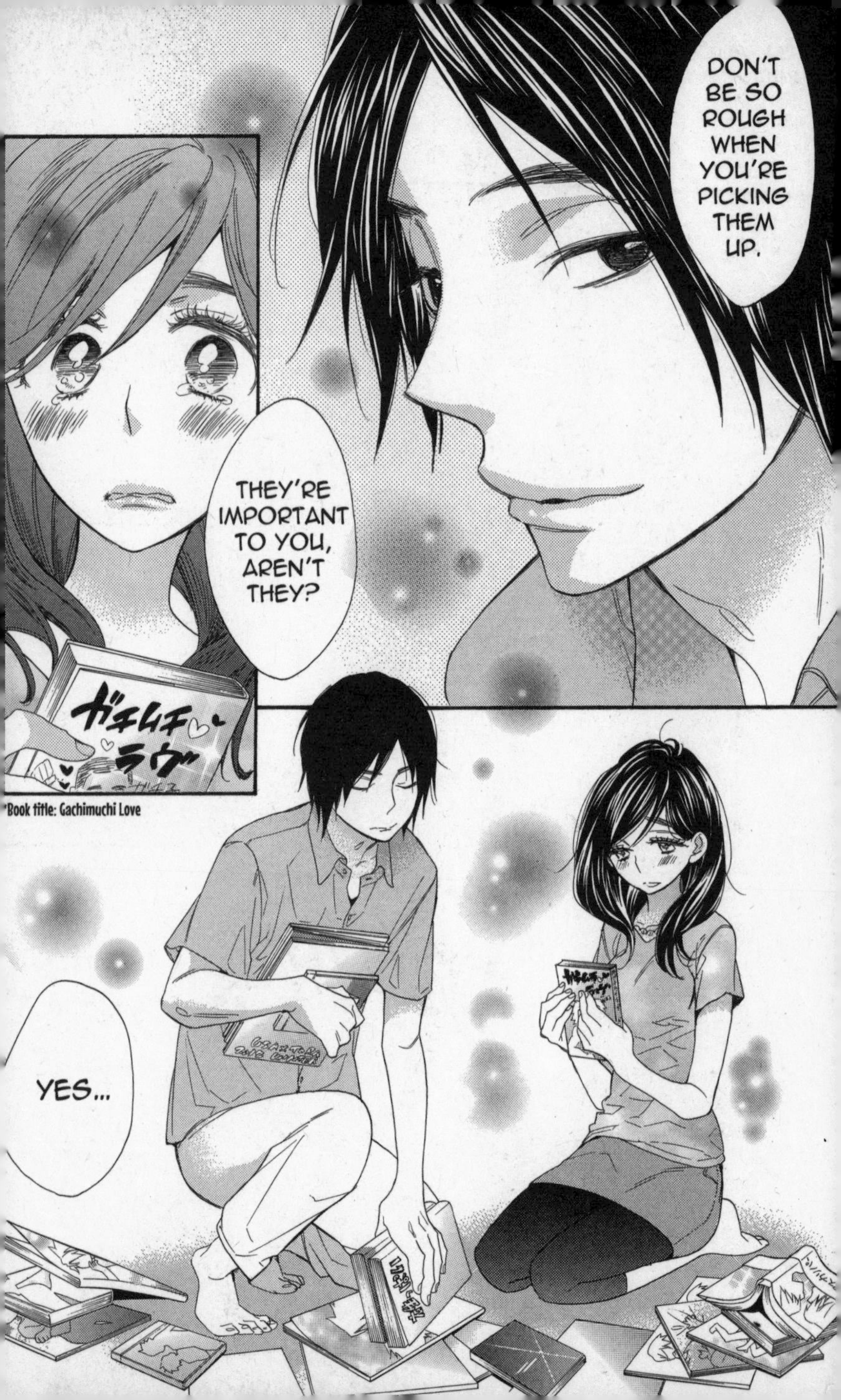
DON'T BE SO ROUGH WHEN YOU'RE PICKING THEM UP.
THEY'RE IMPORTANT TO YOU, AREN'T THEY?
ガチムチ♡ラヴ
YES...
*Book title: Gachimuchi Love

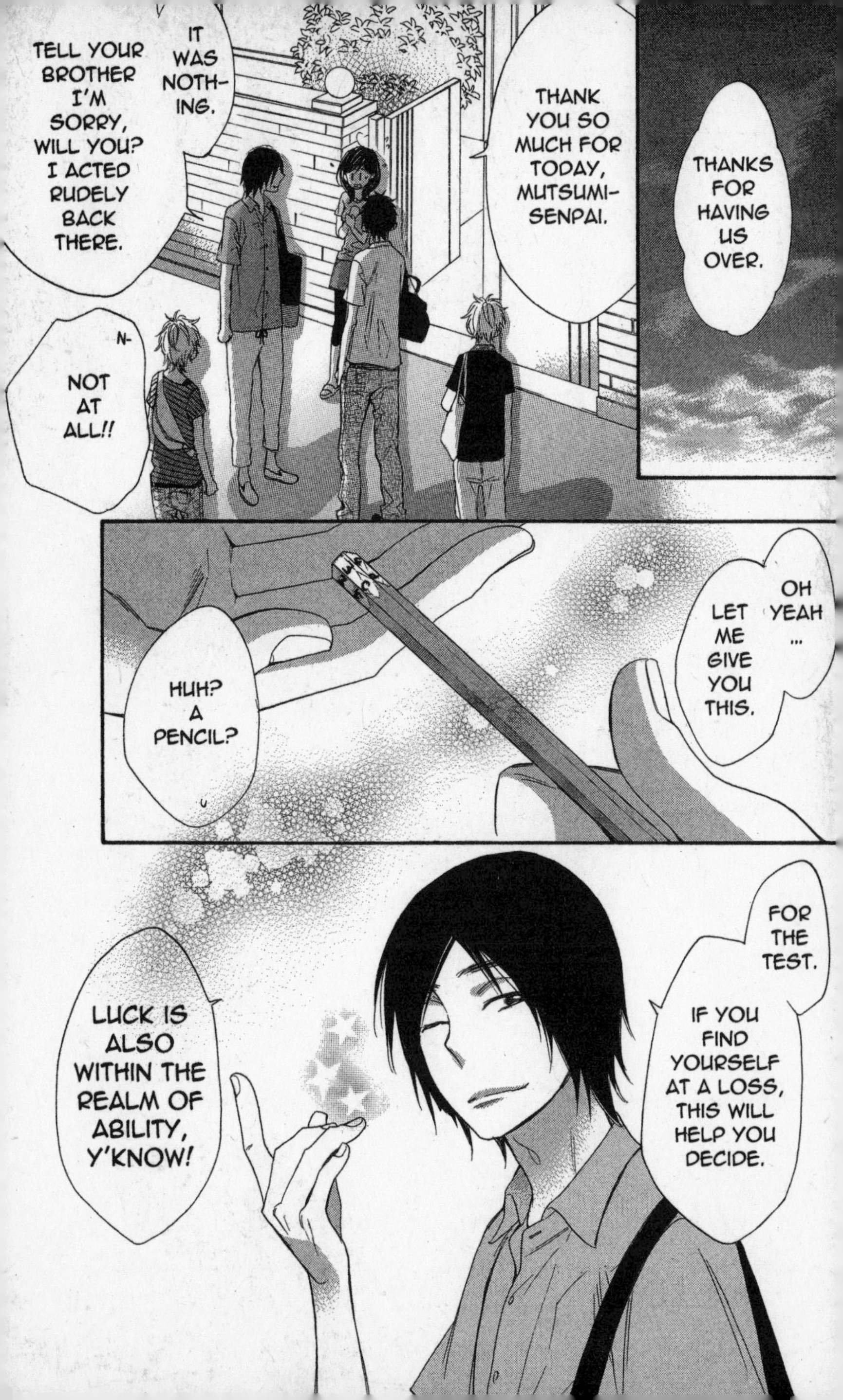
THANKS FOR HAVING US OVER.
THANK YOU SO MUCH FOR TODAY, MUTSUMI-SENPAI.
IT WAS NOTH-ING.
TELL YOUR BROTHER I'M SORRY, WILL YOU? I ACTED RUDELY BACK THERE.
N- NOT AT ALL!!
OH YEAH ... LET ME GIVE YOU THIS.
HUH? A PENCIL?
FOR THE TEST.
IF YOU FIND YOURSELF AT A LOSS, THIS WILL HELP YOU DECIDE.
LUCK IS ALSO WITHIN THE REALM OF ABILITY, Y'KNOW!

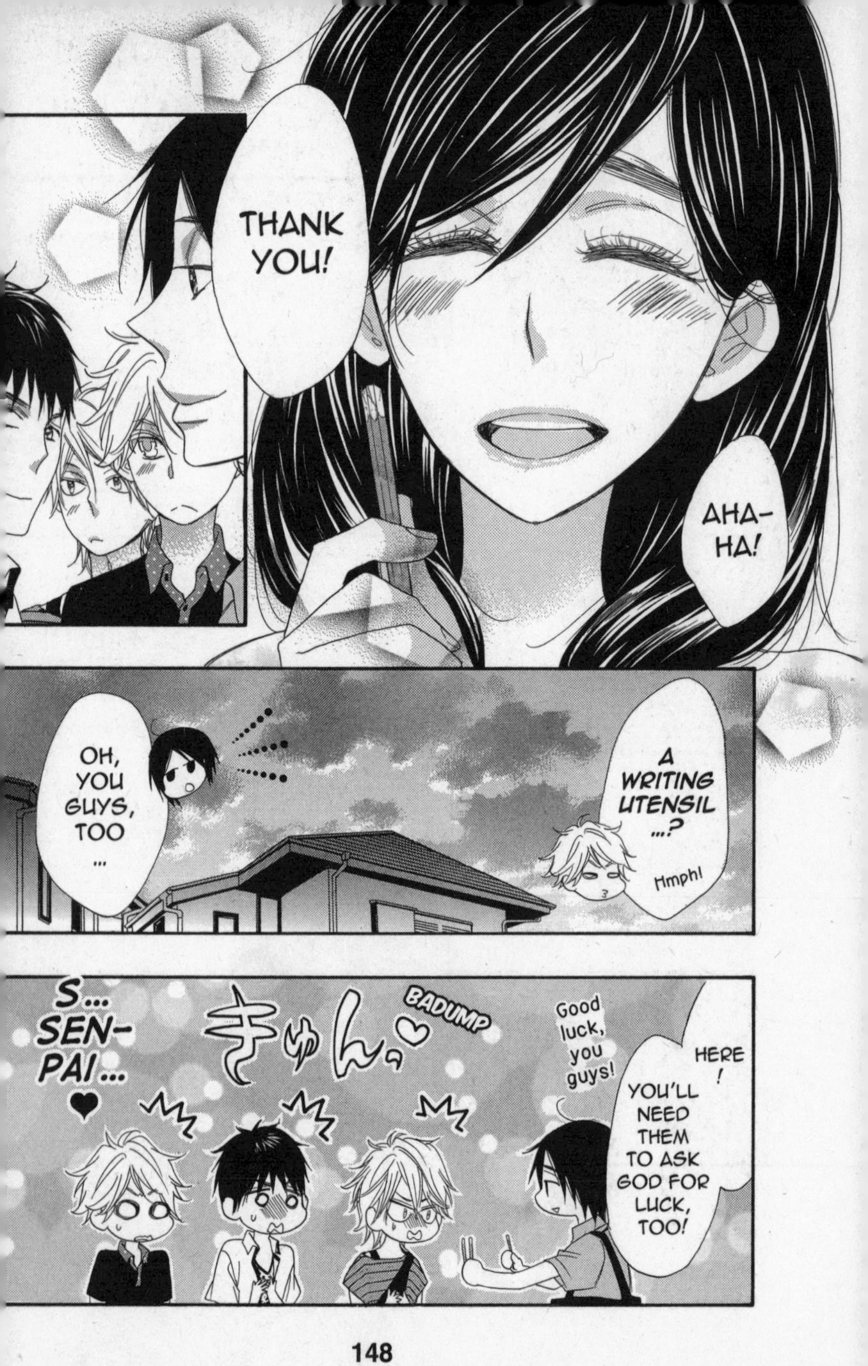
THANK YOU!
AHA-HA!
A WRITING UTENSIL ...?
Hmph!
OH, YOU GUYS, TOO ...
HERE!
YOU'LL NEED THEM TO ASK GOD FOR LUCK, TOO!
Good luck, you guys!
BADUMP
きゅん
S... SEN-PAI...

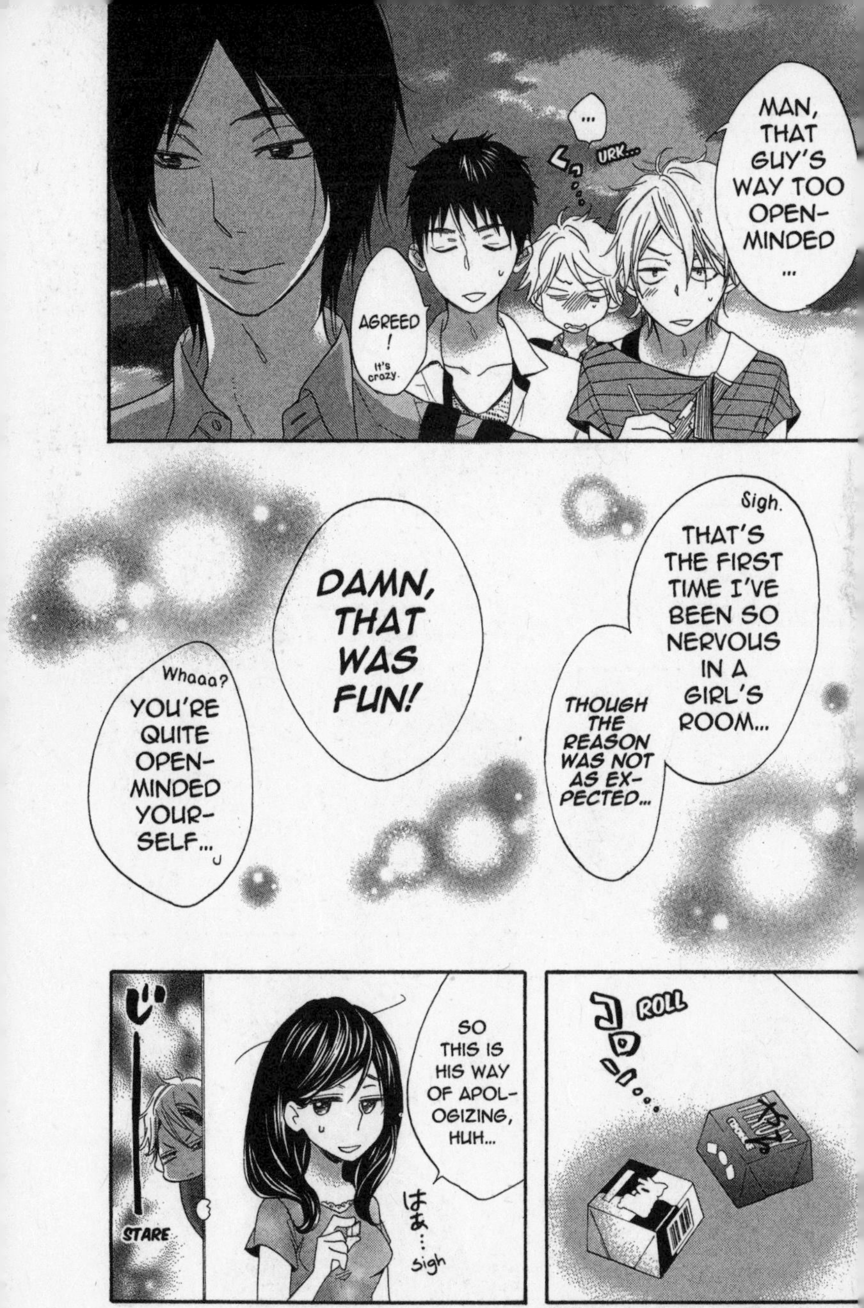
MAN, THAT GUY'S WAY TOO OPEN-MINDED ...
...
URK...
AGREED! It's crazy.
Sigh. THAT'S THE FIRST TIME I'VE BEEN SO NERVOUS IN A GIRL'S ROOM...
THOUGH THE REASON WAS NOT AS EXPECTED...
DAMN, THAT WAS FUN!
Whaaa? YOU'RE QUITE OPEN-MINDED YOURSELF...
ROLL
SO THIS IS HIS WAY OF APOLOGIZING, HUH...
はあ… Sigh
STARE

*Writing on chocolate wrapper: "I'll give this to you

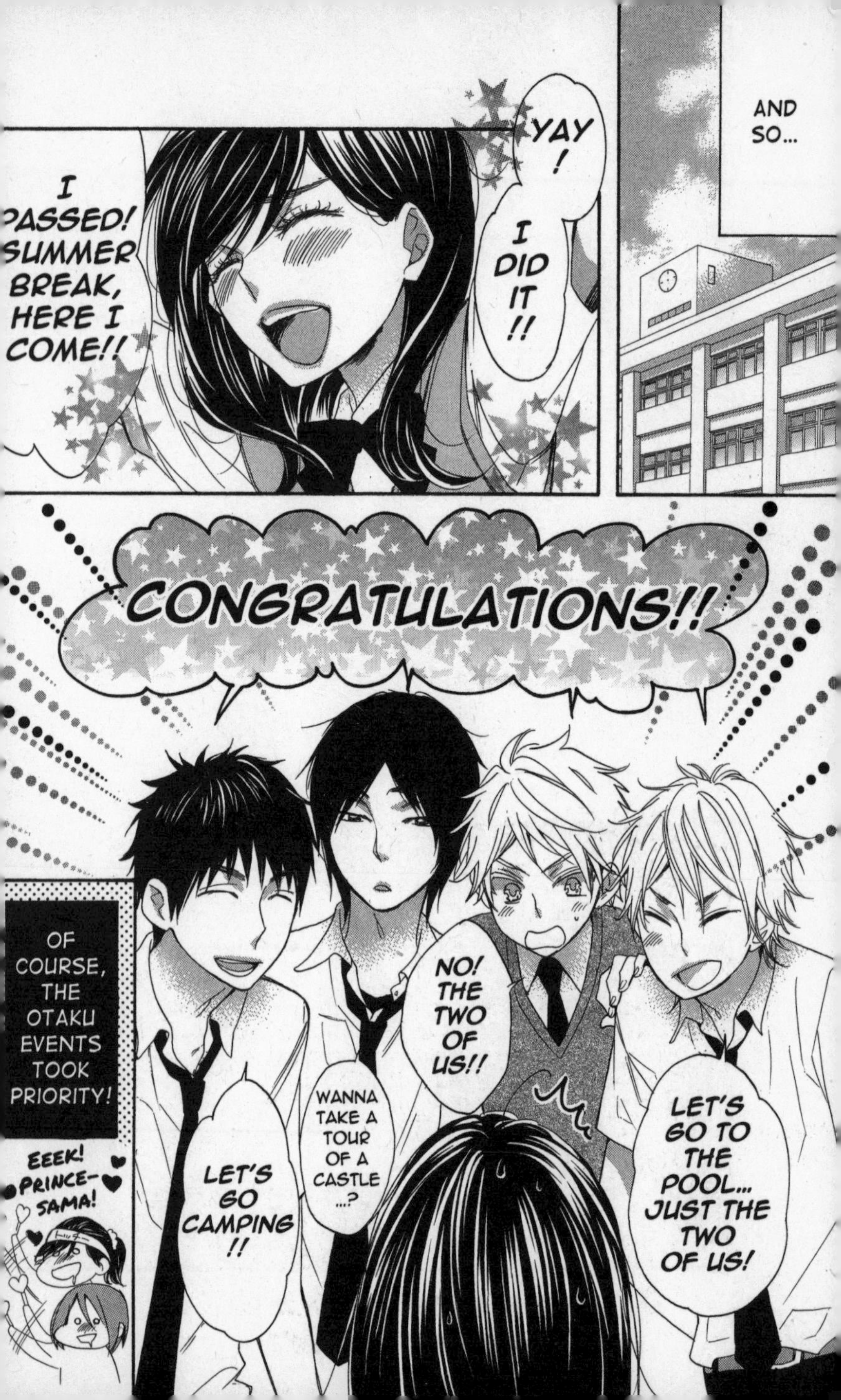
AND SO...
YAY! I DID IT!!
I PASSED! SUMMER BREAK, HERE I COME!!
CONGRATULATIONS!!
LET'S GO TO THE POOL... JUST THE TWO OF US!
NO! THE TWO OF US!!
WANNA TAKE A TOUR OF A CASTLE ...?
LET'S GO CAMPING!!
OF COURSE, THE OTAKU EVENTS TOOK PRIORITY!
EEEK! PRINCE-SAMA!

SUMMER CO-MIKET: 3-HOUR LINE
IT'S SO HOT!
IT'S SO HOT!
MIRAGE SAGA COLLAB-ORATION CAFE: 2-HOUR LINE
IT'S SO HOT!
IT'S SO HOT!
VOICE ACTORS LIVE SHOW: 2-HOUR LINE TO BUY STUFF
IT'S SO HOT!
IT'S SO HOT!
NICE TAN! DID YOU SPEND YOUR SUMMER OUT-DOORS?
NOPE. WE WERE INSIDE THE WHOLE TIME.
??
こんがり
GOLDEN BROWN

TO BE CONTINUED IN VOLUME 2 OF KISS HIM, NOT ME!

KiSS HiM, NOT ME!

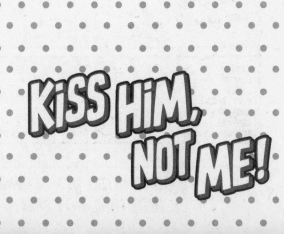

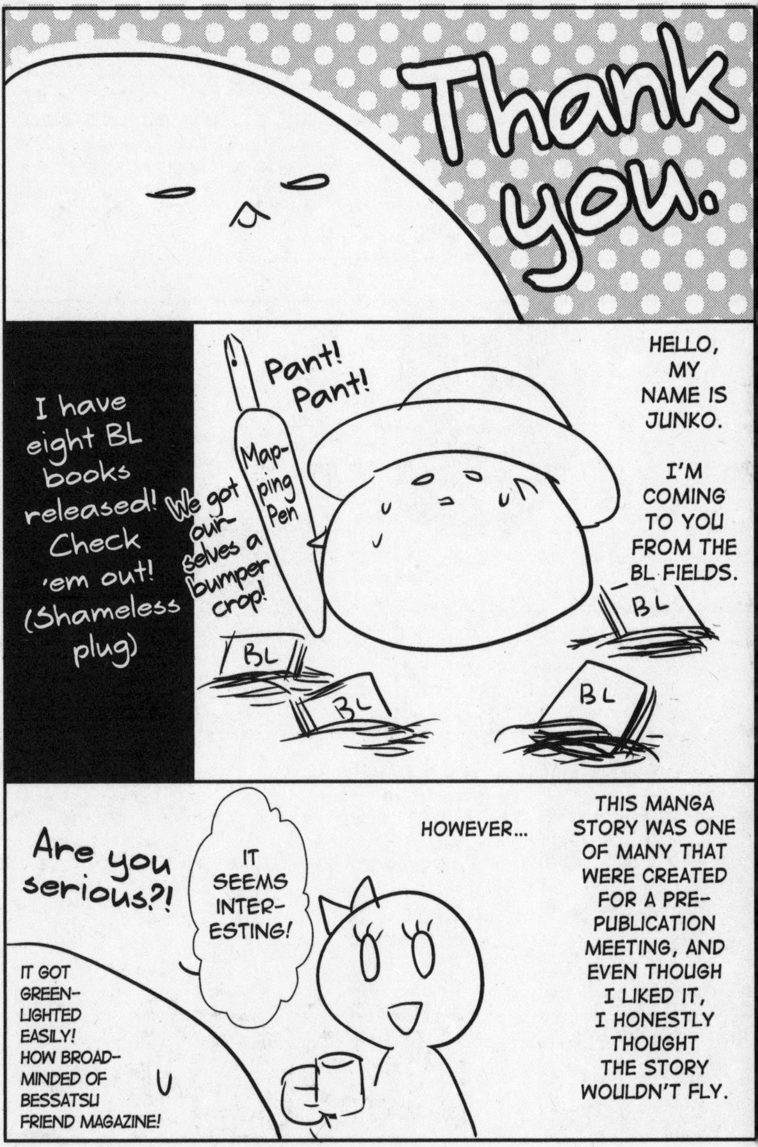
Thank you.
HELLO, MY NAME IS JUNKO.
I'M COMING TO YOU FROM THE BL FIELDS.
Pant! Pant!
Mapping Pen
We got ourselves a bumper crop!
BL
BL
BL
BL
I have eight BL books released! Check 'em out! (Shameless plug)
THIS MANGA STORY WAS ONE OF MANY THAT WERE CREATED FOR A PRE-PUBLICATION MEETING, AND EVEN THOUGH I LIKED IT, I HONESTLY THOUGHT THE STORY WOULDN'T FLY.
HOWEVER...
IT SEEMS INTERESTING!
Are you serious?!
IT GOT GREEN-LIGHTED EASILY! HOW BROAD-MINDED OF BESSATSU FRIEND MAGAZINE!

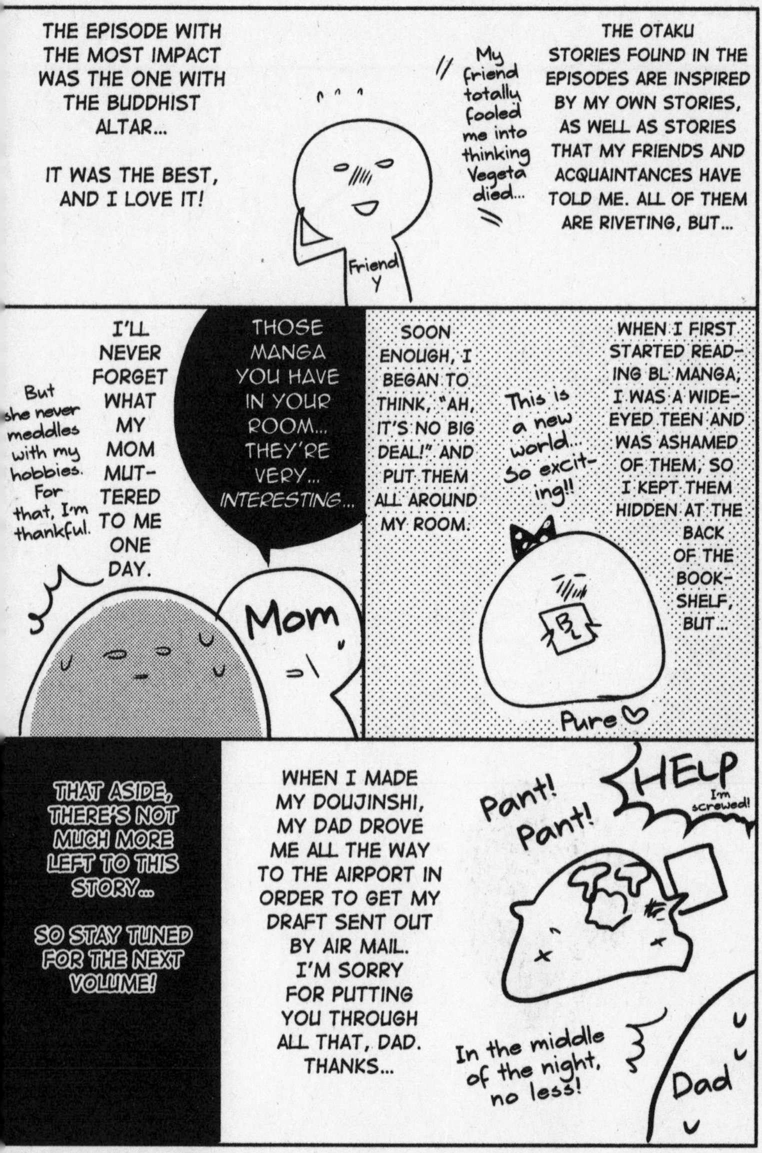
THE OTAKU STORIES FOUND IN THE EPISODES ARE INSPIRED BY MY OWN STORIES, AS WELL AS STORIES THAT MY FRIENDS AND ACQUAINTANCES HAVE TOLD ME. ALL OF THEM ARE RIVETING, BUT...
My friend totally fooled me into thinking Vegeta died...
Friend Y
THE EPISODE WITH THE MOST IMPACT WAS THE ONE WITH THE BUDDHIST ALTAR...
IT WAS THE BEST, AND I LOVE IT!
WHEN I FIRST STARTED READING BL MANGA, I WAS A WIDE-EYED TEEN AND WAS ASHAMED OF THEM, SO I KEPT THEM HIDDEN AT THE BACK OF THE BOOKSHELF, BUT...
This is a new world... So exciting!!
BL
SOON ENOUGH, I BEGAN TO THINK, "AH, IT'S NO BIG DEAL!" AND PUT THEM ALL AROUND MY ROOM.
Pure
THOSE MANGA YOU HAVE IN YOUR ROOM... THEY'RE VERY... INTERESTING...
I'LL NEVER FORGET WHAT MY MOM MUTTERED TO ME ONE DAY.
But she never meddles with my hobbies. For that, I'm thankful.
Mom
HELP
I'm screwed!
Pant! Pant!
WHEN I MADE MY DOUJINSHI, MY DAD DROVE ME ALL THE WAY TO THE AIRPORT IN ORDER TO GET MY DRAFT SENT OUT BY AIR MAIL. I'M SORRY FOR PUTTING YOU THROUGH ALL THAT, DAD. THANKS...
In the middle of the night, no less!
Dad
THAT ASIDE, THERE'S NOT MUCH MORE LEFT TO THIS STORY...
SO STAY TUNED FOR THE NEXT VOLUME!

o everyone who helped, Eiki Eiki-sensei, my supervisor, everyone else ho was involved, and all the readers, thank you so much!!

AUTHOR'S NOTE

AT FIRST, I WAS WORRIED ABOUT WHAT I WOULD ACTUALLY DRAW FOR THIS MANGA, BUT WHEN IT COMES DOWN TO IT, I'M AN ACTUAL FEMALE OTAKU AND KNEW THAT I COULD COME UP WITH THE MATERIAL. WITH THAT ATTITUDE IN MIND, AND WITH CONSIDERABLE HELP FROM THOSE AROUND ME, I WAS ABLE TO COMPLETE THIS MANGA! THANK YOU SO MUCH!

-JUNKO

I ♥ BL

Translation Notes

Moe, page 8

Moe originally described a person or character who is undeniably cute, endearing, and attractive. The Japanese character for "moe" means "to bud" or "sprout," perhaps because these objects of affection are often youthful. It is also homonym for "to burn," so it is equally used as a verb when one's passion "burn for a character, as is the case here.

5x7 versus 7x5, page 12

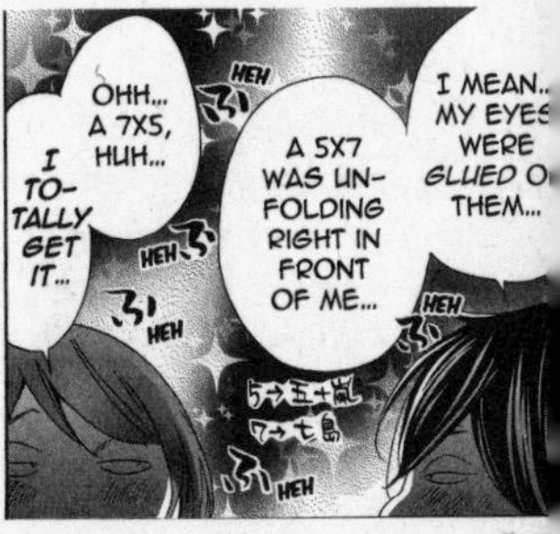
I MEAN.. MY EYES WERE GLUED O THEM...
HEH
A 5X7 WAS UN-FOLDING RIGHT IN FRONT OF ME...
HEH
OHH... A 7X5, HUH...
HEH
I TO-TALLY GET IT...
HEH
5→五十嵐
7→七島
HEH

In the Japanese, Igarashi's name is spelled with the character for the number five, and Nanashima's is spelled with the character for seven. Many fans, especially in BL (Boys Love), take into account which character's name comes first in the shipping notation. Here, Kae and Ah-chan debate over the ordering, pitting Igarashi x Nanashima (5 x 7) against Nanashima x Igarashi (7 x 5). The name that comes first denotes the dominant partner and the latter signifies the submissive partner.

Fujoshi, page 12

Fujoshi in Japanese translates to "rotten woman," referencing how these women self-identify as individuals opposite from Japan's patriarchal definition of what a "good woman" is—a helpful wife and a wise mother. Fujoshi indulge their desire as women, regardless of the purity and innocence that is expected of them. Thu it is considered unladylike and unattractive to be one, and many women (like Ah chan) must keep it a secret. Most commonly, fujoshi refers to a passionate fangir of anime and manga that objectifies male characters and male-to-male sexuality.

Shipping, page 13

"Shipping," as Kae explains, is a devotion to a fictional or potential relationship. "Ships" (short for "relationships") can range from actual relationships shown in th source material, to inferences taken from subtext, to just plain fantasy—even if th characters hate each other or have never interacted.

Bishonen, page 15

The literal translation of bishonen is "beautiful boy," not to be confused with "pretty boy" in English. The term refers to a young man who is seen as both elegant and deeply desirable with an androgynous beauty.

OTP, page 19

In fandom terminology, OTP stands for One True Pairing, where "pairing" means the same thing as a couple, or the aforementioned "ship." It is the ideal and ultimate couple as seen by the fan. Here, initially in the Japanese, Kae used the ɔanese transliteration of the English word, "couple," which is a similar stand-in r OTP and "ship" in Japan's fujoshi circles.

ome game, page 53

ı otome game is a video game directed at a female audience, in which the ayer is able to navigate a narrative with various options of male in-game love terests. Mostly, the player character in otome games will be female, but BL (Boys ve) otome games with male love interests and male player characters exist as ell. In Japanese, "otome" refers to a maidenly, young girl.

aku, page 55

ften mistakenly appropriated in English as "nerd/geek", an otaku is an obsessive ı who hoards information and merchandise of their favorite things—there are in otaku, camera otaku, and most famously, anime and manga otaku. The word taku" in Japanese is a formal and honorific pronoun that the speaker uses to ldress "you," reflecting their insider culture. In general, the term "otaku" connotes inability to function "normally" in society, so Japanese otaku are shamed for it d might try to hide it in their public lives.

cket tissues, page 60

ı the streets of Japan, pocket tissues are often given out with advertisements aced on the back.

rikura, page 63

rikura (short for "print club") are photo booths in Japan where you can stomize and put cute frames and stickers around selfies taken in the booth, and en print them on the spot.

ptain Tsubasa, page 89

ptain Tsubasa is a popular shonen soccer manga-turned-anime from the)s that was also the seminal text for the first doujinshi (unofficial fan magazine or anga) ever made. Female fans drew new stories, putting members of the soccer am in romantic relationships with ch other. The doujinshi industry s expansively grown since, and s homage is quite fitting for the *ss Him, Not Me* series. Captain ıbasa's motto is, "The ball is my end!"

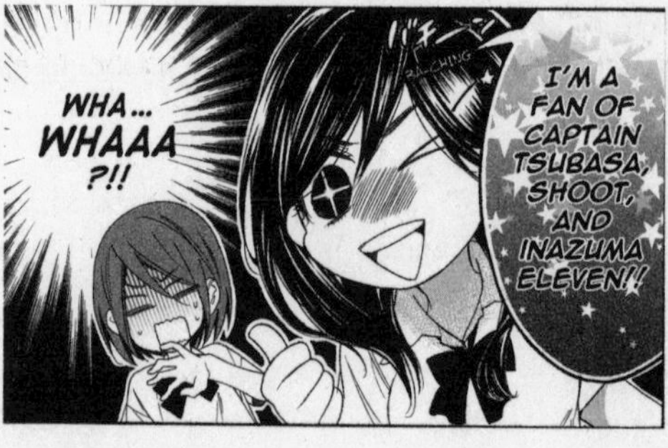
I'M A FAN OF CAPTAIN TSUBASA, SHOOT, AND INAZUMA ELEVEN!!
WHA... WHAAA ?!!

Inazuma Eleven, page 89

Inazuma Eleven, or "Ina-Ele" for short, is a popular soccer video game franchise that started in 2008. It has a manga spin-off that was made into an anime.

Uke (bottom), page 127

"Uke" is a term in BL which is used to refer to whichever character in a ship is the submissive party. The dominant counterpart to this is "seme." "Uke" is short for "ukeru," which means "to receive" in Japanese. "Seme," is short for "semeru," which means "to chase." "Seme" and "uke" are roughly equivalent to the slang terms "top" and "bottom" in English.

┌(┌ ^o^)┐ (Homo emoji), page 127

This is an emoji which originated on Twitter as a meme with the purpose of mocking fujoshi. This is supposed to depict a vaguely humanoid figure crawling along on all fours, with its mouth open saying, "homoooo." It's since been taken up by fujoshi for use in fanart and online postings.

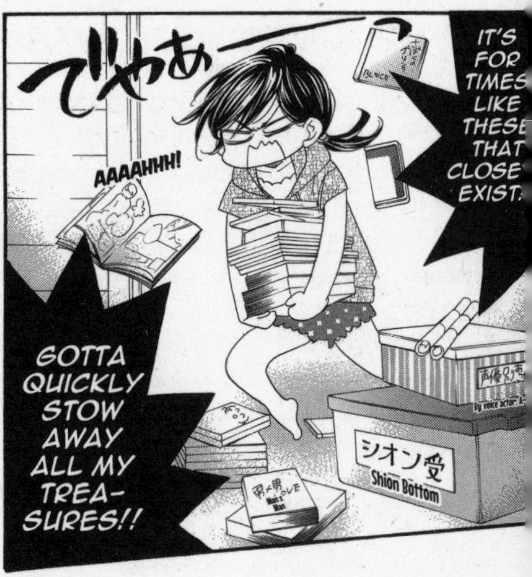

IT'S FOR TIMES LIKE THESE THAT CLOSE EXIST.
でやあーー
AAAAHHH!
GOTTA QUICKLY STOW AWAY ALL MY TREA-SURES!!
シオン受
Shion Bottom

Bessatsu Friend, page 153

The monthly manga magazine in which Kiss Him, Not Me is published; its target audience is teenage girls.

Doujinshi, page 154

Doujinshi are fan-made comics based on existing media. They fill the same niche of fanworks as fan fiction and fan art, with the main difference being that fanfiction doesn't get printed and sold, but doujinshi comics do. The other main difference is that doujinshi are almost exclusively about shipping, whereas fanfiction tends to cover a much broader range of genres.

Kiss Him, Not Me volume 1 is a work of fiction. Names, characters, places, and incidents are the products of the author's imagination or are used fictitiously. Any resemblance to actual events, locales, or persons, living or dead, is entirely coincidental.

A Kodansha Comics Trade Paperback Original.

Published in the United States by Kodansha Comics,
an imprint of Kodansha USA Publishing, LLC, New York.

Publication rights for this English edition arranged through Kodansha Ltd., Tokyo.

First published in Japan in 2013 by Kodansha Ltd., Tokyo, as *Watashi Ga Motete Dousunda* volume 1.

ISBN 978-1-63236-202-5

Printed in the United States of America.

www.kodanshacomics.com

9 8 7 6 5 4 3 2

Translation: David Rhie
Lettering: Hiroko Mizuno
Editing: Ajani Oloye
Kodansha Comics edition cover design: Phil Balsman
Research: Haruko Hashimoto, Nat Kent, & Kiara Valdez